Windows in the Wall

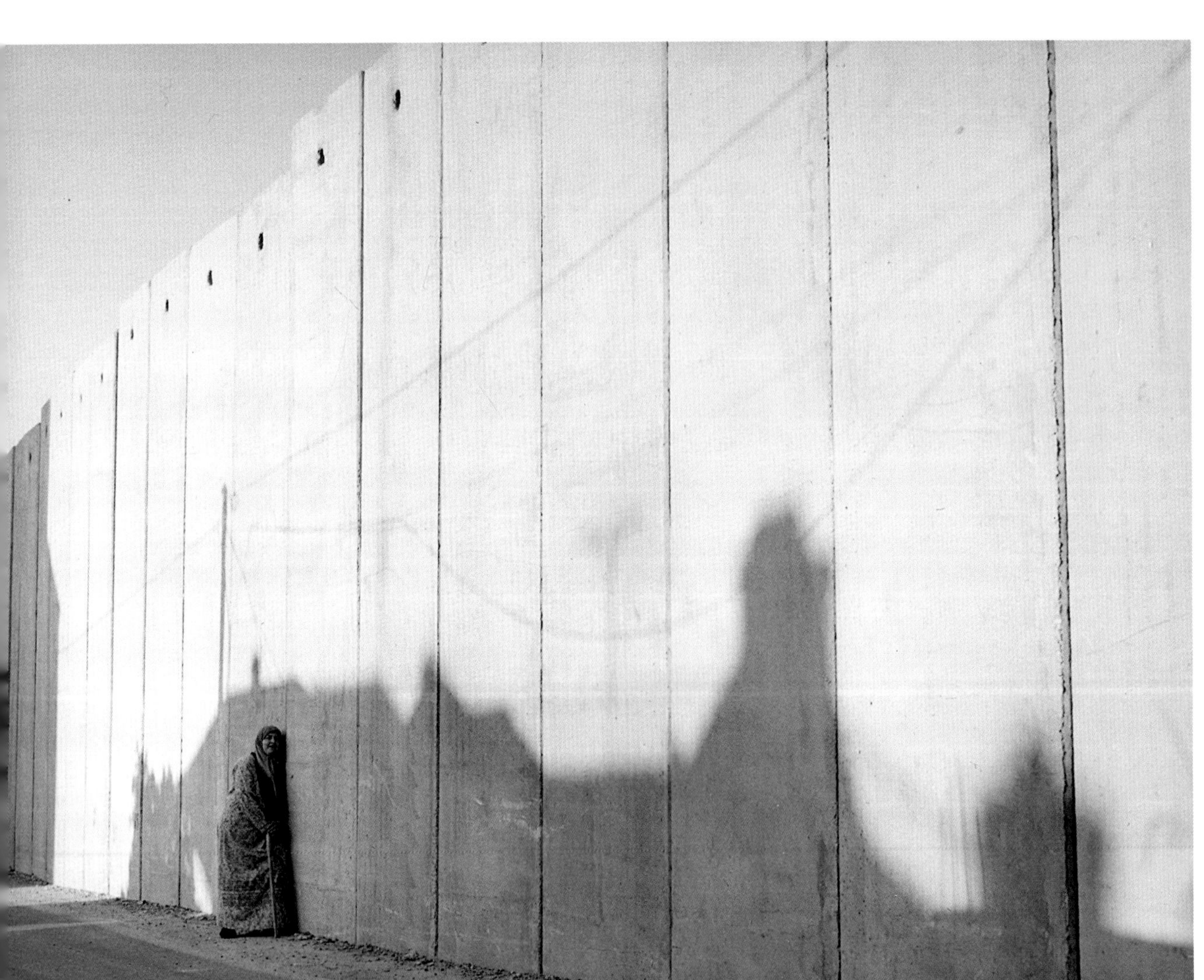

Rebecca Heyl

Windows in the Wall

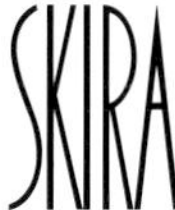

Design
Marcello Francone

Copy Editor
Emanuela Di Lallo

First published in Italy in 2007
by Skira Editore S.p.A.
Palazzo Casati Stampa
via Torino 61
20123 Milano
Italy
www.skira.net

Printed and bound in Italy.
First edition

ISBN-13: 978-88-6130-202-0

Distributed in North America by
Rizzoli International Publications,
Inc., 300 Park Avenue South,
New York, NY 10010.
Distributed elsewhere in the world
by Thames and Hudson Ltd., 181A
High Holborn, London WC1V
7QX, United Kingdom.

Contents

"Land Without People for a People Without Land"

Growing up Jewish in the United States, albeit within the Reformed Jewish movement, the narrative of Israel as a "Land Without People for a People Without Land" was sold to me early. We studied maps of Israel, learned about the Holocaust and sent pocket change off to plant trees in the deserts of Israel. After my *Bat Mitzvah* I can't say I gave much thought to Israel, other than knowing of a distant relative or two who had moved there.

It was not until I lived in Italy as a young adult that I began to identify myself with being Jewish. For the first time I was exposed to the Palestinian cause, and to criticism of Israel. Many people asked me about my views on Israel, and I came to understand that being Jewish directly connected me to that land I had never seen.

In 2001 I moved to Israel, not as a religious or ideological return to the Promised Land, but because my husband had a post-doctoral fellowship in Archaeology. I lived on the beautiful, peaceful, and safe campus of the Weizmann Institute for more than a year before I made my first journey into the occupied territories. But I wanted to know what existed on the other side of the Green Line. For months I researched the various Israeli and Palestinian peace organizations, and participated in my first peace action in December 2002 with the Ta'ayush (Arab-Jewish Partnership). Our group of about twenty Israelis and internationals left from Tel Aviv and entered the West Bank through an Israeli checkpoint. Yacov, our leader, pointed out the rubble of the Baqa Al Gharbia market stalls that had just been demolished to make way for the soon to be built wall. We drove through the Palestinian countryside until we reached the gates of the Mevo Dotan Israeli settlement. Yacov greeted the Palestinian leader, a group of about two dozen farmers began to emerge from the olive groves below us, and we descended into the groves to meet them.

Picking olives side by side we learned the farmers' story. They were from the nearby village of Arabeh. The previous year they had lost their entire olive crop — the mainstay of their livelihood. They had attempted the harvest many times, but each time they were attacked by the settlers of Mevo Dotan. Afraid that the same would happen this year, they had asked Ta'ayush to assist in the olive harvest — not only to help with the actual picking, but, more importantly, to act as a buffer between the Jewish settlers and the Palestinian farmers. Fortunately, the plan succeeded, there were no altercations with the people of Mevo Dotan, and the day turned out to be surprisingly peaceful.

During the next two years I underwent an intensive learning process as my eyes were opened to what was going on around me. Ideas linked to my own cultural identity, as an American and a Jew, were now being challenged. It was an emotional yet exciting experience as I began to understand that almost all I had learned about the Israeli/Palestinian conflict was a load of rubbish. This not only angered me, it also empowered me to get out there to photograph and tell this story.

As I worked with a number of joint Israeli–Palestinian organizations I learned that there were two distinct narratives of history. In Israel I met some Jews who were so identified with the tragedies of history and the need for a homeland and for security that their hearts had no room to consider Palestinian claims or Palestinian humanity; they had no understanding of Palestinians except as enemy. But when I went to the occupied territories those Palestinians, the people whose very existence was denied in the myth of "a Land Without People for a People Without Land" from my childhood, welcomed me — a Jew, an American, living in Israel — into their homes and their lives. There I learned of the tragedies of their history, of their need for a homeland and security. And there too I met many Israelis who call these Palestinians friends, and who call Israel their only home. As a peace activist and photographer traveling between Israel and the West Bank I began to weave the two histories into my own narrative.

This is a book about the wall that separates Palestinians and Israelis. When I began photographing the new barrier, in December 2002, little was known about the construction, either within the Israeli public or abroad. Only the Palestinians whose land had been confiscated understood its importance. They found land confiscation notices — not delivered in person, or by mail, but pinned by the Israeli Army to their trees. And then they watched as those trees were cut down, burned, bulldozed, or uprooted — as the groves which their families had cultivated for generations. Some trees planted in Roman times and still bearing fruit were destroyed in a single day.

Now, more than four years later, 400 plus miles of electronic fencing combined with 5–8 meter high concrete wall slabs make up this Barrier. Although it is still not complete, the Barrier has affected the life of every Palestinian, separating them from loved ones, schools, land, markets, universities, jobs, and medical services. Not only has the Barrier affected contact among Palestinians, it also has made the already difficult contact between Palestinians and Israelis nearly impossible.

As we go to press Israel and Palestine have seen two years of cataclysmic changes: the death of Yasser Arafat, the Gaza disengagement, Ariel Sharon's departure from the Likud party and soon thereafter from politics, and the election of Hamas. Each event has opened windows of opportunity and hope, albeit briefly, to many on both sides of the conflict. But the question remains — what has changed on the ground for the average people of both sides? The suicide bombings continue to occur on streets of Israeli cities. The Palestinians are no closer to having a State, the Israeli occupation of Palestinian land continues, settlements are rapidly expanding, restriction of movement within the West Bank has not lifted. The immense project of the Barrier continues to level hundreds of miles of land, bulldozing the trees, houses, livelihoods, and histories in its path.

This new enormous physical barrier between the Palestinian and Israeli peoples has made the other, older, wall that separates them all the more apparent — the invisible wall of fear, distrust, paranoia, and separation. This is the wall that is the subject of my photographic work. This is the wall that fascinates me — this wall, and the courageous people on both sides who continue to penetrate the barriers between them.

Rebecca Heyl
Boston, January 2007

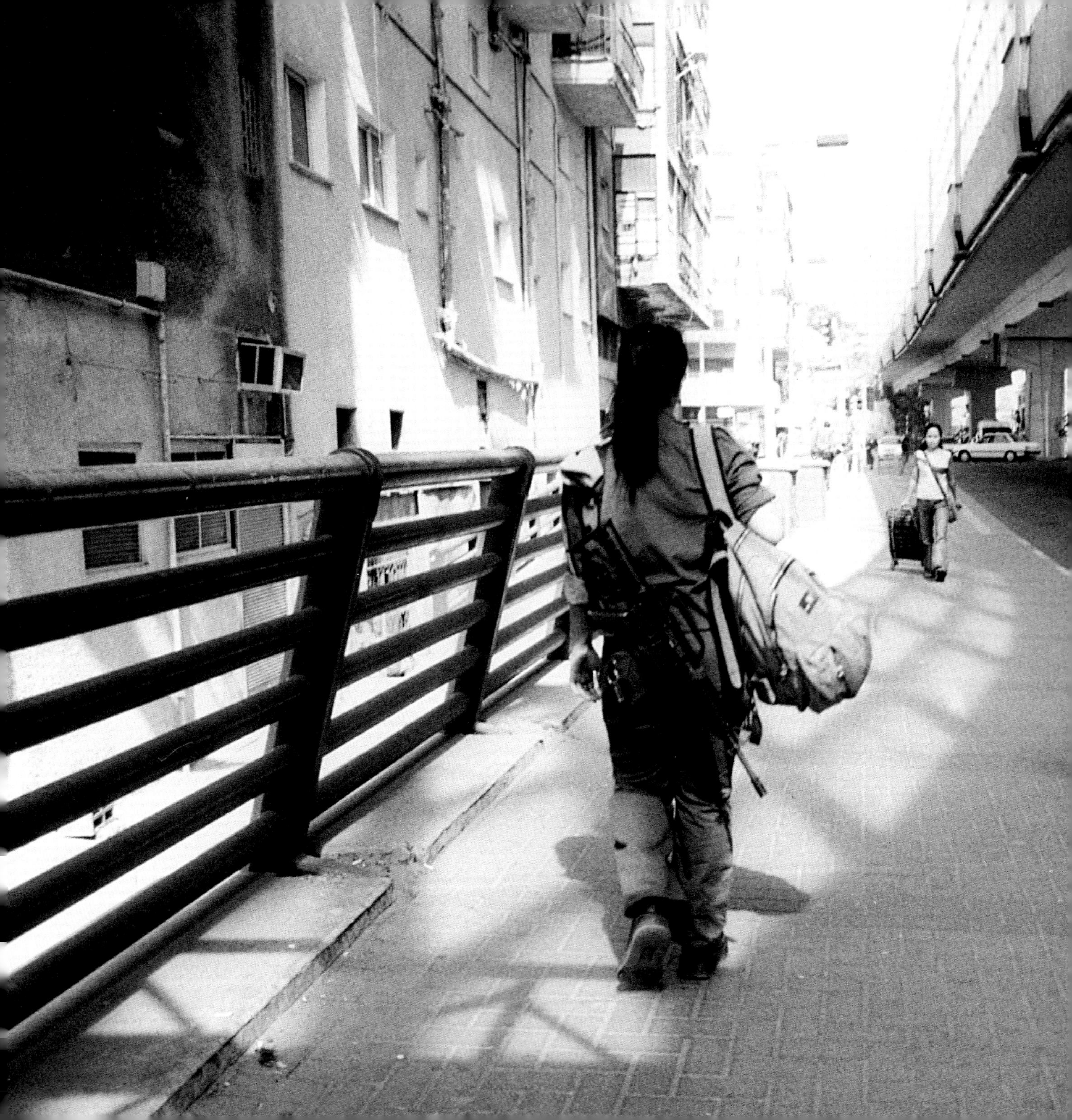

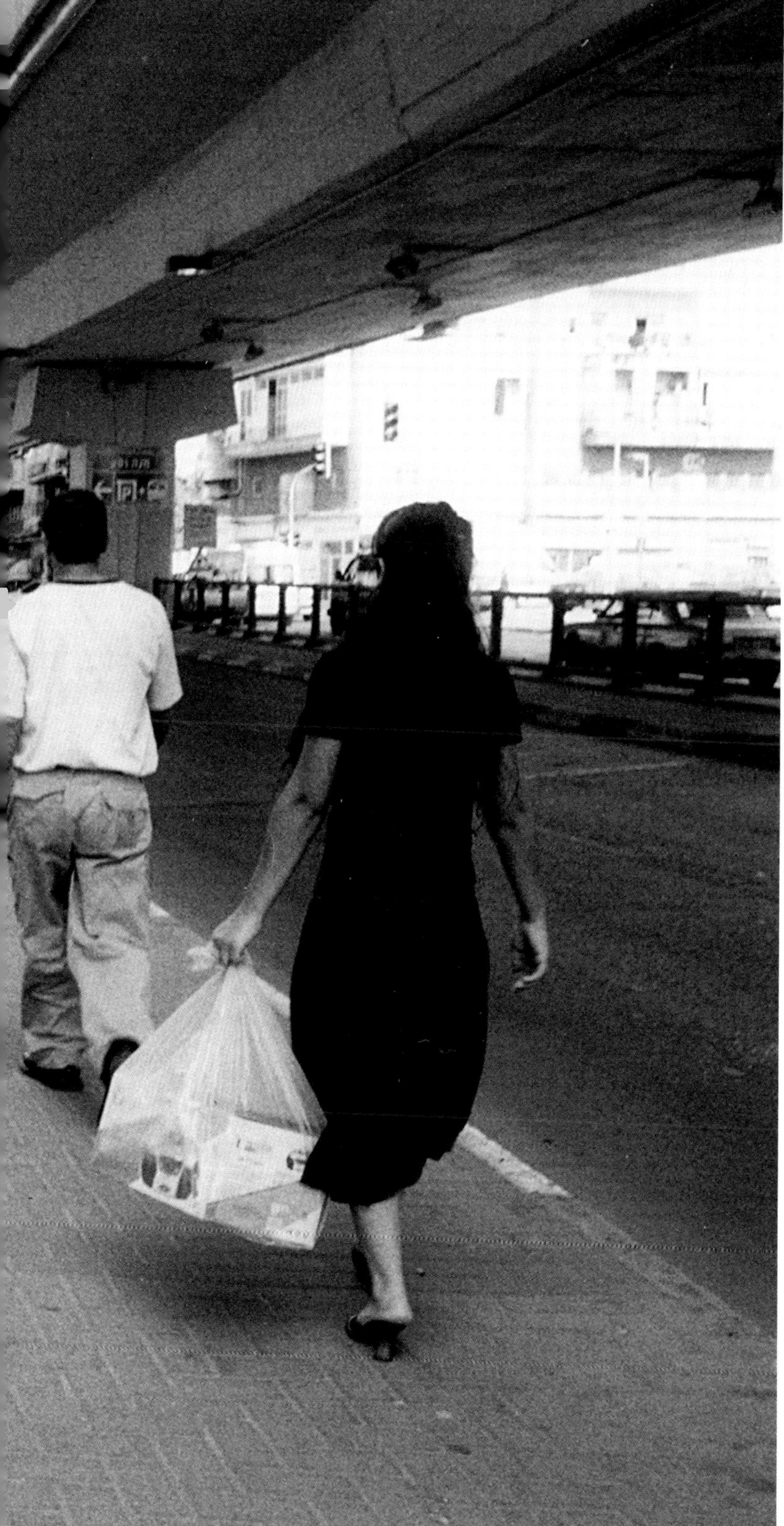

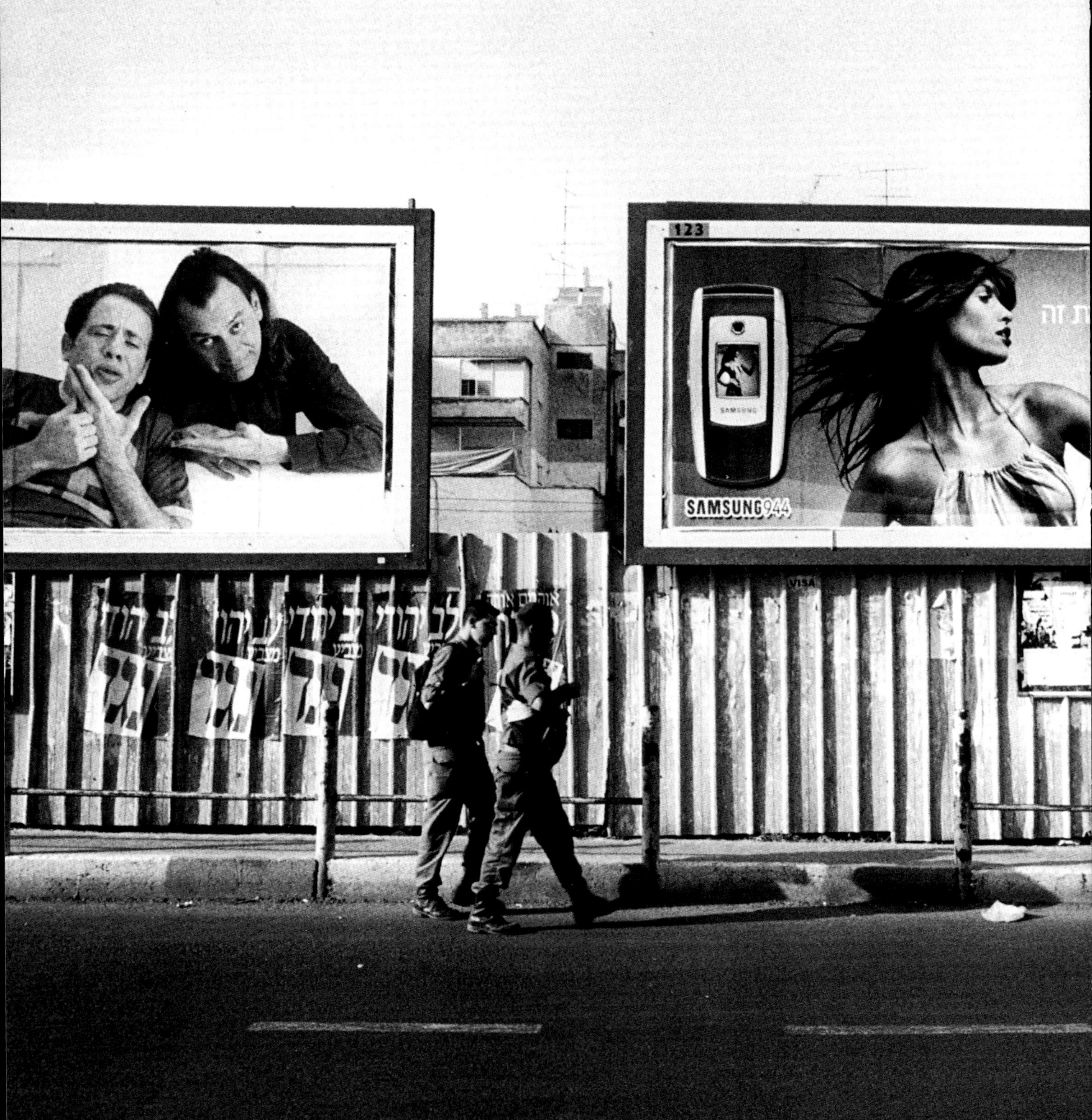

123
SAMSUNG
SAMSUNG 944
VISA

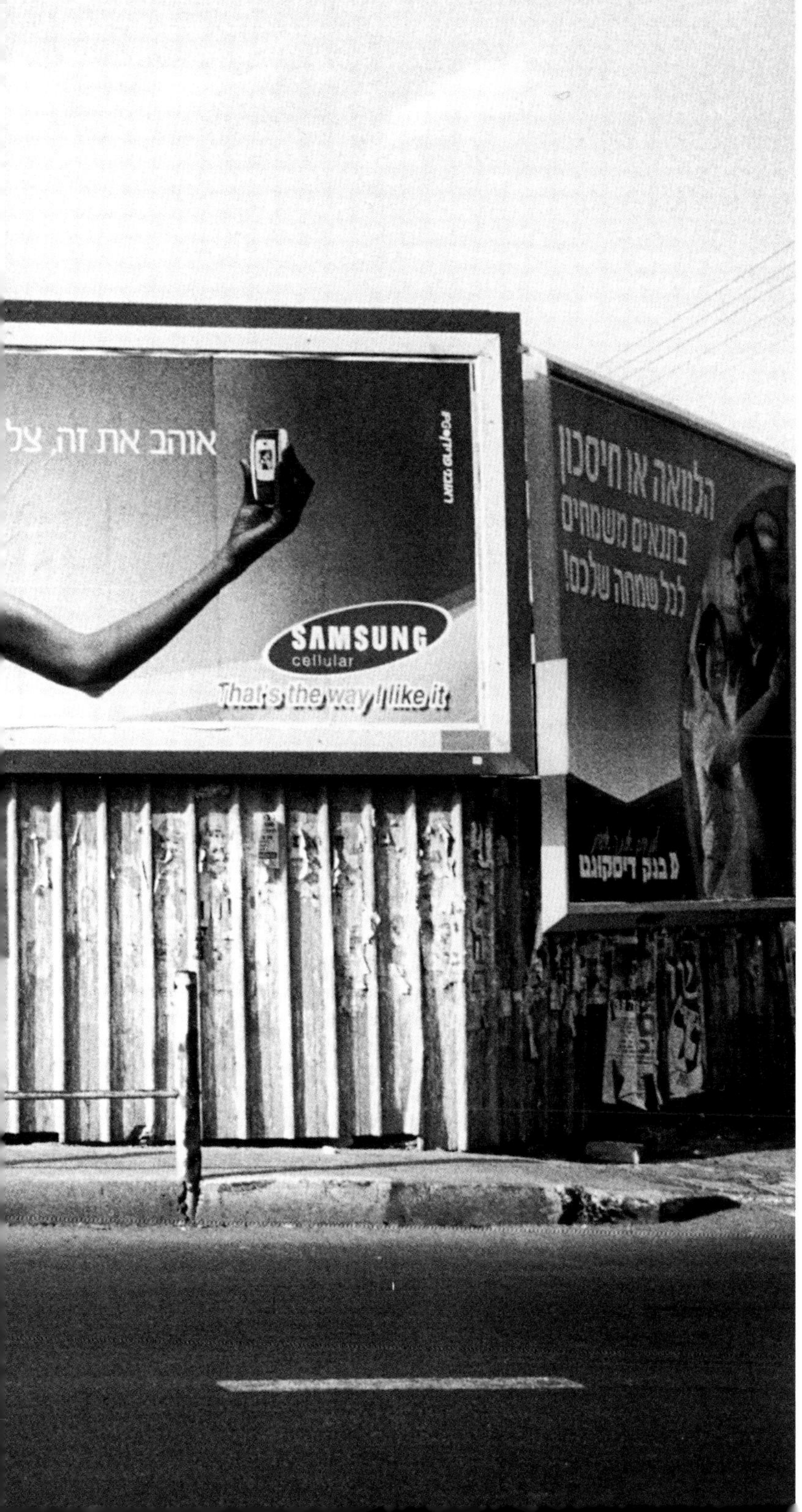
אוהב את זה, צל
SAMSUNG
cellular
That's the way I like it
הלוואה או חיסכון
בתנאים משמחים
לכל שמחה שלכם!
בנק דיסקונט

Busy shopping district,
Allenby Street, Tel Aviv.

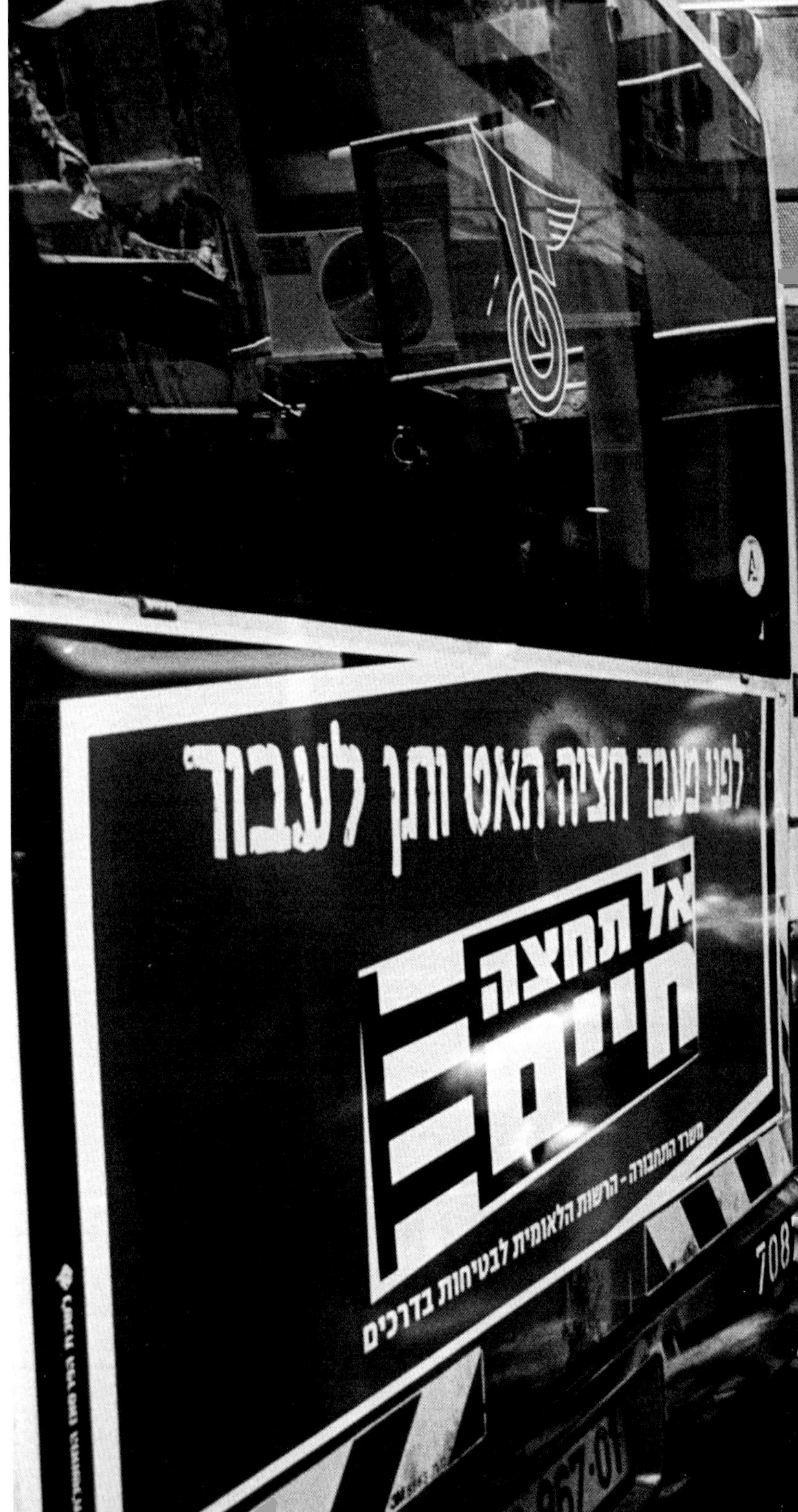

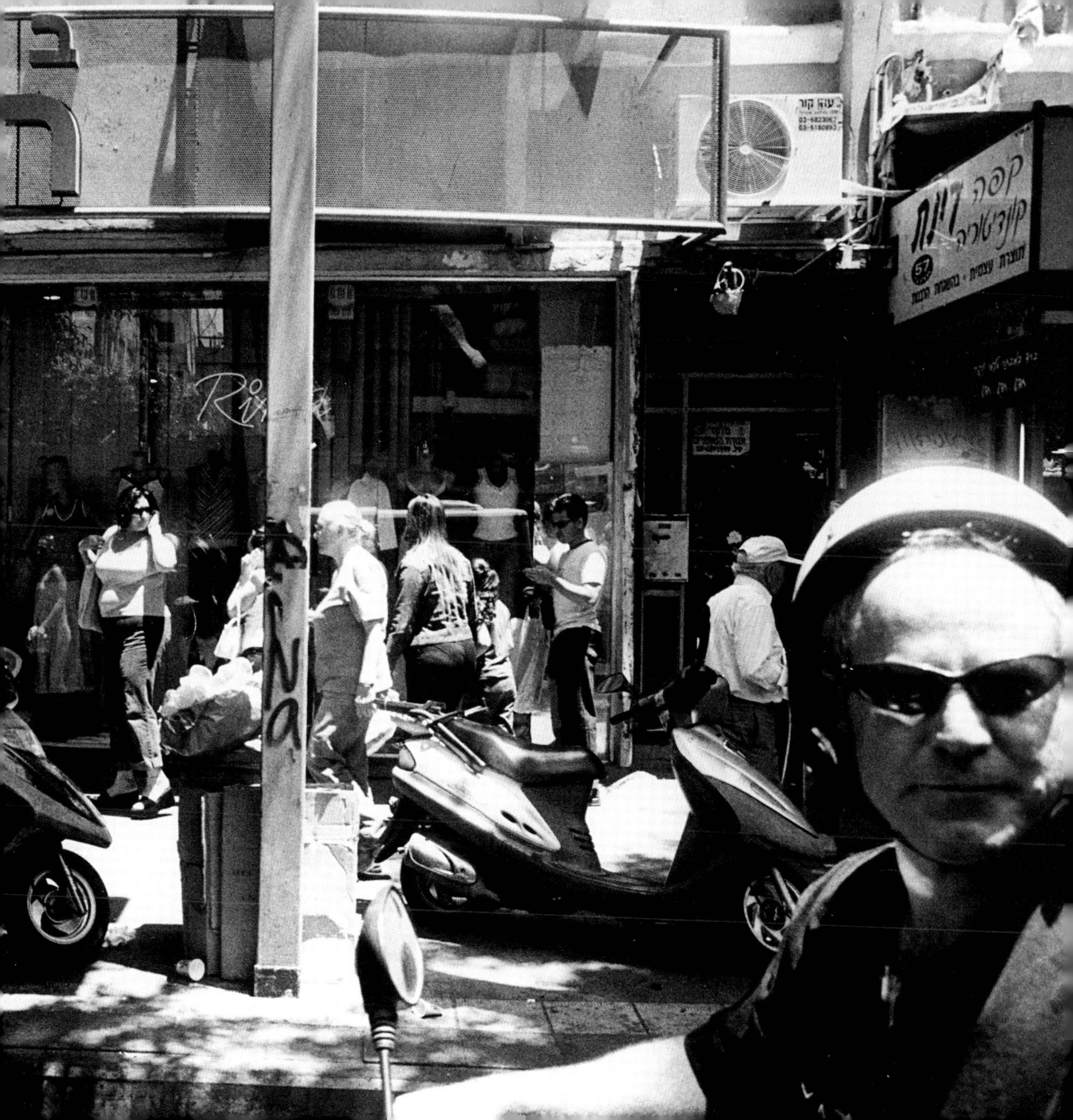

עוה קור
03-6823067
03-6180893
קפה קונדיטוריה זוית
תוצרת עצמית בטעמה הישנה
של פעם 57

Sami, Jaffa
Palestinian Israeli.

The State of Israel was founded in 1948 after a war which the Israelis call the War of Independence and the Palestinians call the *Nakba*, or catastrophe. Before the war of 1948, the Palestinian population was 1,380,000 people, more than half (730,000) were driven off their land by the Israeli army.[1]

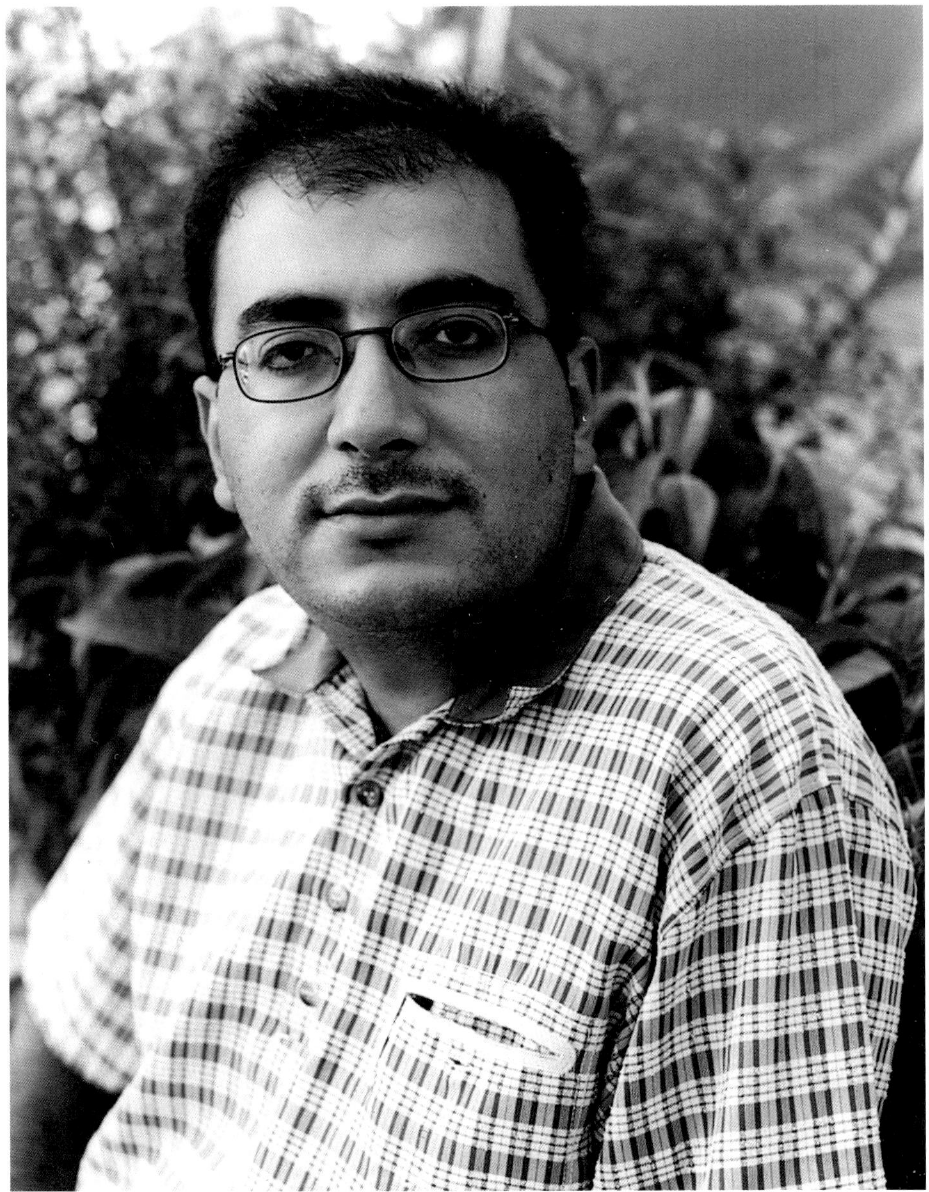

"Israel is the most dangerous
country for the Jewish people. We
are behaving in a terrible way, not
only to the Palestinians, but to
ourselves. To be realistic, my hope
is to still be alive when there
are better times. Yet, I fear to
see the end of this country and
the beginning of another Diaspora."

Manuela Dviri, Tel Aviv
Jewish Israeli.

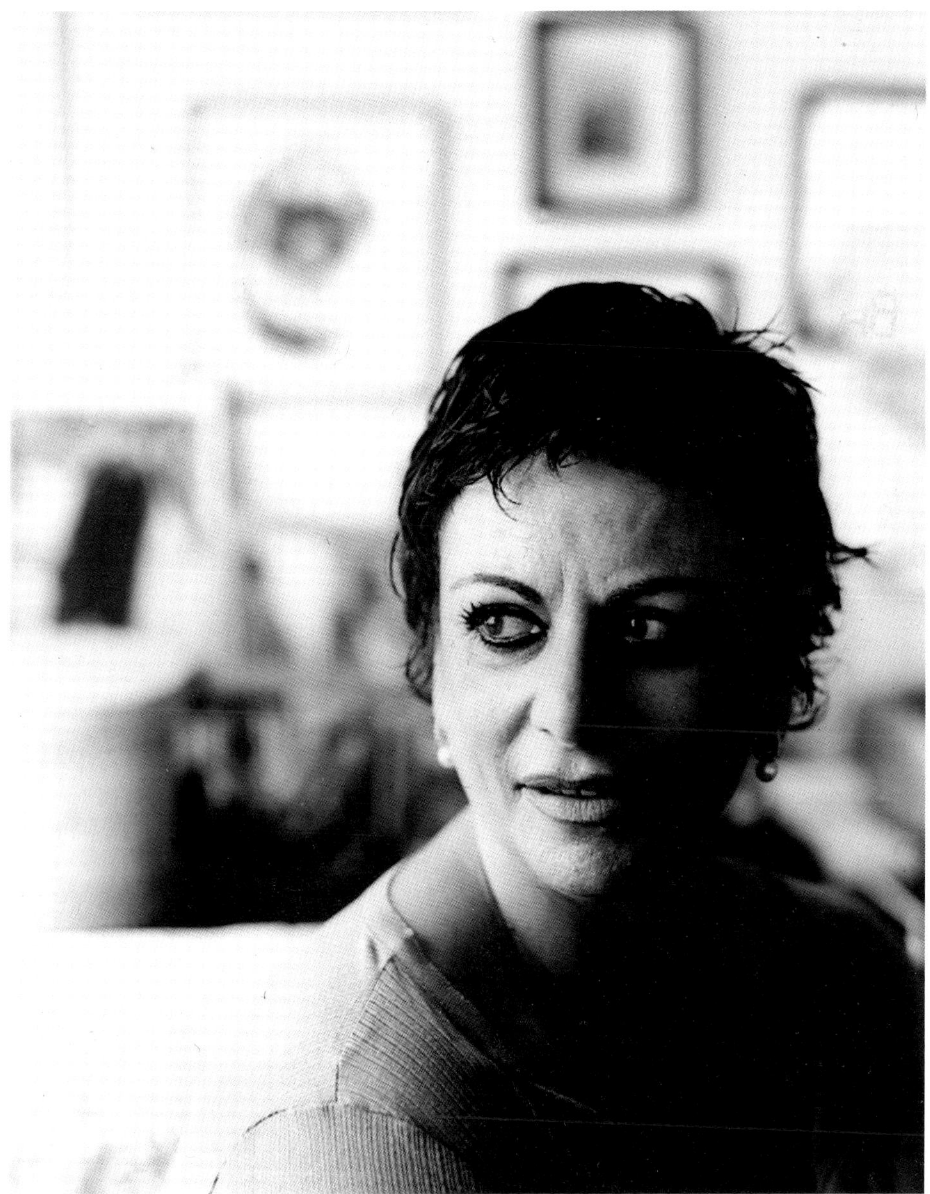

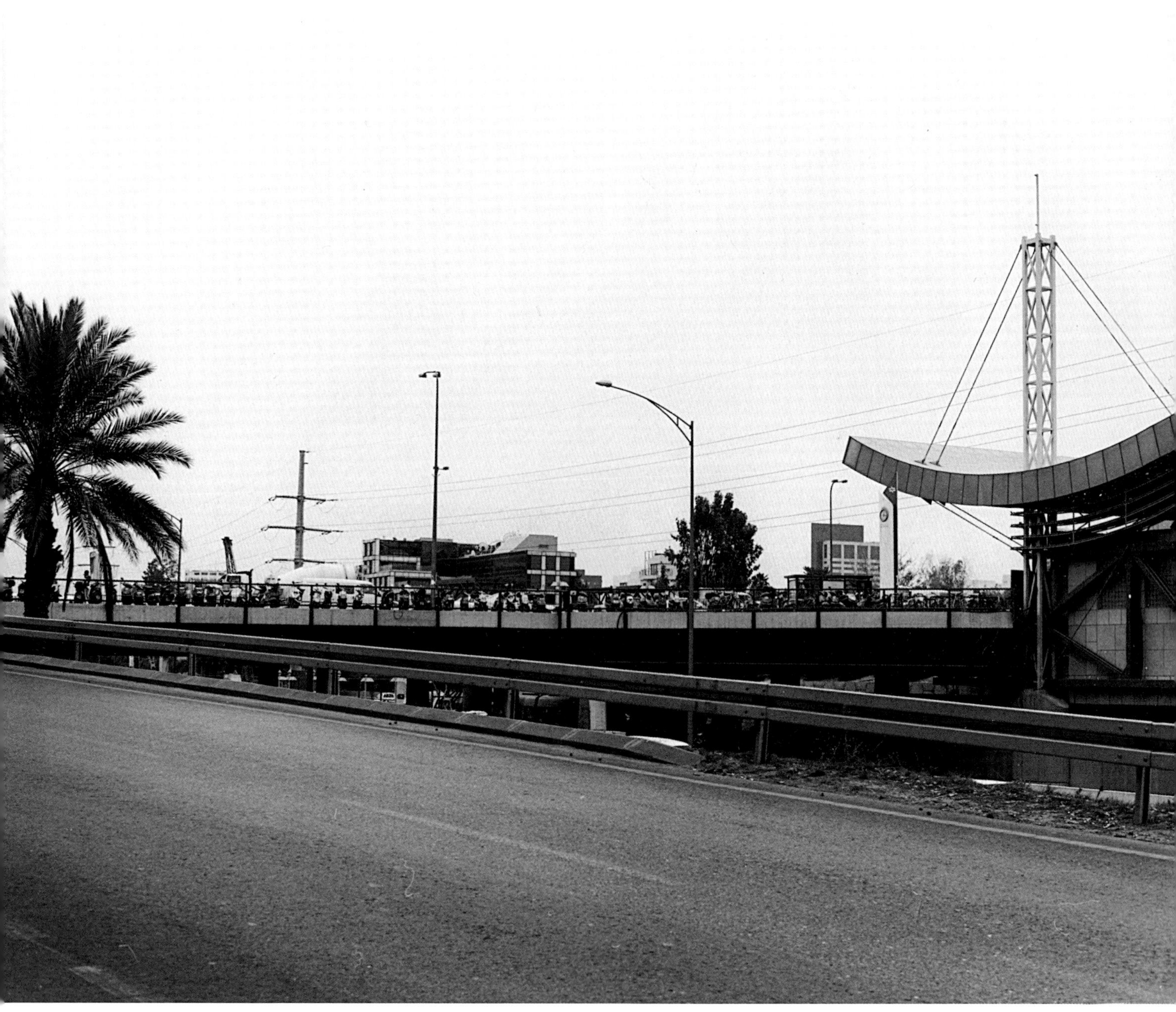

Tel Aviv cityscape,
Hashalom train station.

Rush hour at the
Haganah train station,
Tel Aviv.

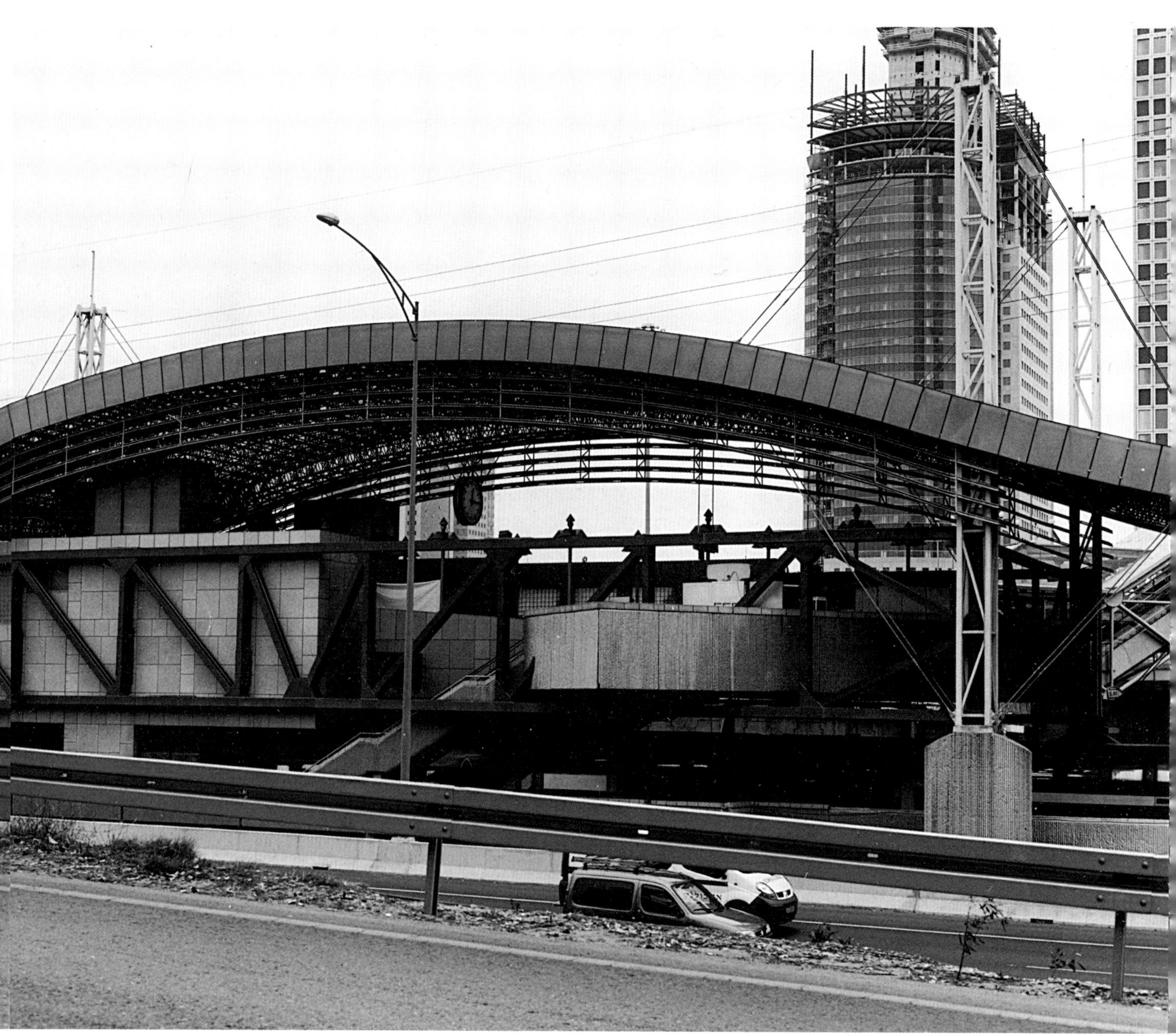

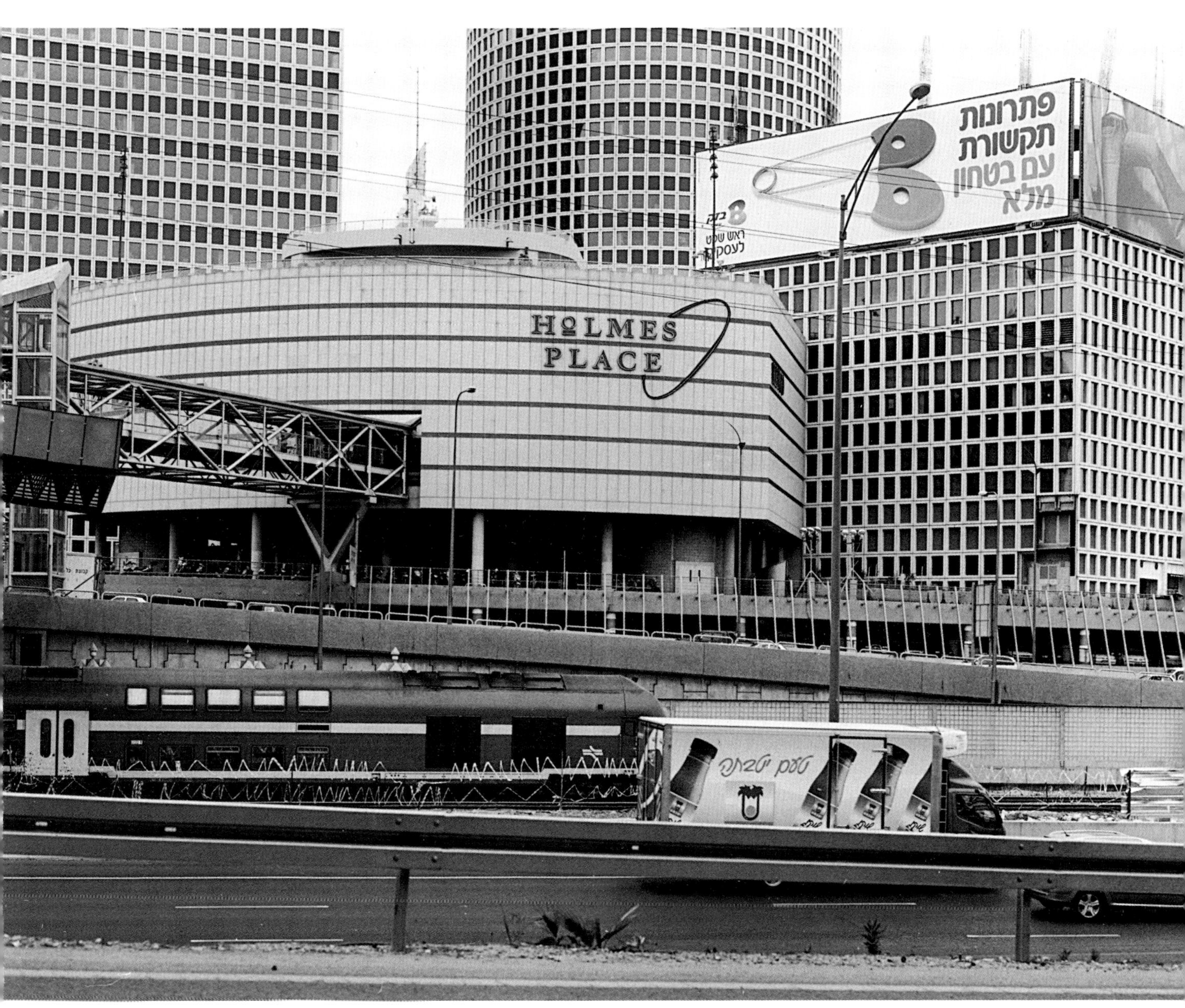

HOLMES
PLACE
פתרונות
תקשורת
עם בטחון
מלא
B
טעם יטעם

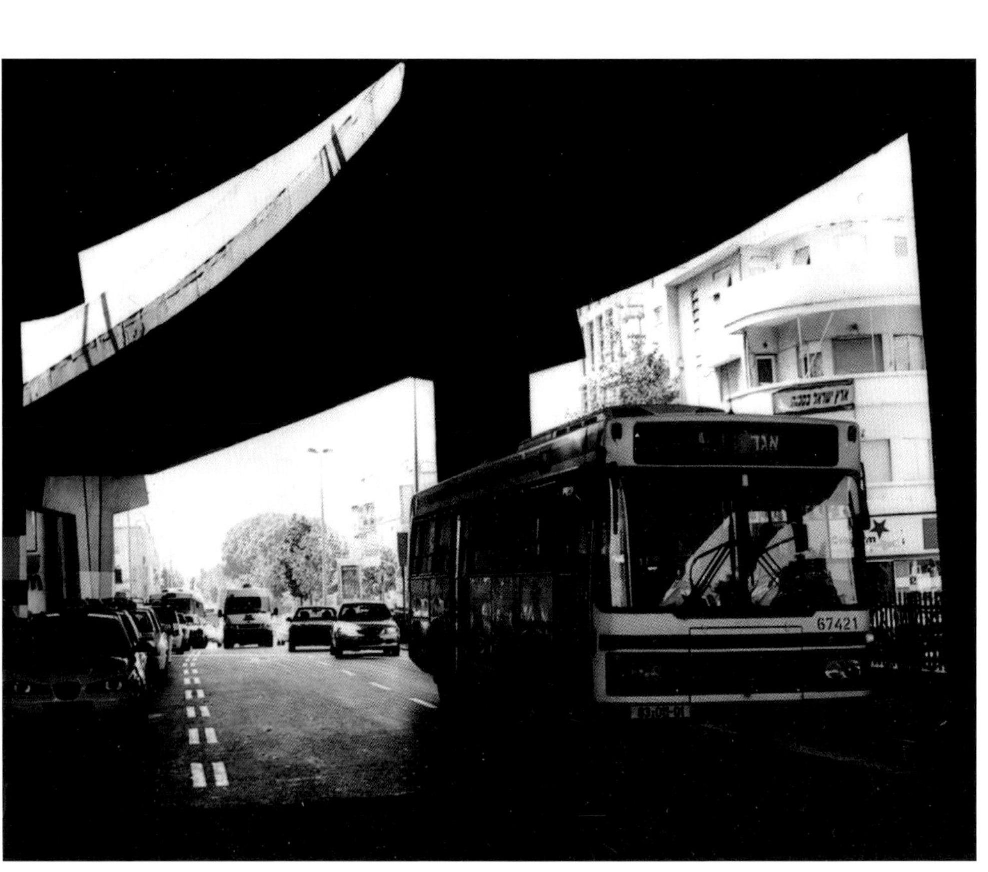
67421

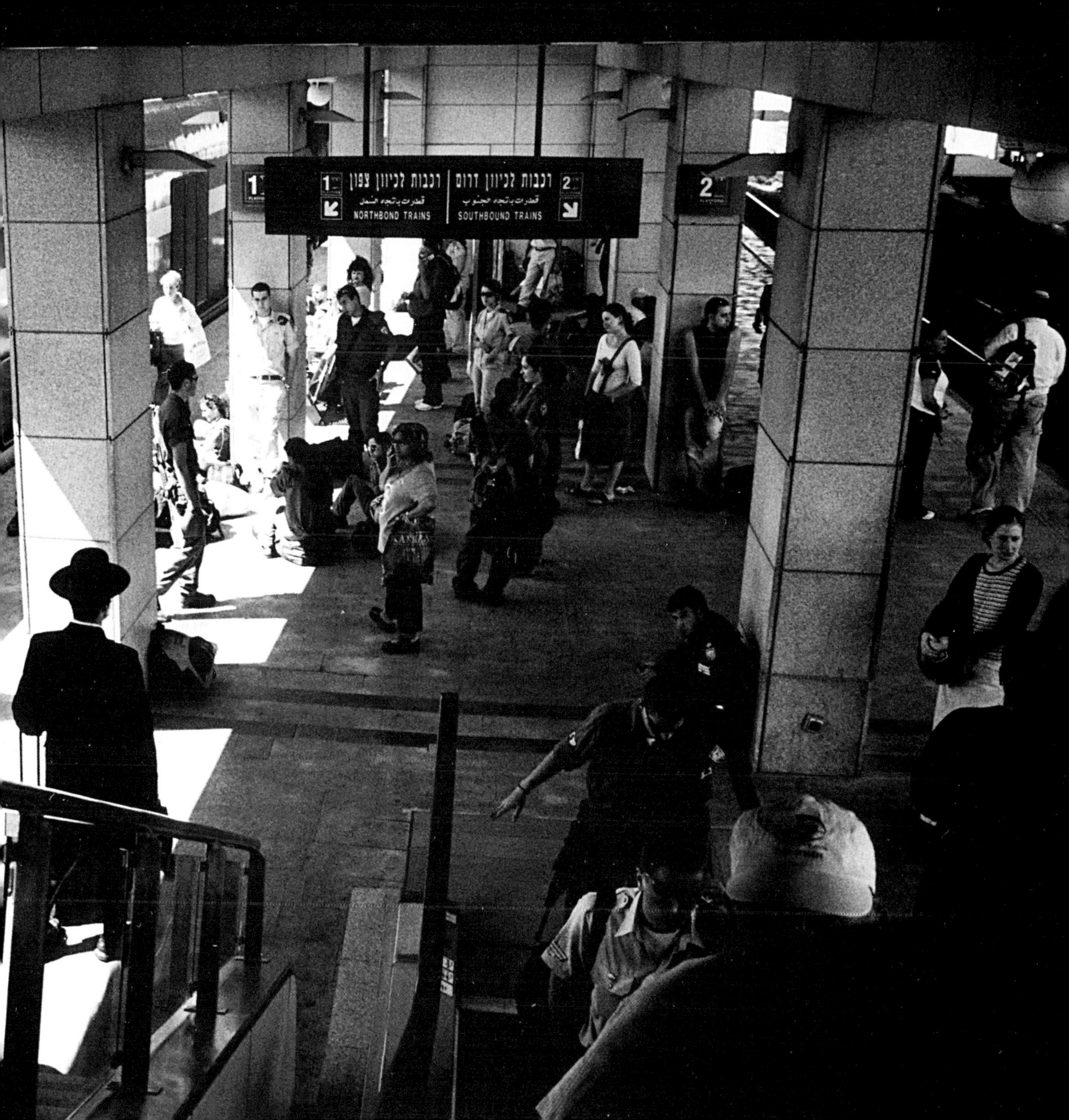
1 רכבות לכיוון צפון
قطارات باتجاه الشمال
NORTHBOND TRAINS
2 רכבות לכיוון דרום
قطارات باتجاه الجنوب
SOUTHBOUND TRAINS

My first trip to Israel was in July 2000, at the same time as the Camp David peace talks hosted by President Clinton with Arafat and Barak. There was an air of optimism in Jerusalem. Within two months all this optimism was shattered as the second *Intifada* (Palestinian uprising) erupted in late September.
I returned to Israel about one year later to live in what I had imagined would be a war zone. Instead, I was surprised by what I found: life continued and there was no visible war zone. The bombings also continued but we witnessed them at a distance, the same way everyone throughout the world saw them, on television. The ubiquitous security checks soon became normal to me, opening one's bag or purse was almost a reflex upon entering any shop or restaurant. It was not until many months later that I began to see and understand the fear underlying Israeli society because on the surface everything seemed normal. Most Israelis would not openly discuss the fear. Many had no choice but to ride buses or walk on the street and they somehow managed to put this fear in a place far in the back of their minds.
My friend Iris volunteered her time twice a week answering phones at a trauma hotline in Tel Aviv. She said that she never imagined that there were so many people who were terribly traumatized by the bombings and learned that many of them would no longer leave their homes, or were terrified to walk on the streets after witnessing a bombing.

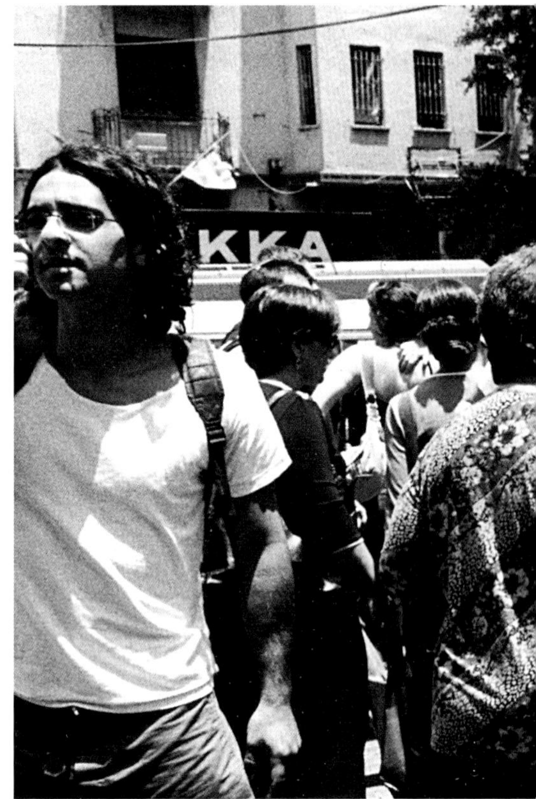

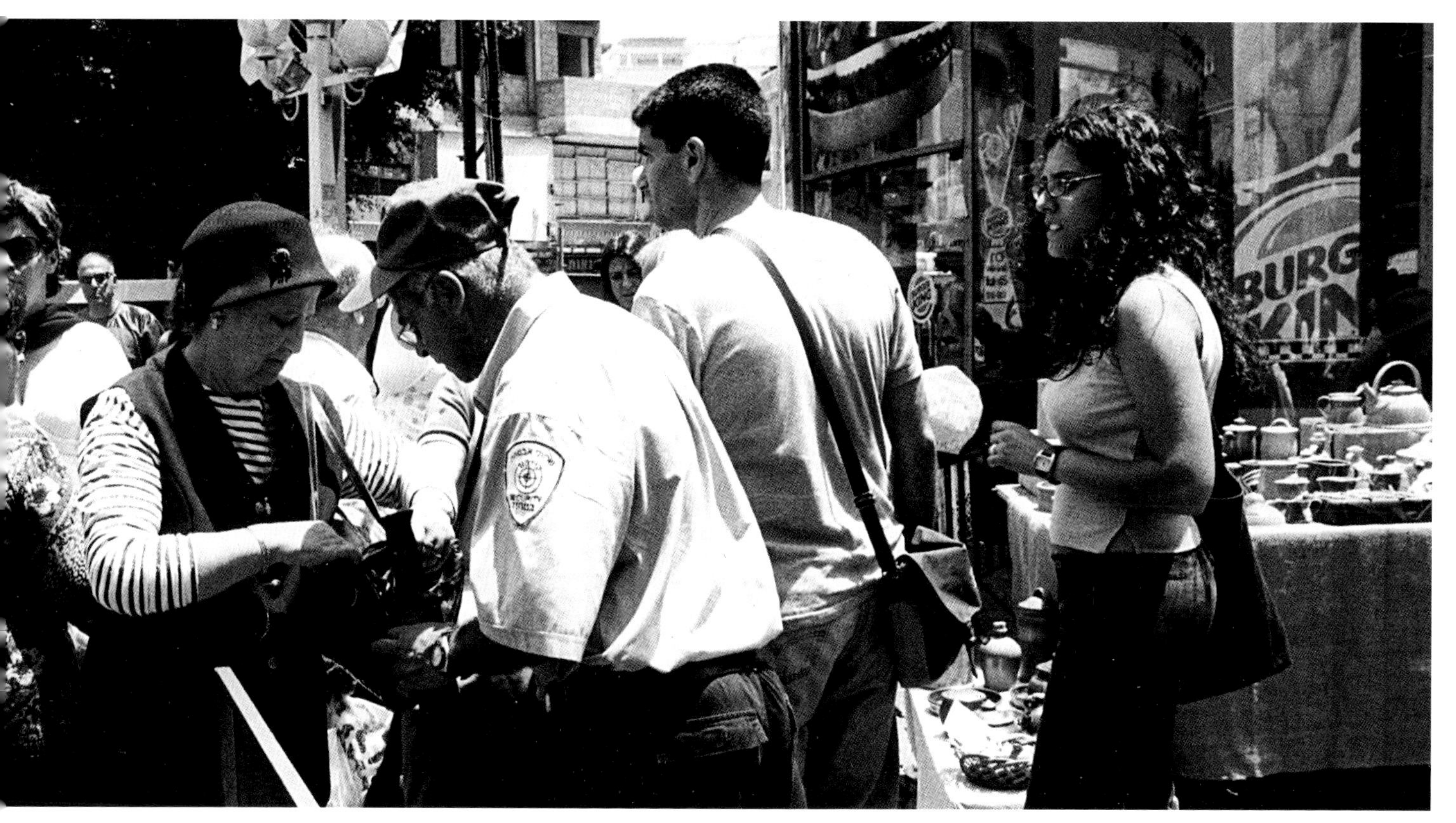

Women at bus stop,
Rehovot.

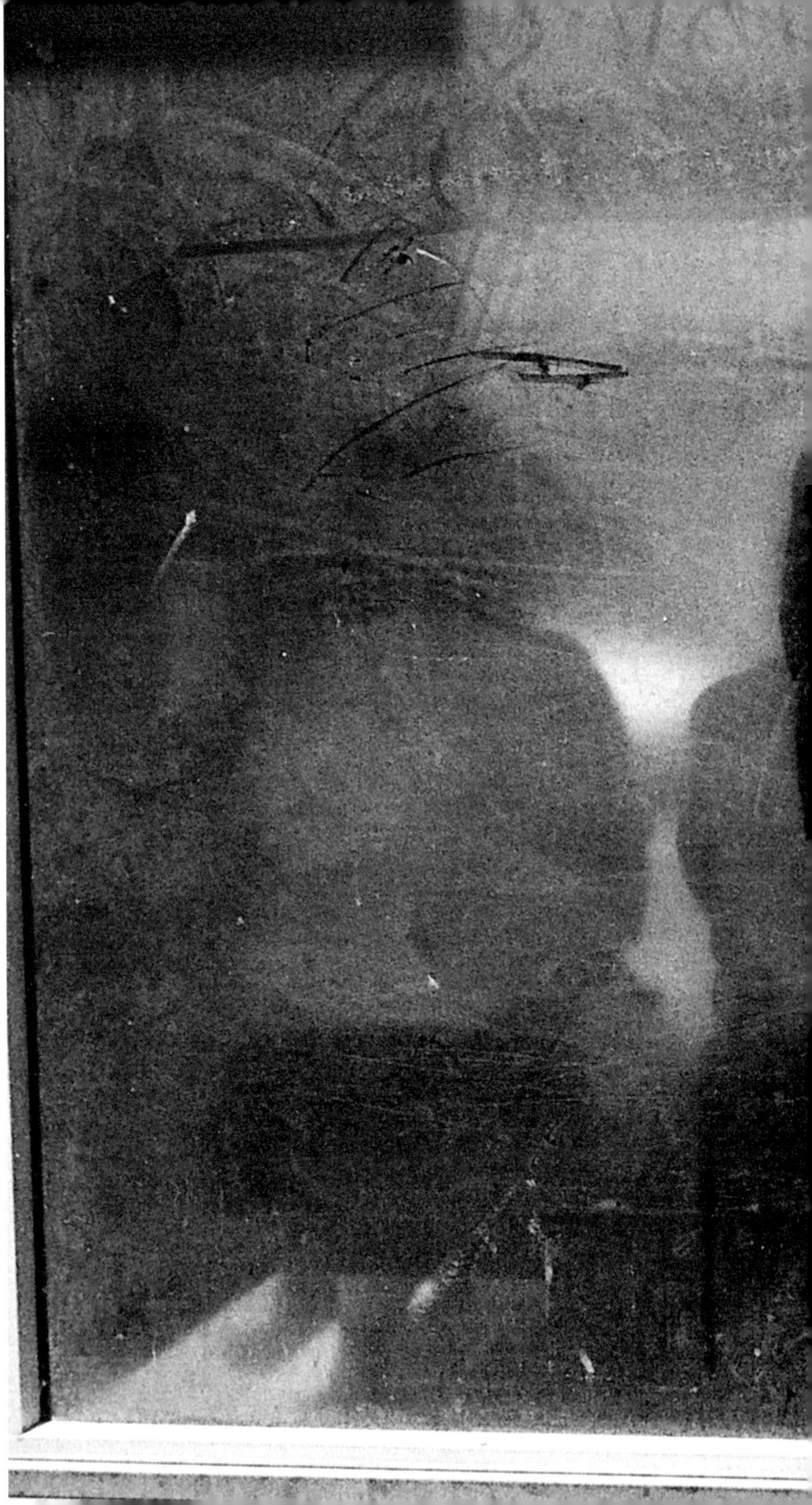

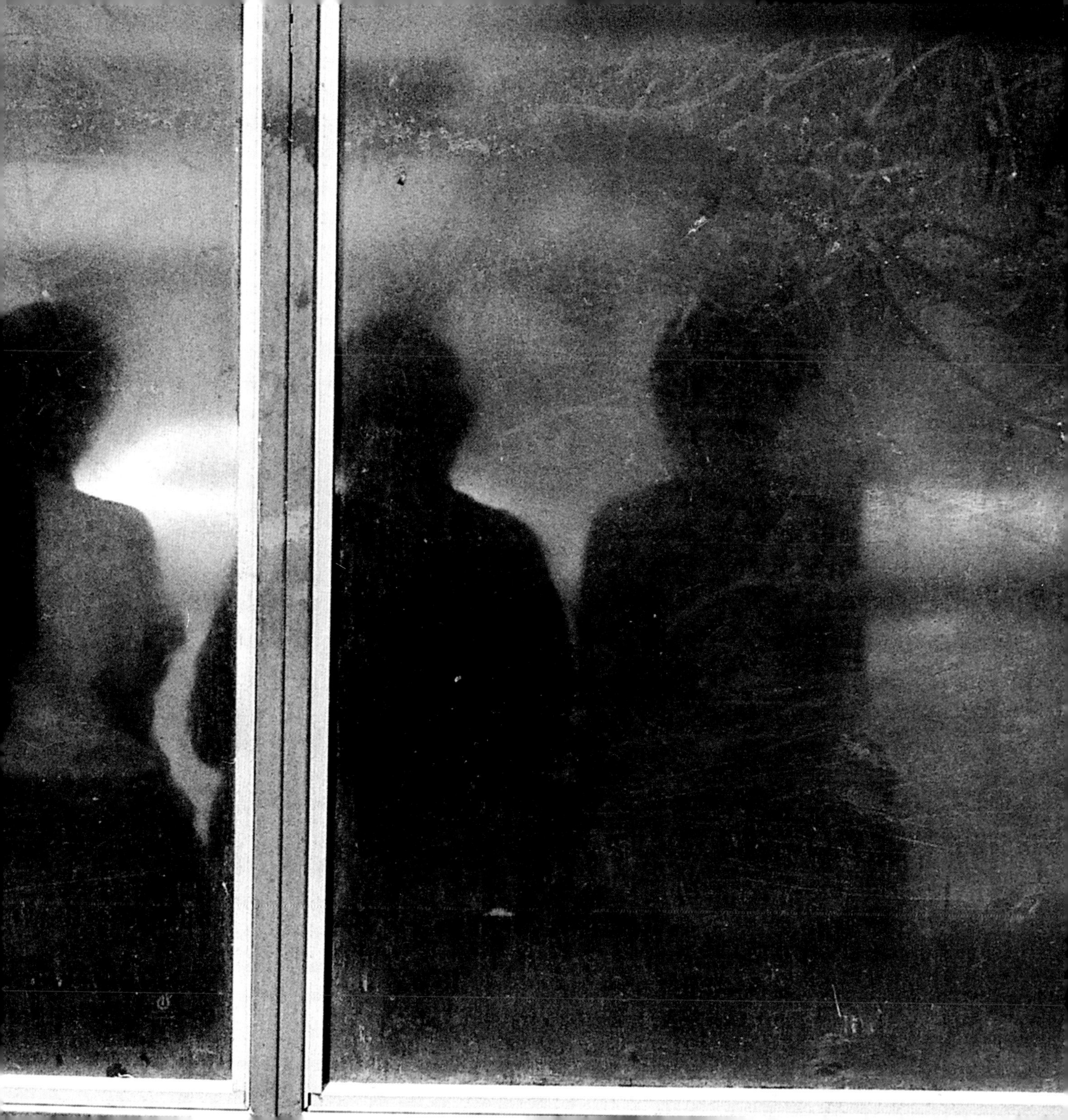

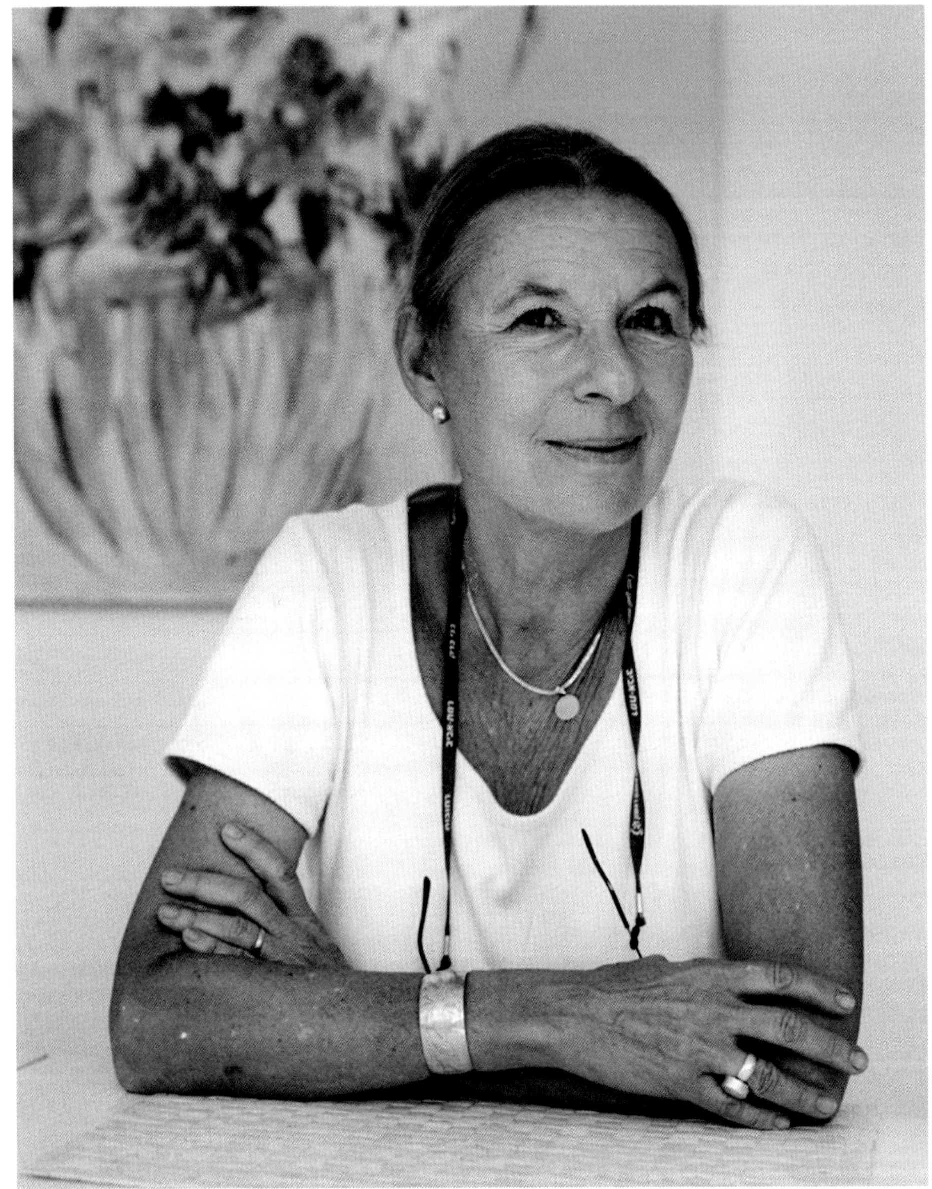

"I fear that the moderate people on both
sides will give up hope and leave
the country, leaving the field open to
the extremists."

Ricki, Rehovot
Jewish Israeli.

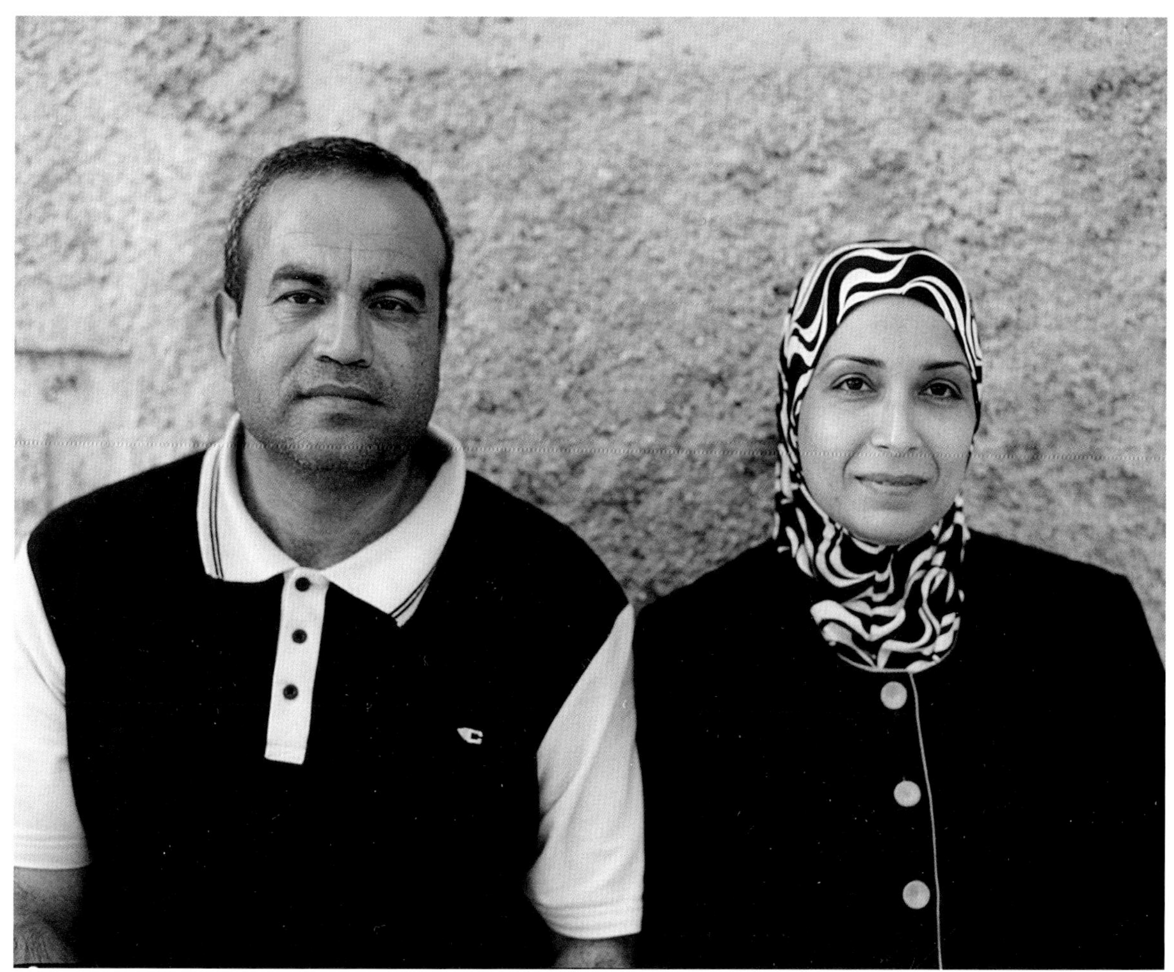

"My hope is for peace in the world and
especially with our neighboring countries."

"I'm afraid of how the situation we live
in will affect my children."

Ziad & Salam, Lod
Palestinian Israelis.

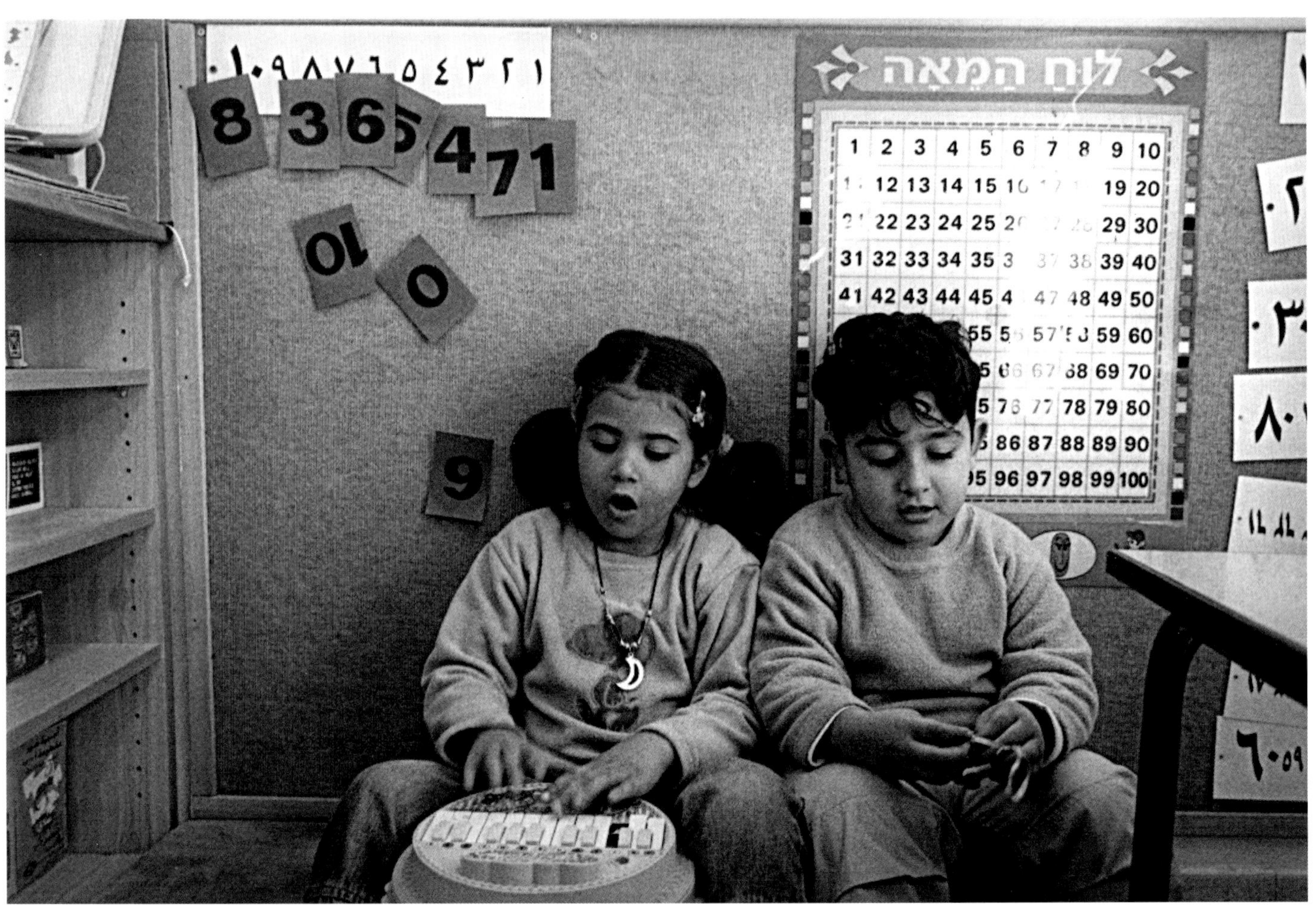

לוח המאה
1 2 3 4 5 6 7 8 9 10
11 12 13 14 15 16 17 18 19 20
21 22 23 24 25 26 27 28 29 30
31 32 33 34 35 36 37 38 39 40
41 42 43 44 45 46 47 48 49 50
51 52 53 54 55 56 57 58 59 60
61 62 63 64 65 66 67 68 69 70
71 72 73 74 75 76 77 78 79 80
81 82 83 84 85 86 87 88 89 90
91 92 93 94 95 96 97 98 99 100

Christian, Jewish and
Muslim children play
together at the
kindergarten of Neve
Shalom - Wahat al
Salam meaning "Oasis
of Peace". Neve
Shalom is a village in
Israel established
jointly by Israeli
Palestinians and Jews
that is engaged in
educational work for
peace, equality and
understanding between
peoples.

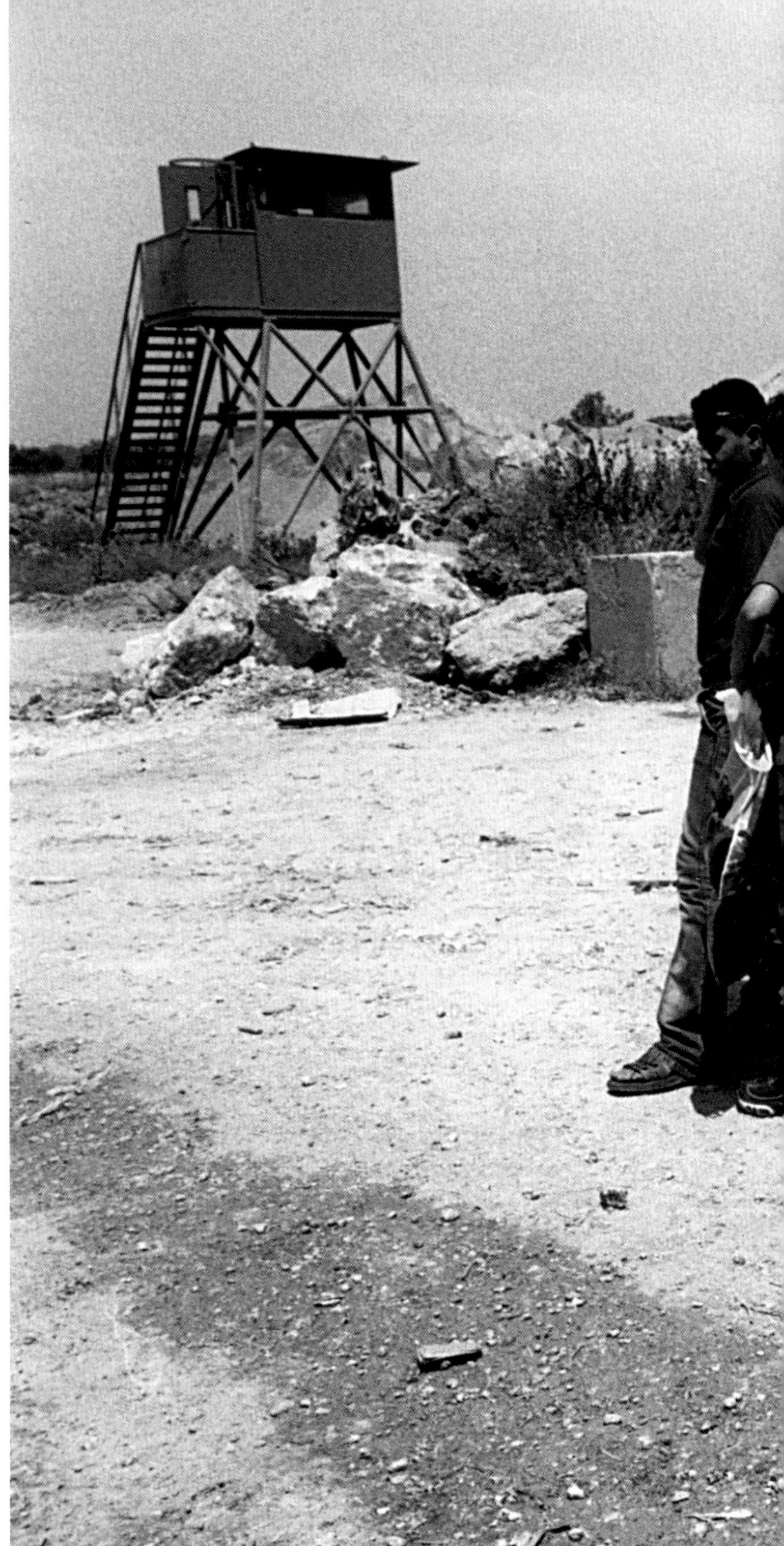

The young Palestinian journalists from *Windows* magazine (a Hebrew–Arabic magazine written by Israeli and Palestinian youth) wait at the Tulkarem checkpoint to enter Israel and participate in a dialogue with their Israeli counterparts in Tel Aviv.

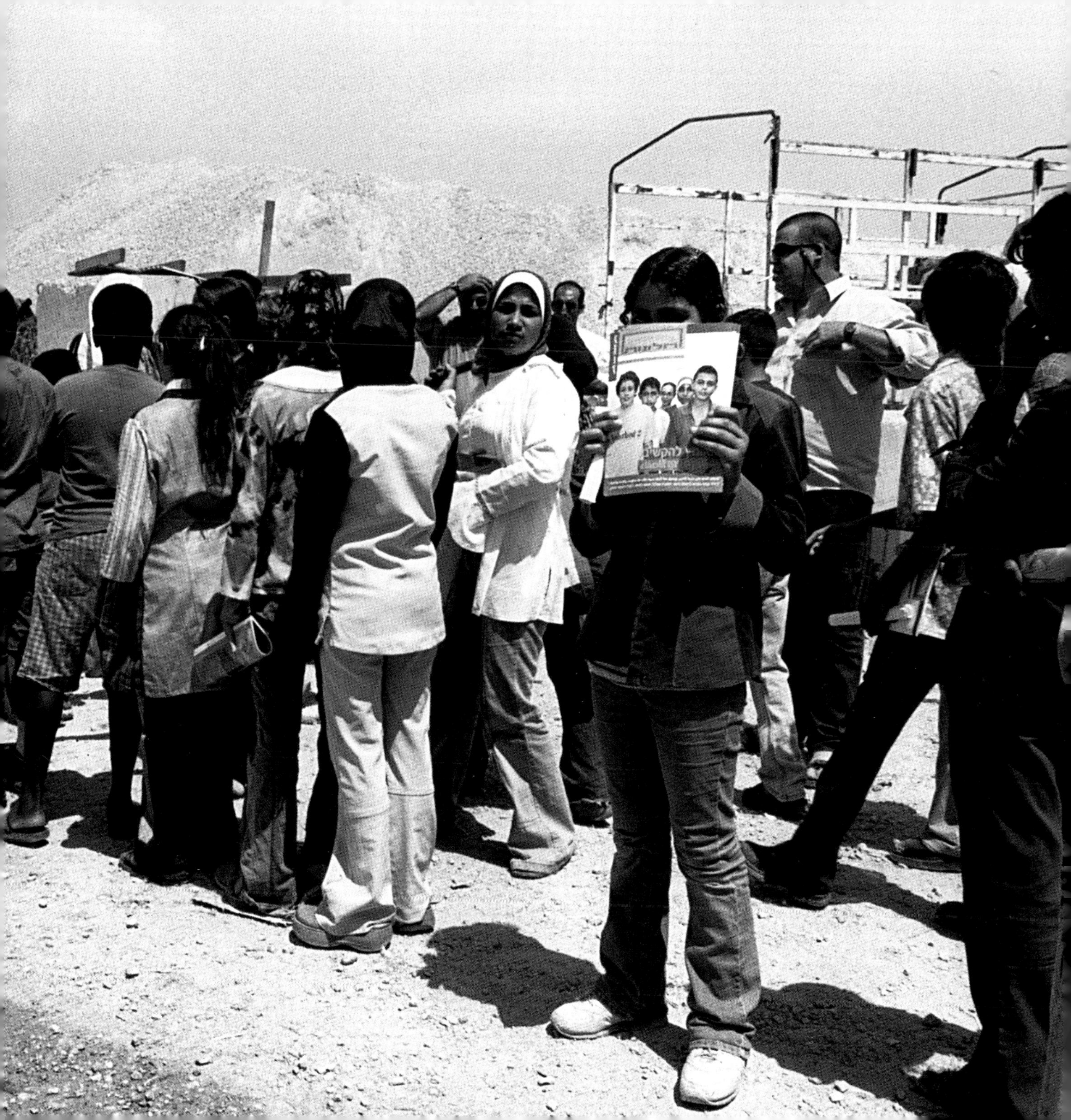

Israeli and Palestinian
children from *Windows*
share their lunch
together on the beach
of Tel Aviv.

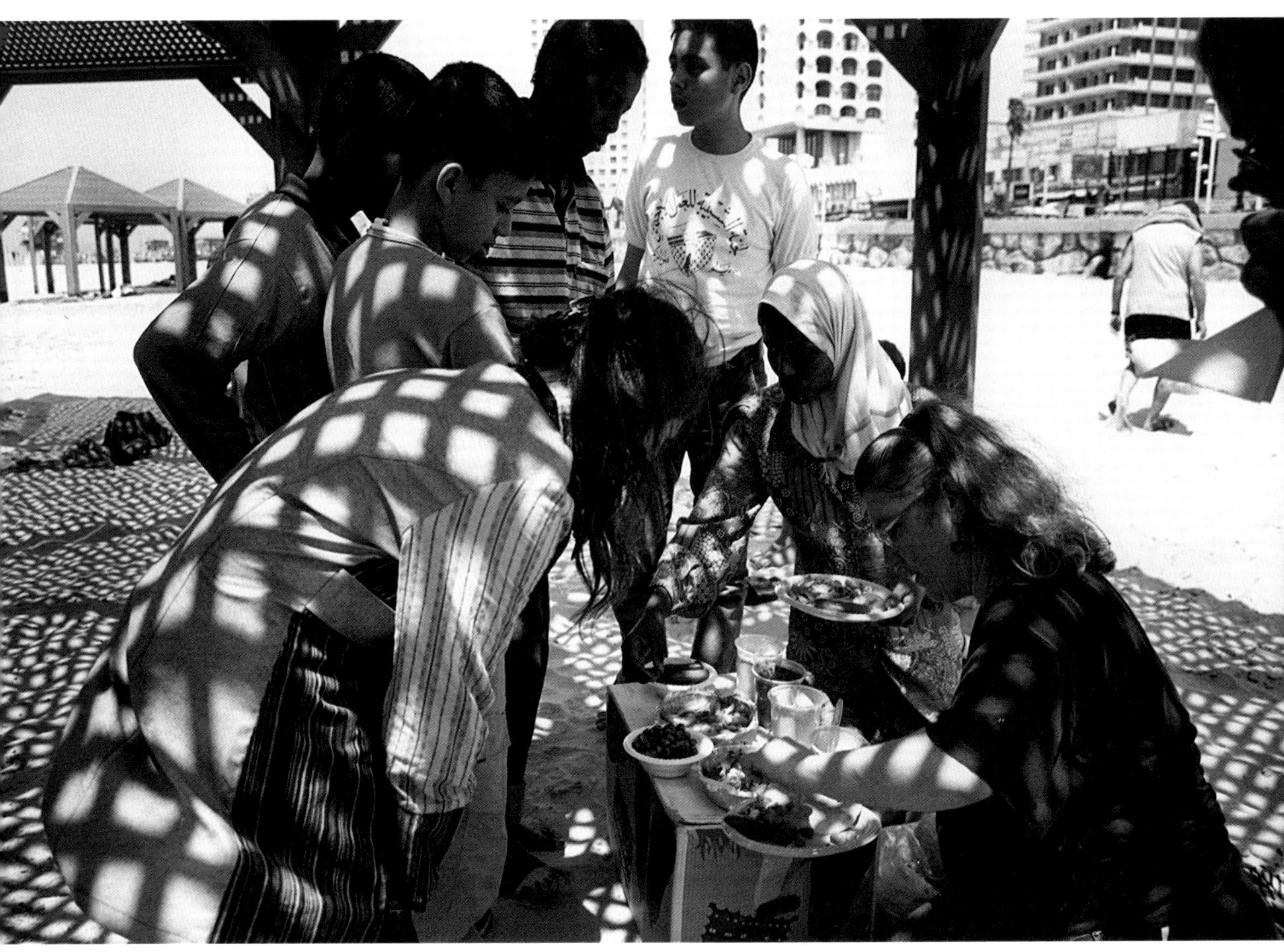

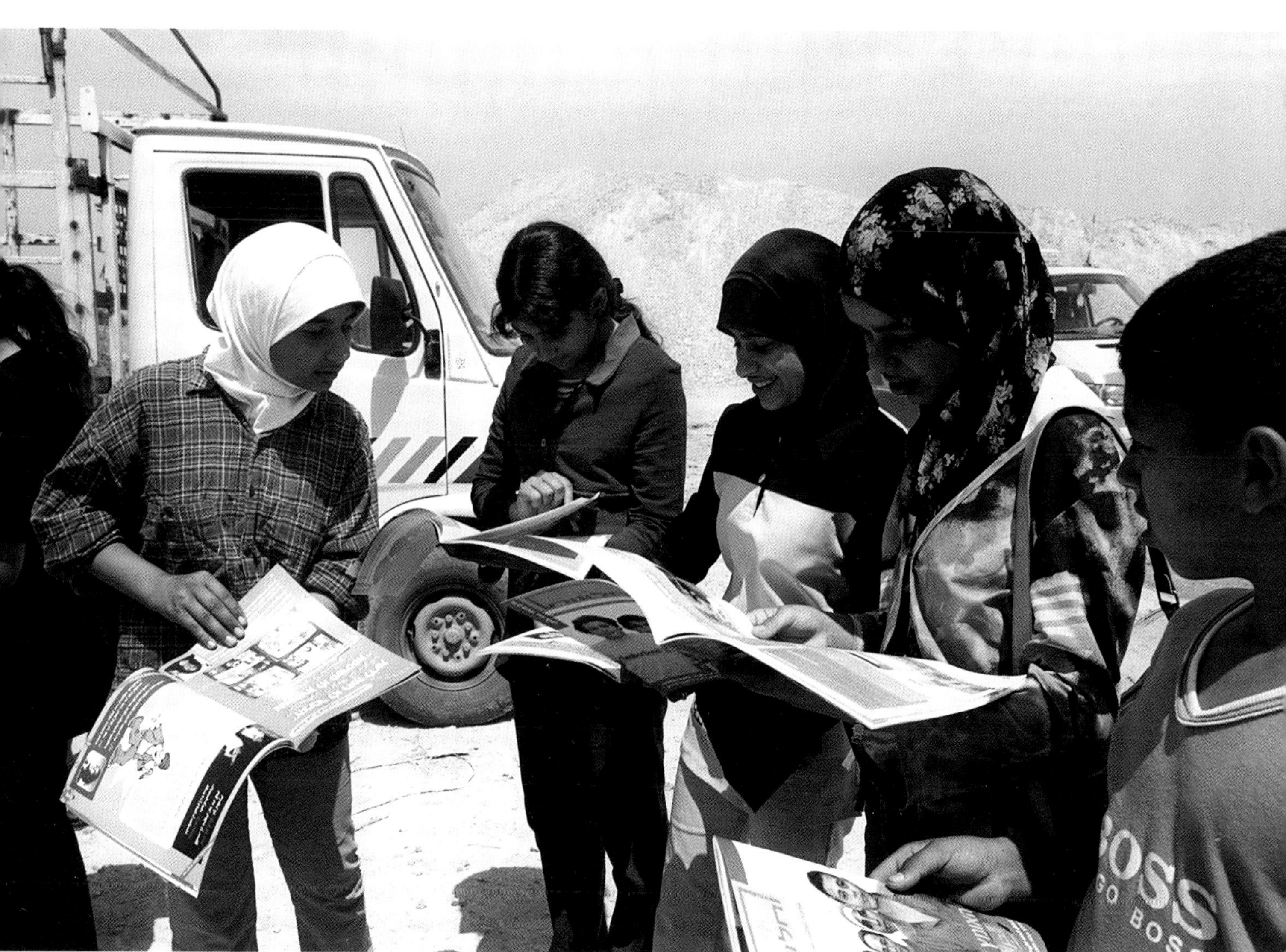

Palestinian girls get their first look at the articles they have written in *Windows* magazine.

For the Palestinian
children to enter Israel
it is necessary to
request permits from
the Israeli army well
in advance of the visit.
In the rare case that a
permit is obtained, it is
only valid from dawn
to dusk. After the day
in Tel Aviv, the children
must go through this
checkpoint on the
outskirts of Tulkarem
before sunset.

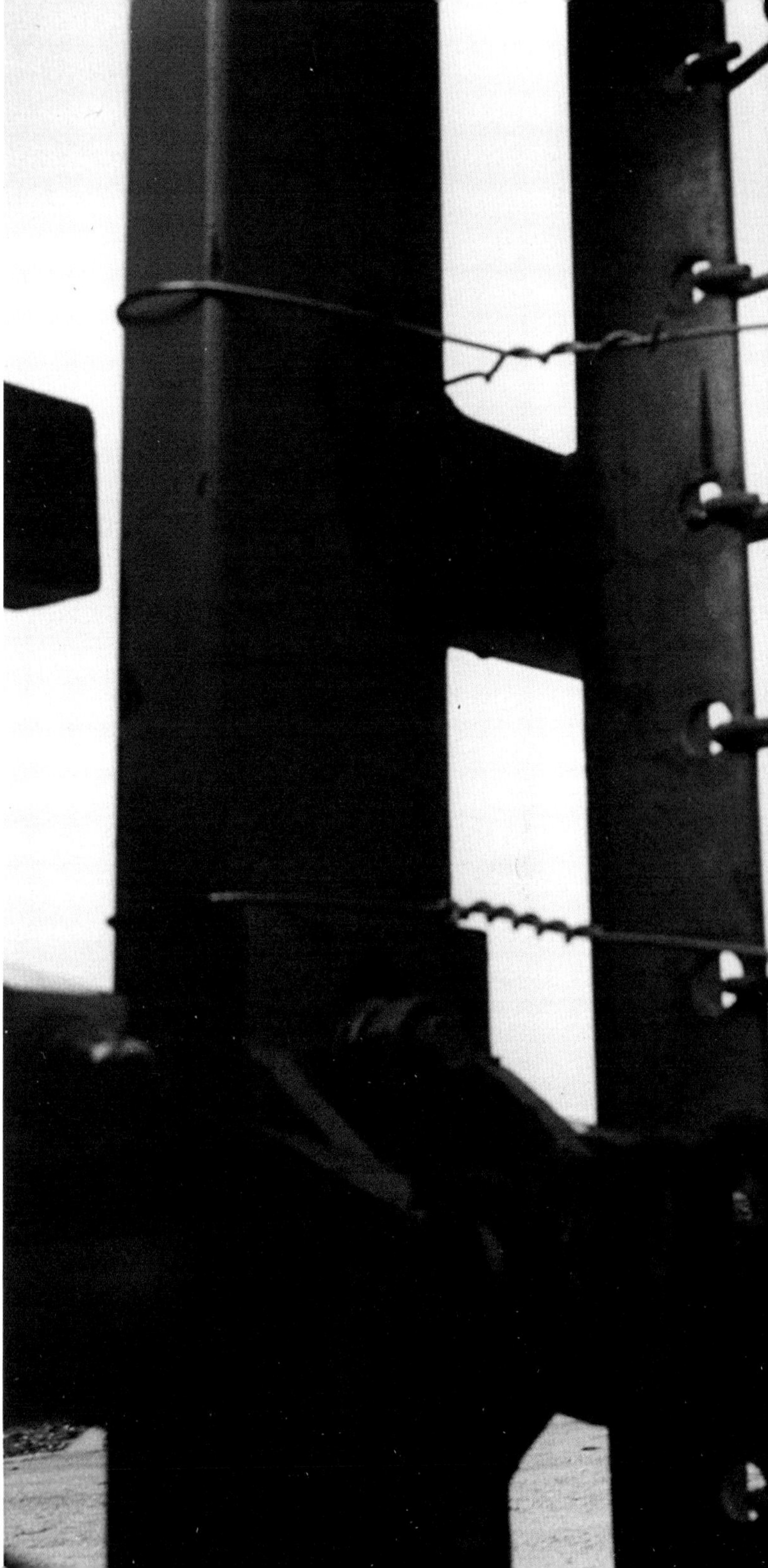

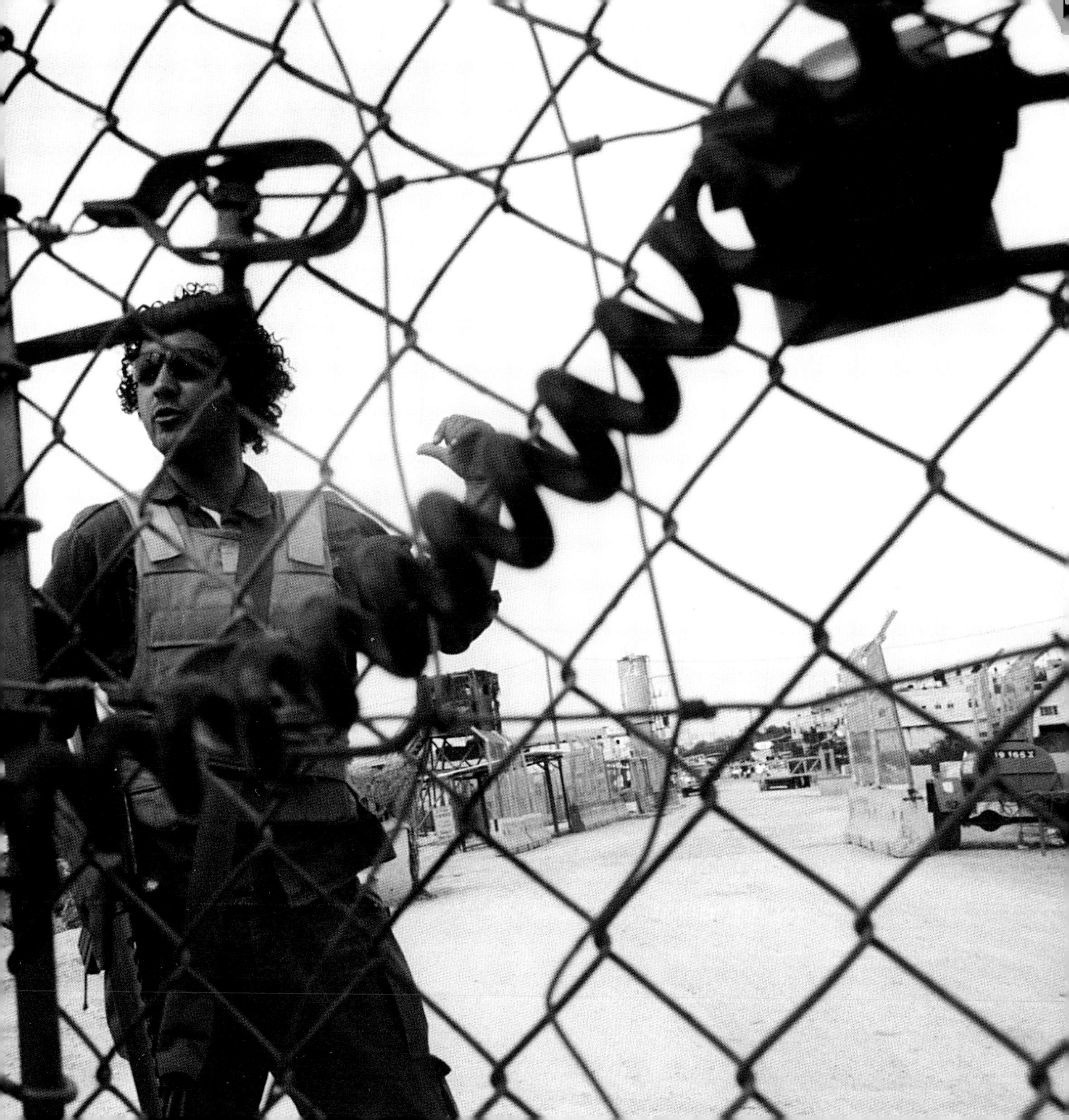

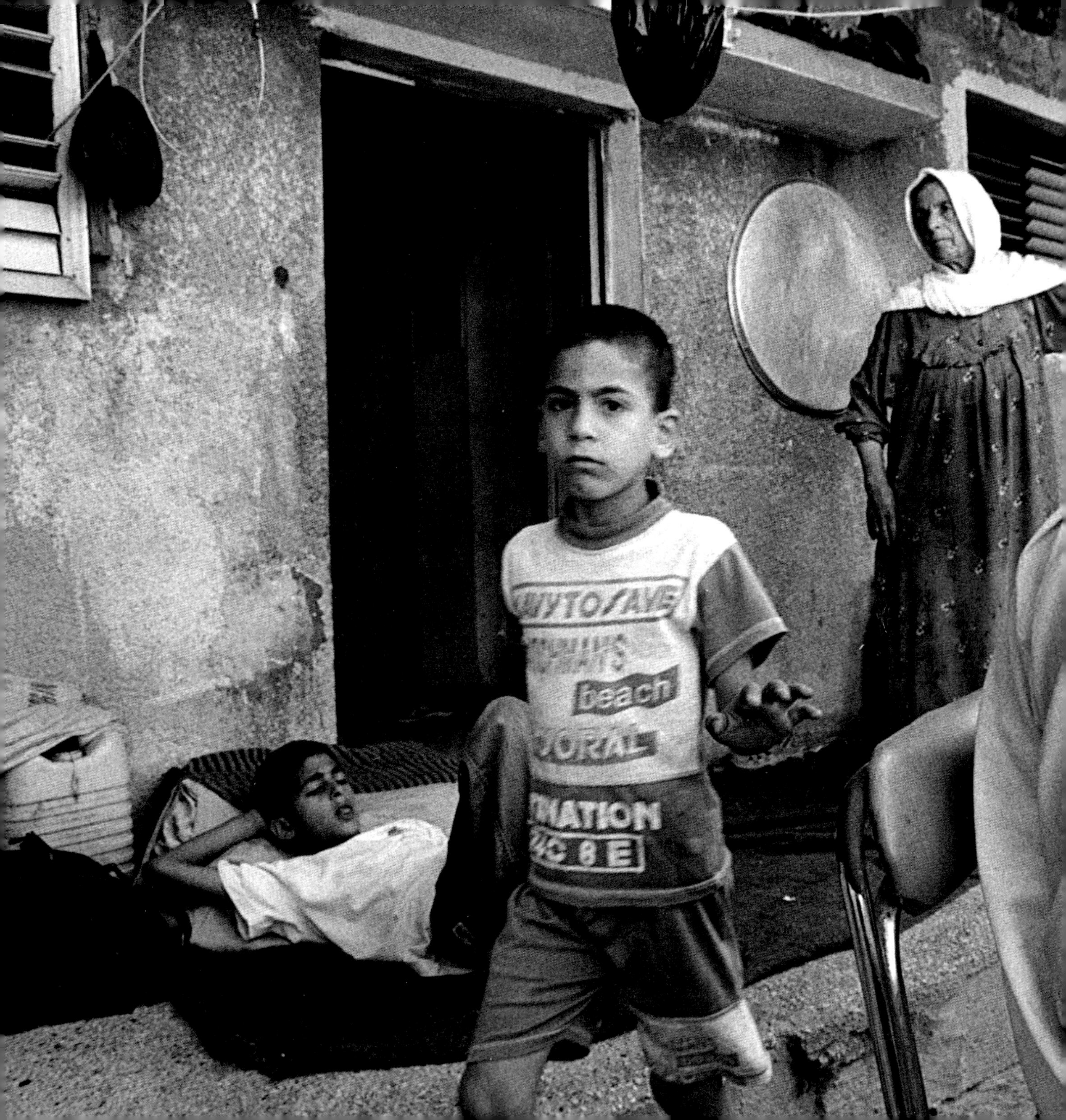
BUYTOSAVE
beach
MATION
BE

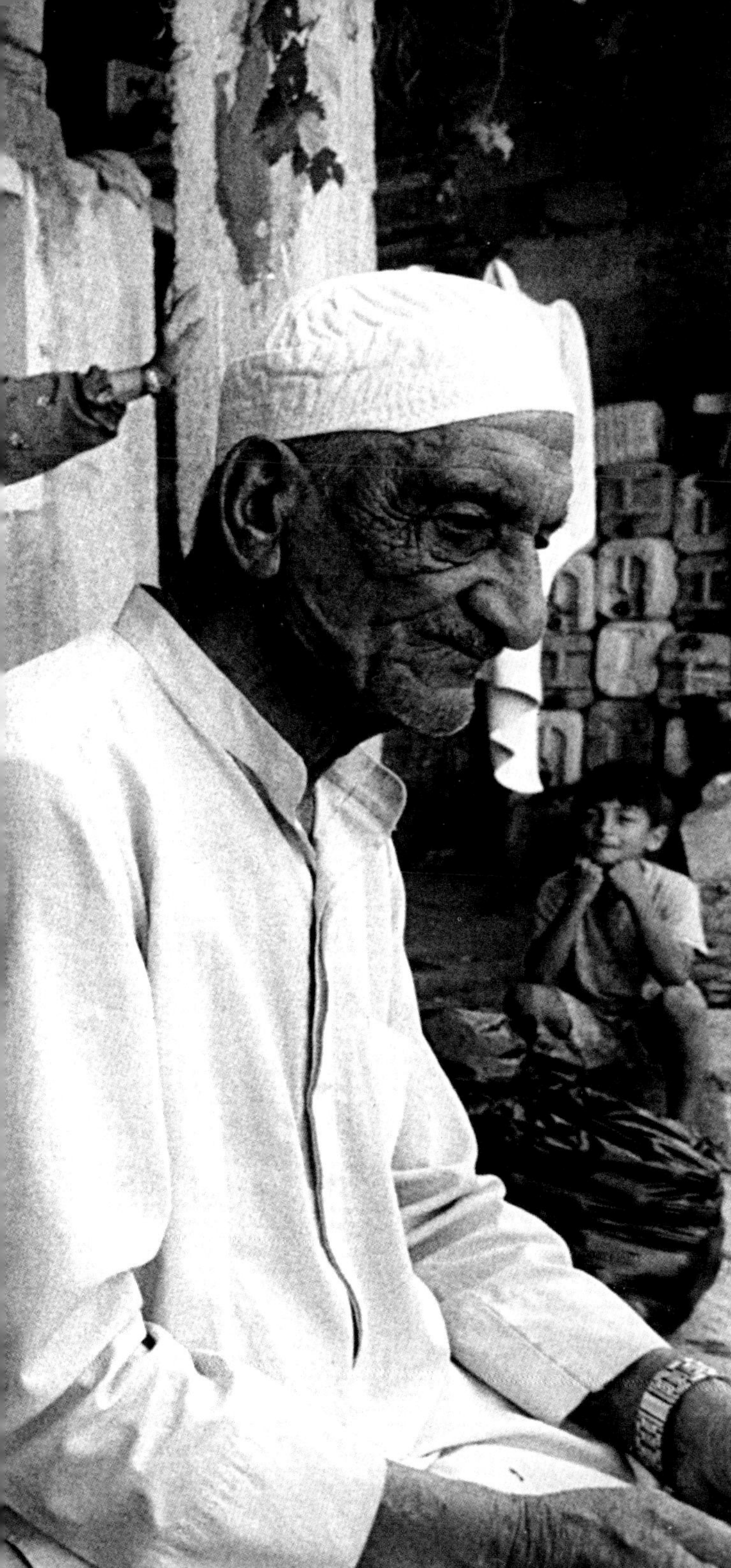

The Tanji family at their modest home in the Tulkarem refugee camp that lies just outside the city of Tulkarem (northern West Bank) and houses approximately 20,000 refugees.

The UN agency UNRWA (United Nations Relief and
Works Agency) as of March 2005 records more than
4 million registered Palestinian refugees in Jordan,
Lebanon, Syria, the West Bank and the Gaza Strip.
Of the 4 million refugees, 1,259,813 are living in the
59 officially recognized Palestinian refugee camps in
the above-mentioned countries or territories.[2]

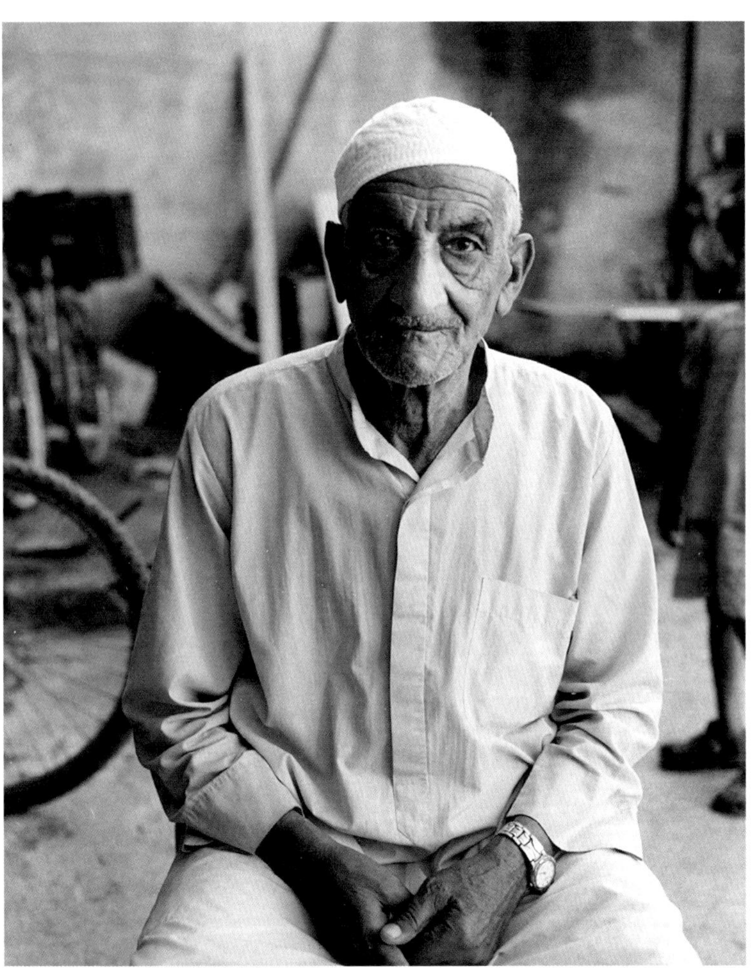

Ramzi, 15 years old,
was born in the
Tulkarem camp and has
lived there his entire
childhood.

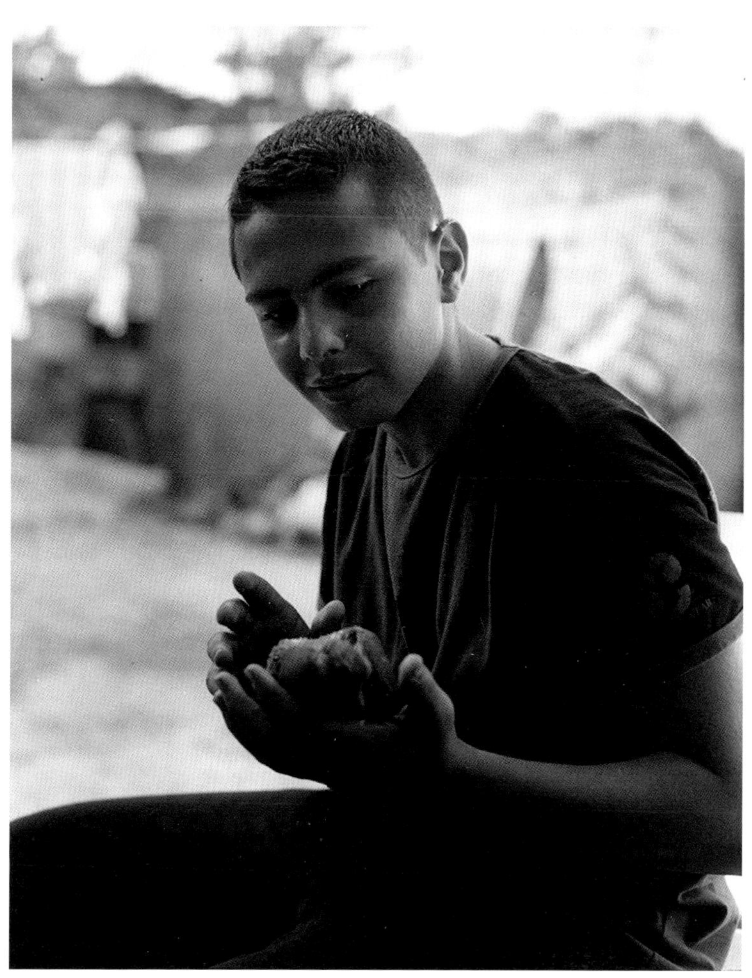

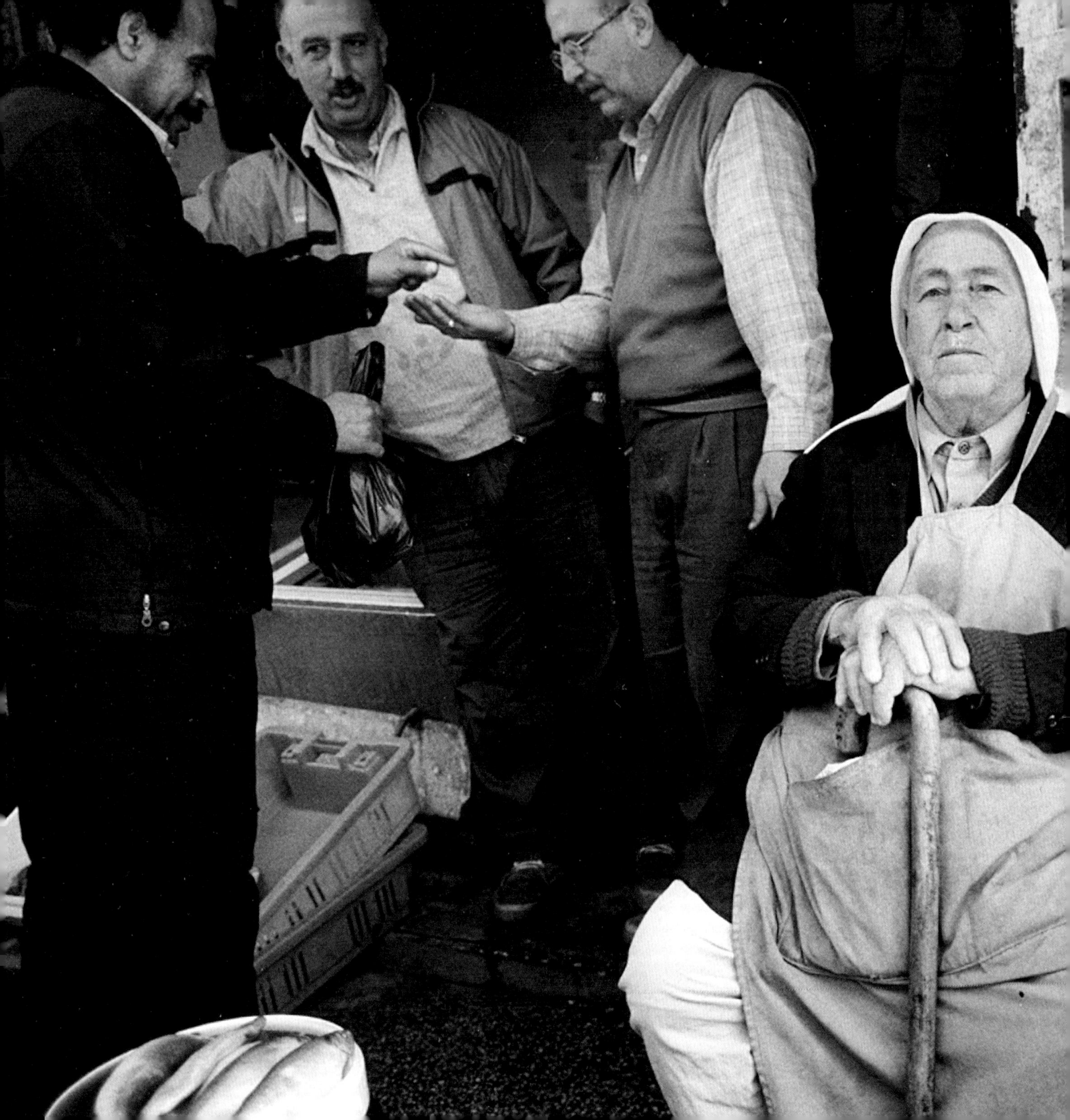

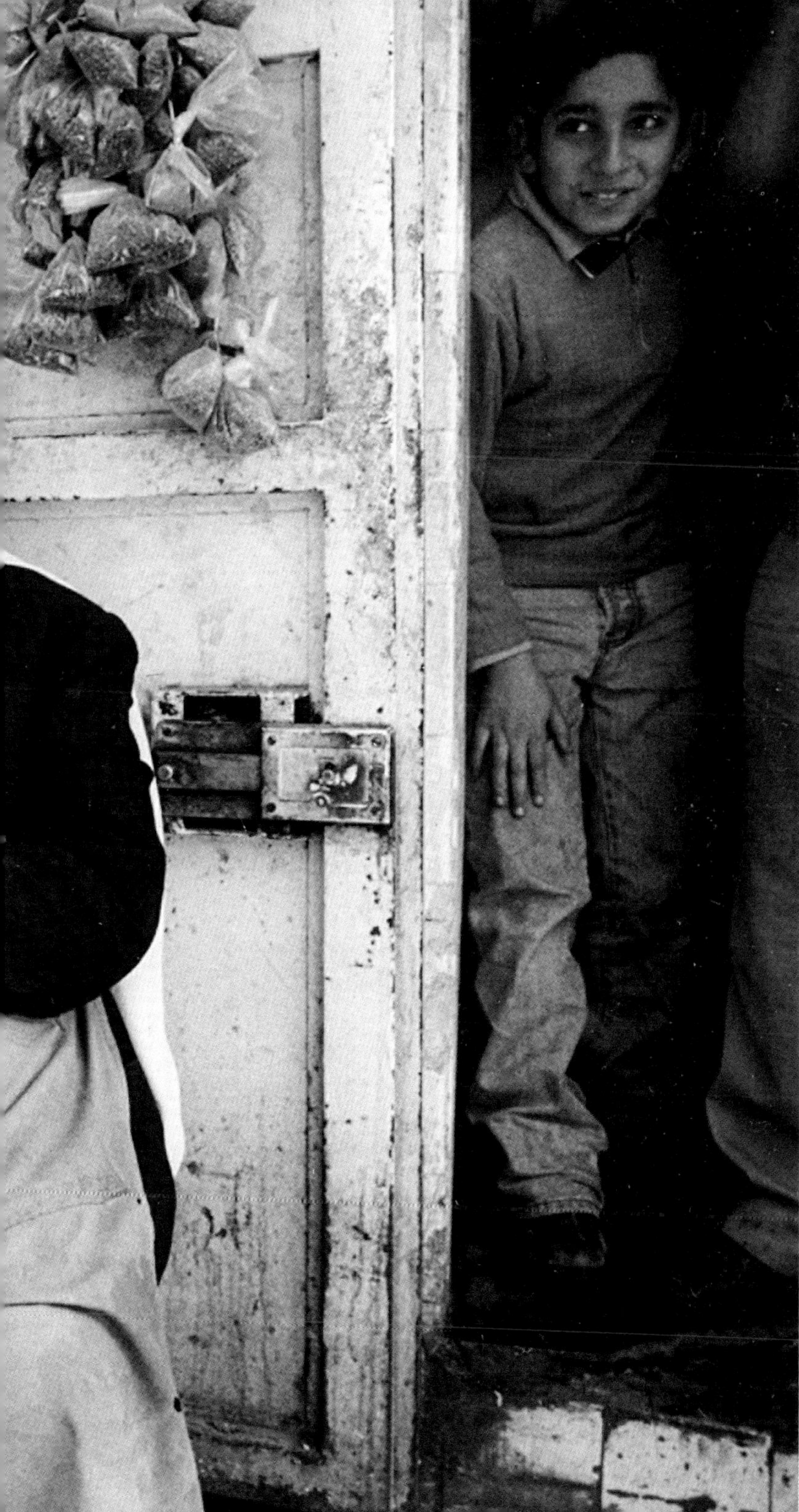

People shopping
for fish along the street
market of Tulkarem,
West Bank.

The view over the Nur
Shams refugee camp,
8,500 residents, the
smaller of the two
camps located just
outside of Tulkarem,
the West Bank.

UNRWA figures from March 2005 show 181,241 registered Palestinian refugees living in refugee camps in the West Bank and 471,555 living in refugee camps in the Gaza Strip.[3]

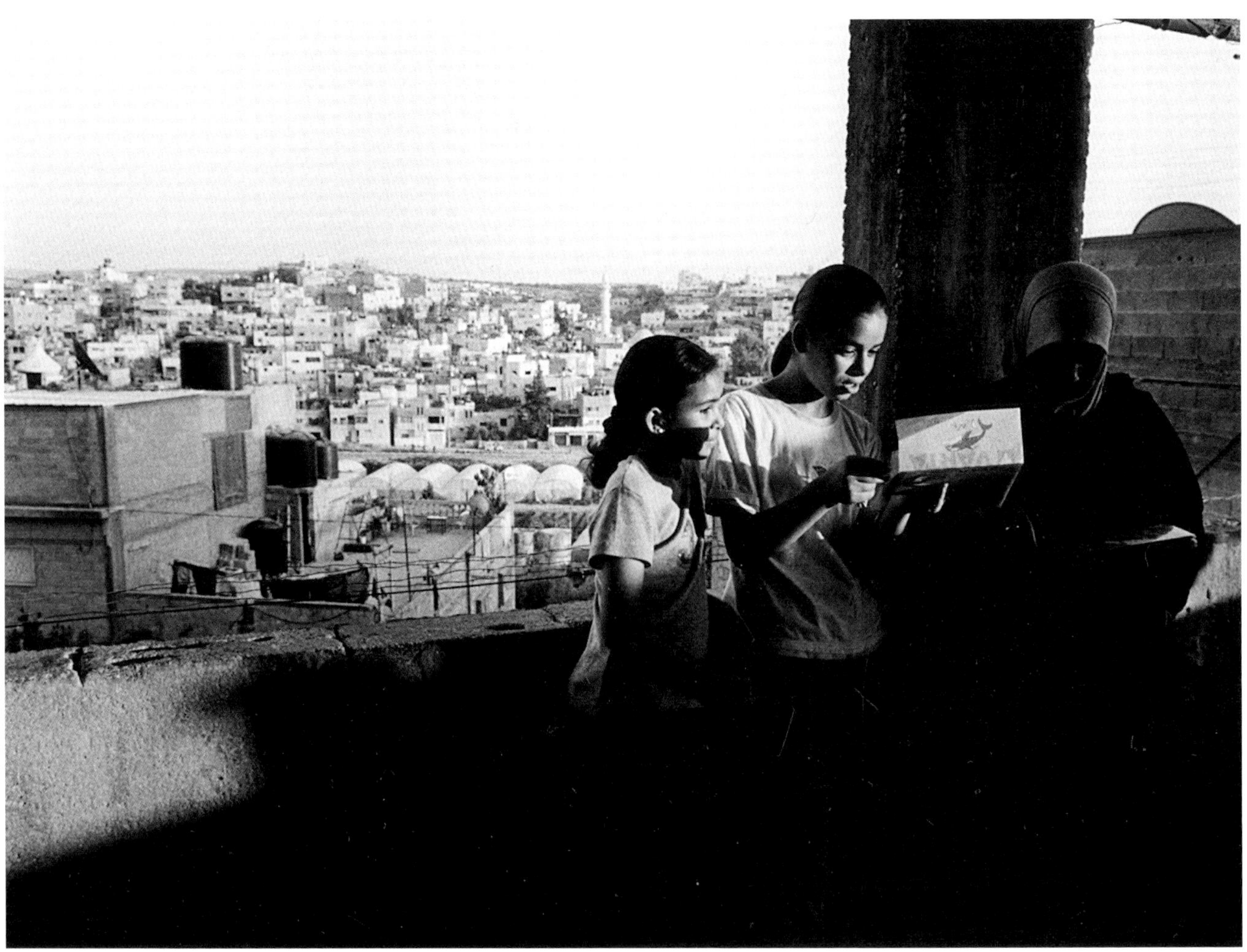

Traveling by car to
the rural areas of the
Tulkarem district.

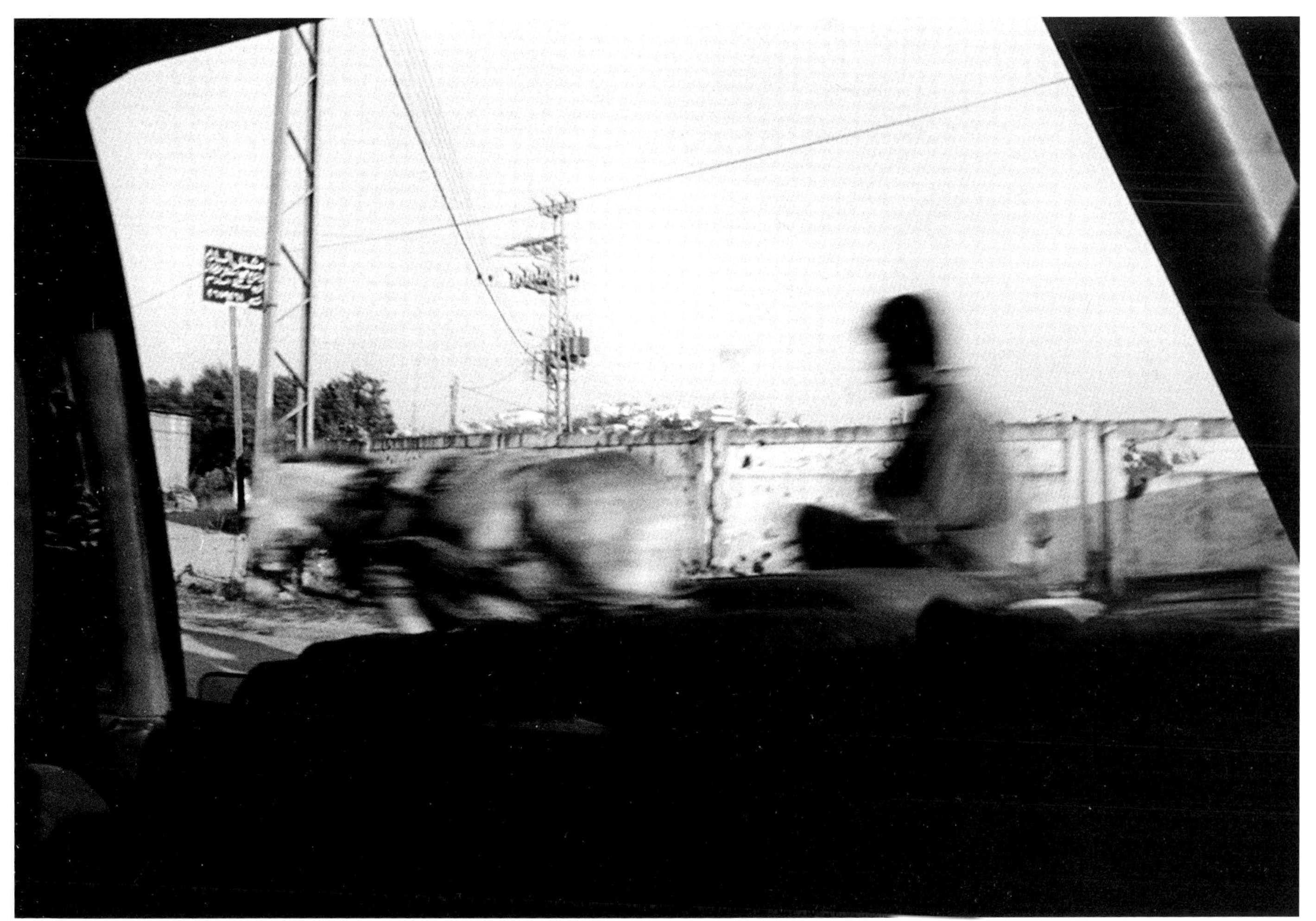

Wall murals in the
village of Ilar
celebrating the return
of those who have
made the pilgrimage
to Mecca.

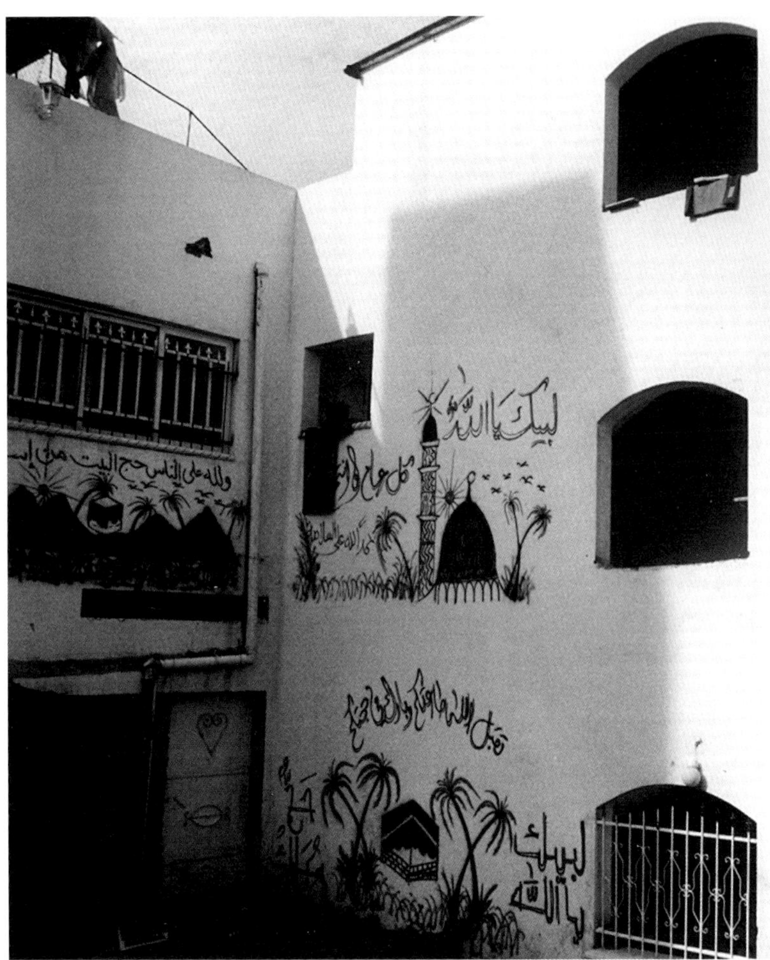
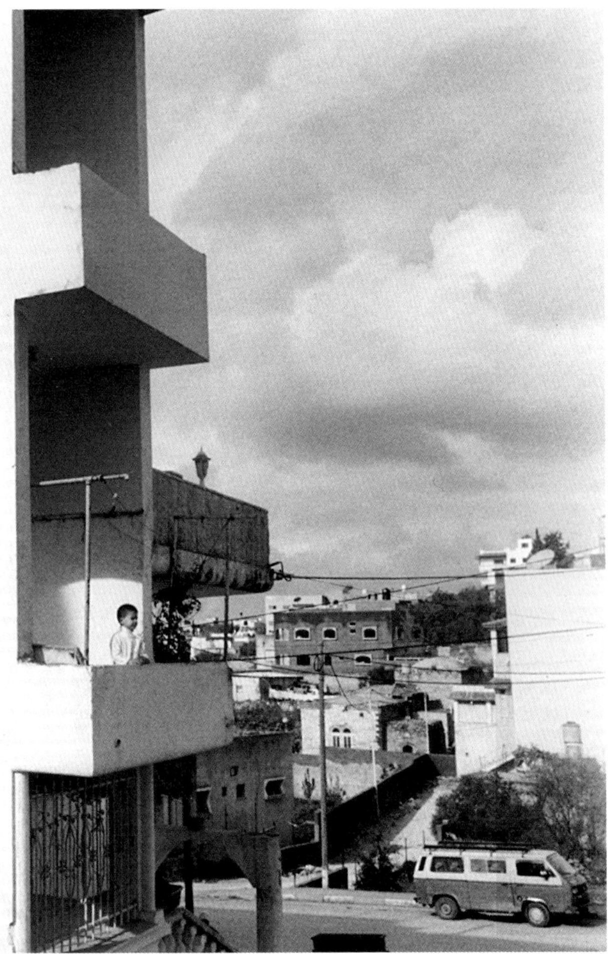

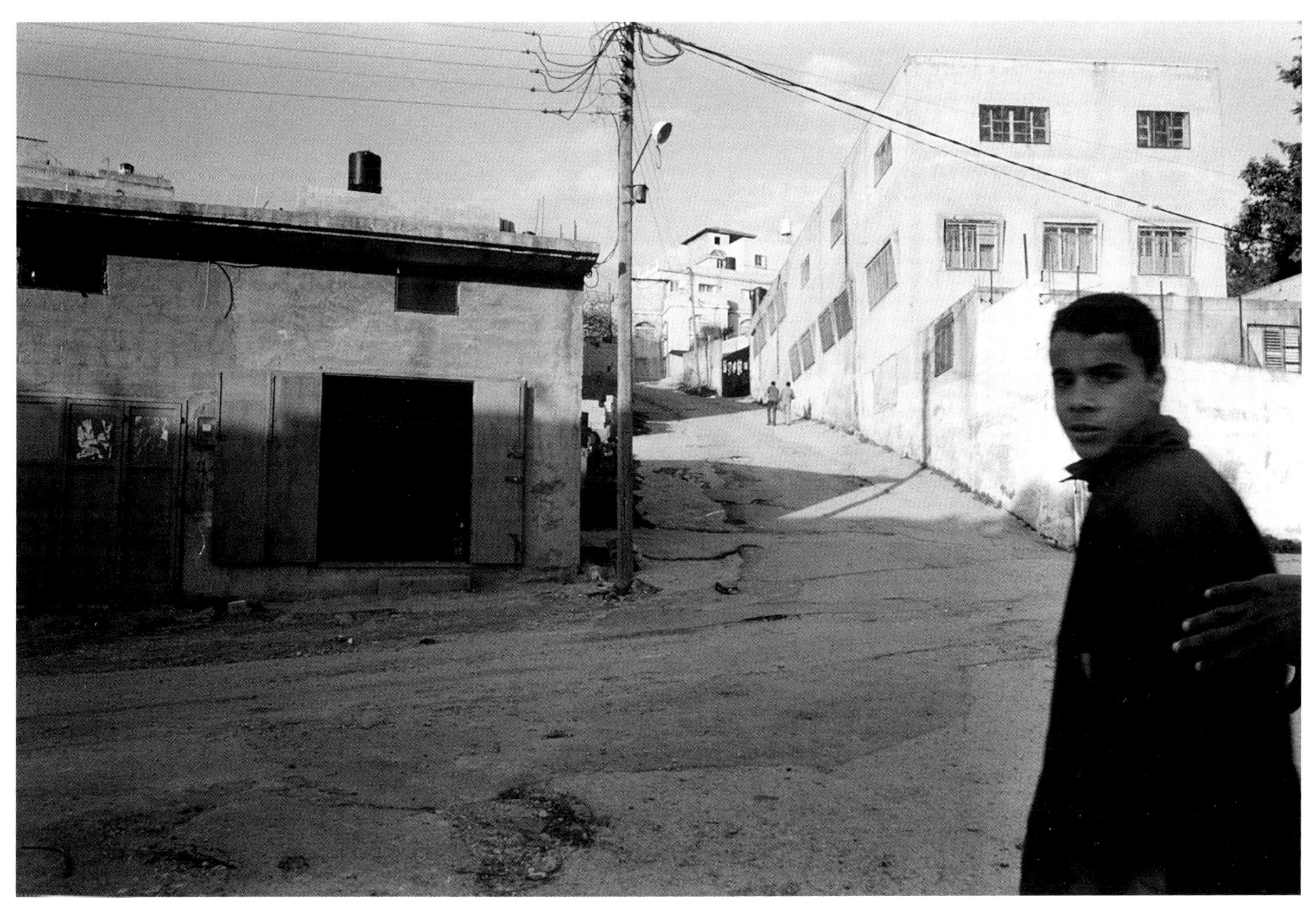

A boy walks on the
street of Qaffin, a
village in the northern
West Bank.

Townspeople visit
the graves of martyrs
on the *Eid* holiday,
Tulkarem.

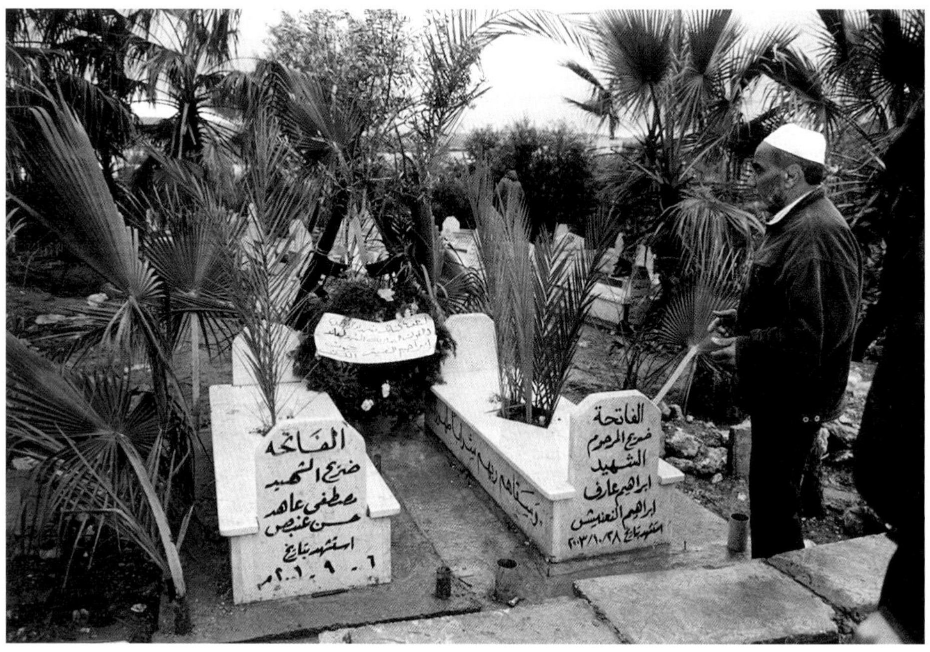

A family prepares for
the *Eid* holiday feast
in the Tulkarem refugee
camp.

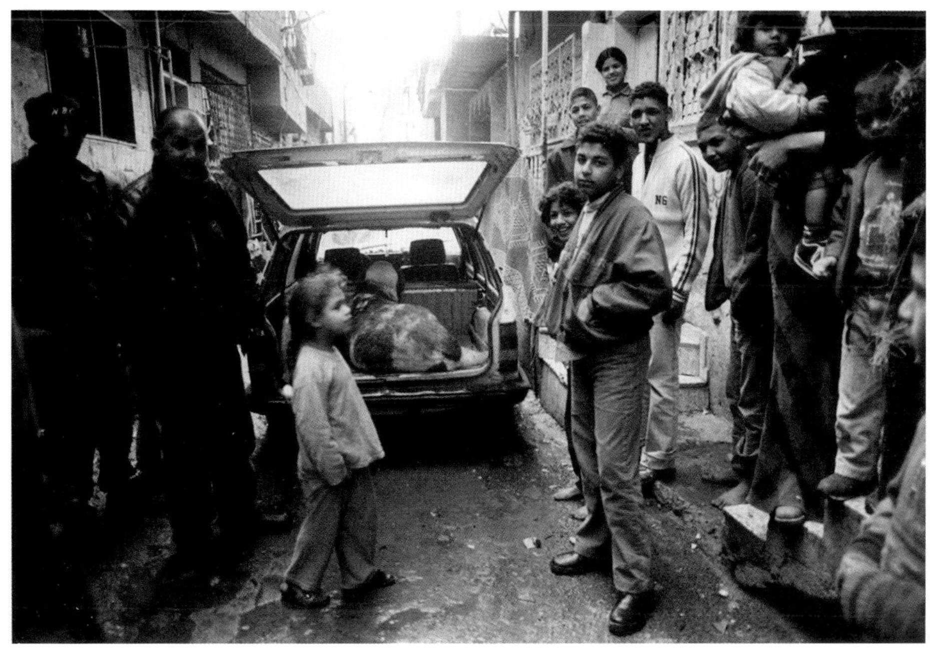

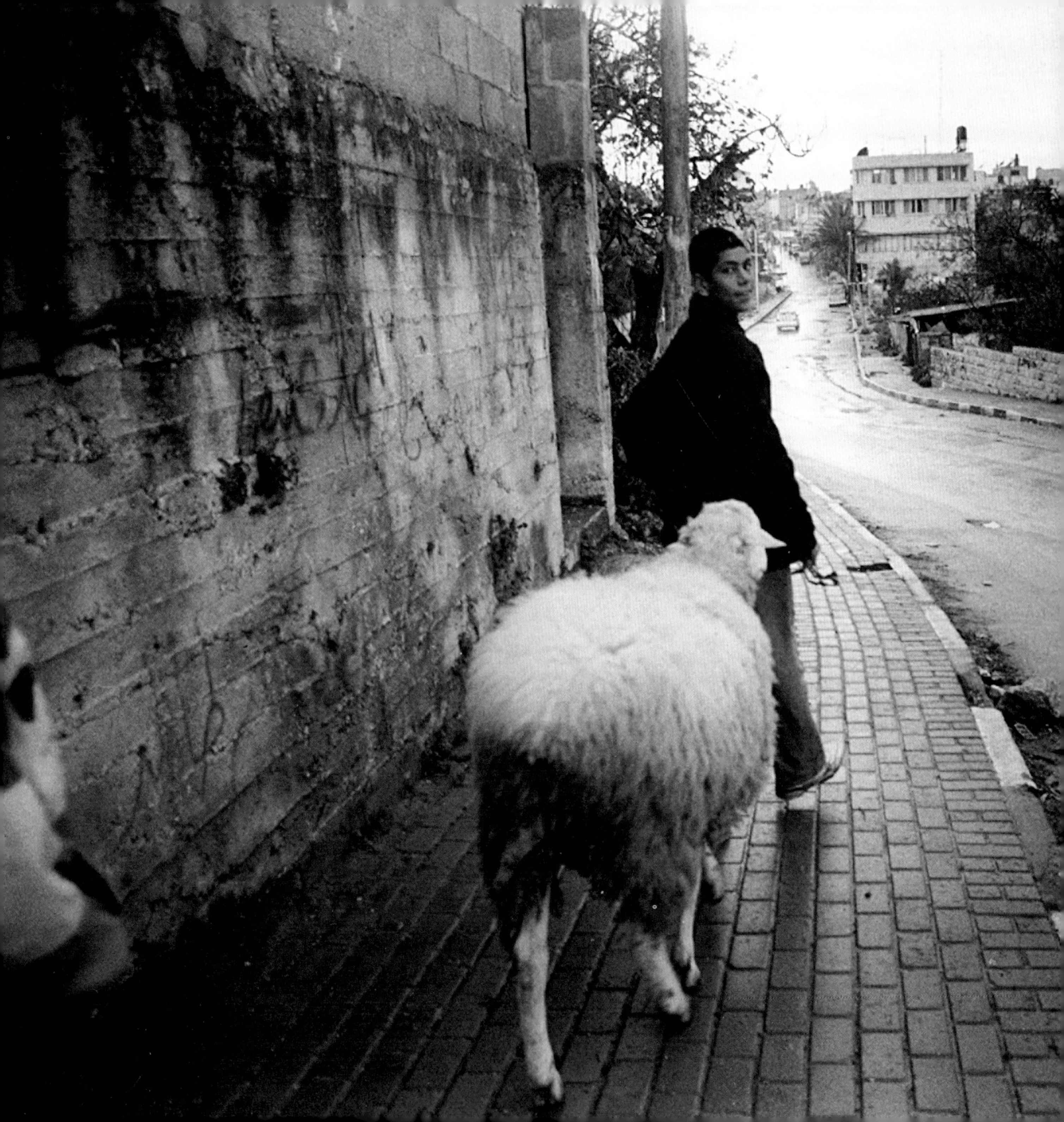

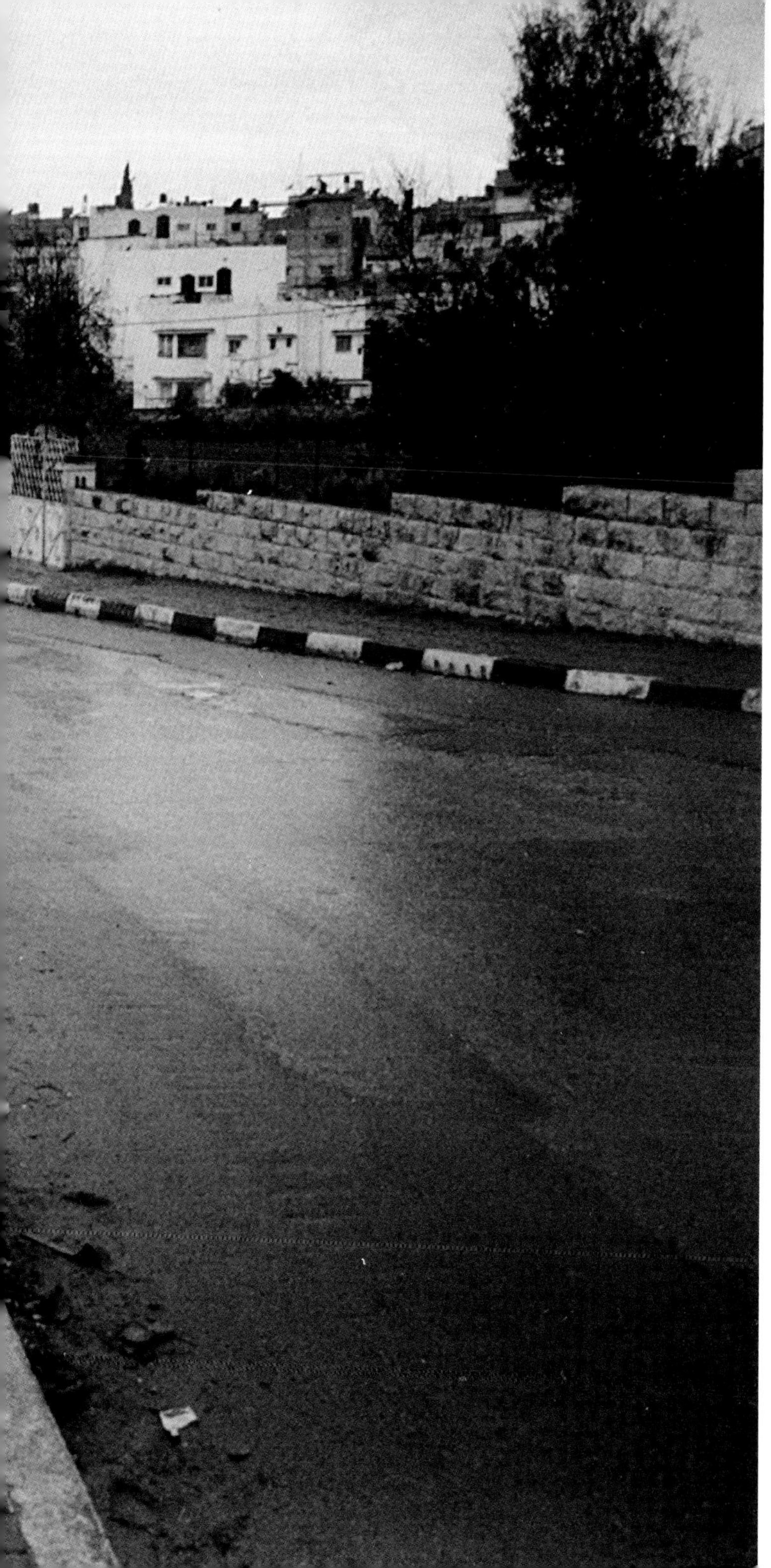

Tulkarem, West Bank.

49

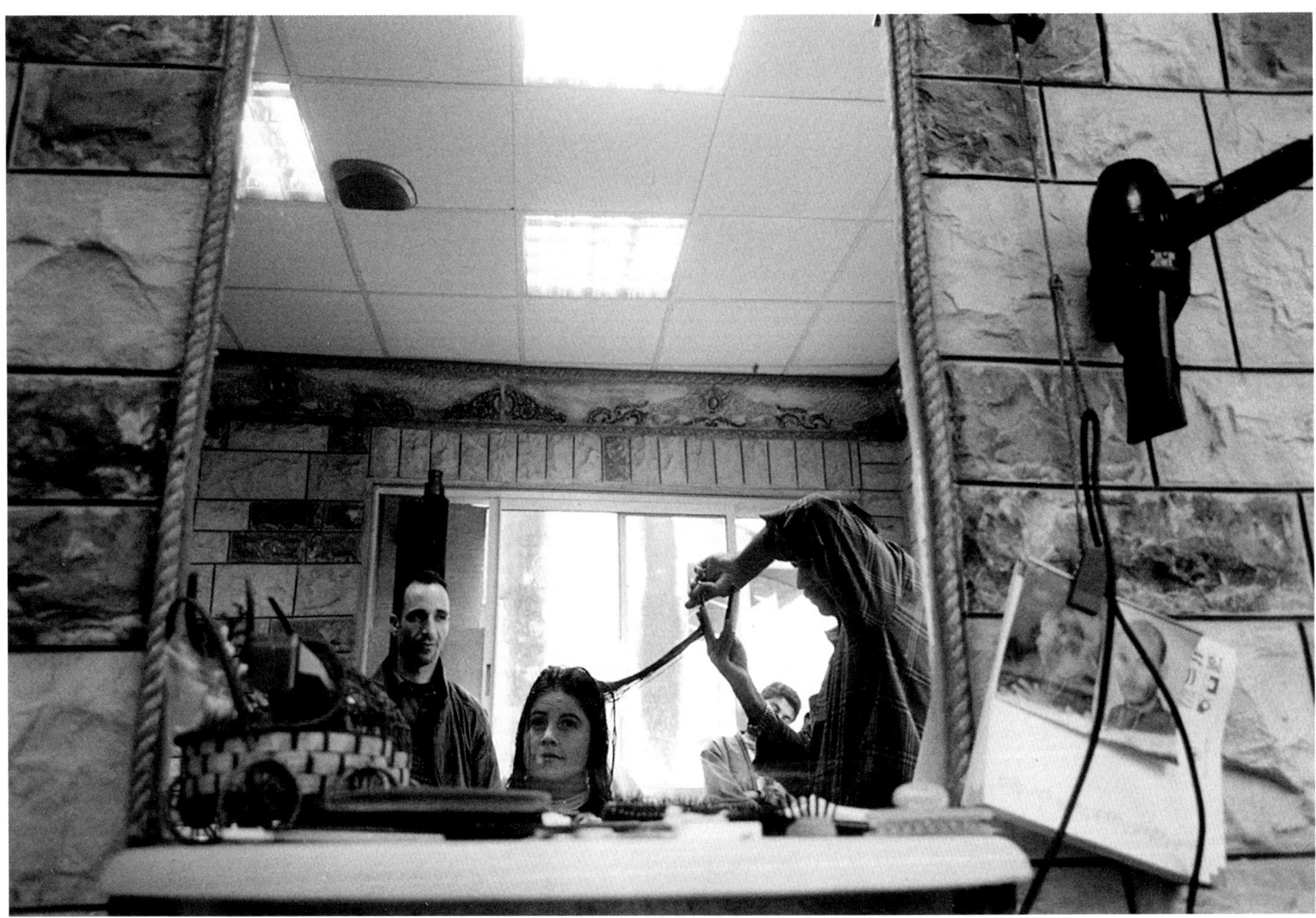

The barber cuts my
hair for the holiday,
Tulkarem refugee
camp.

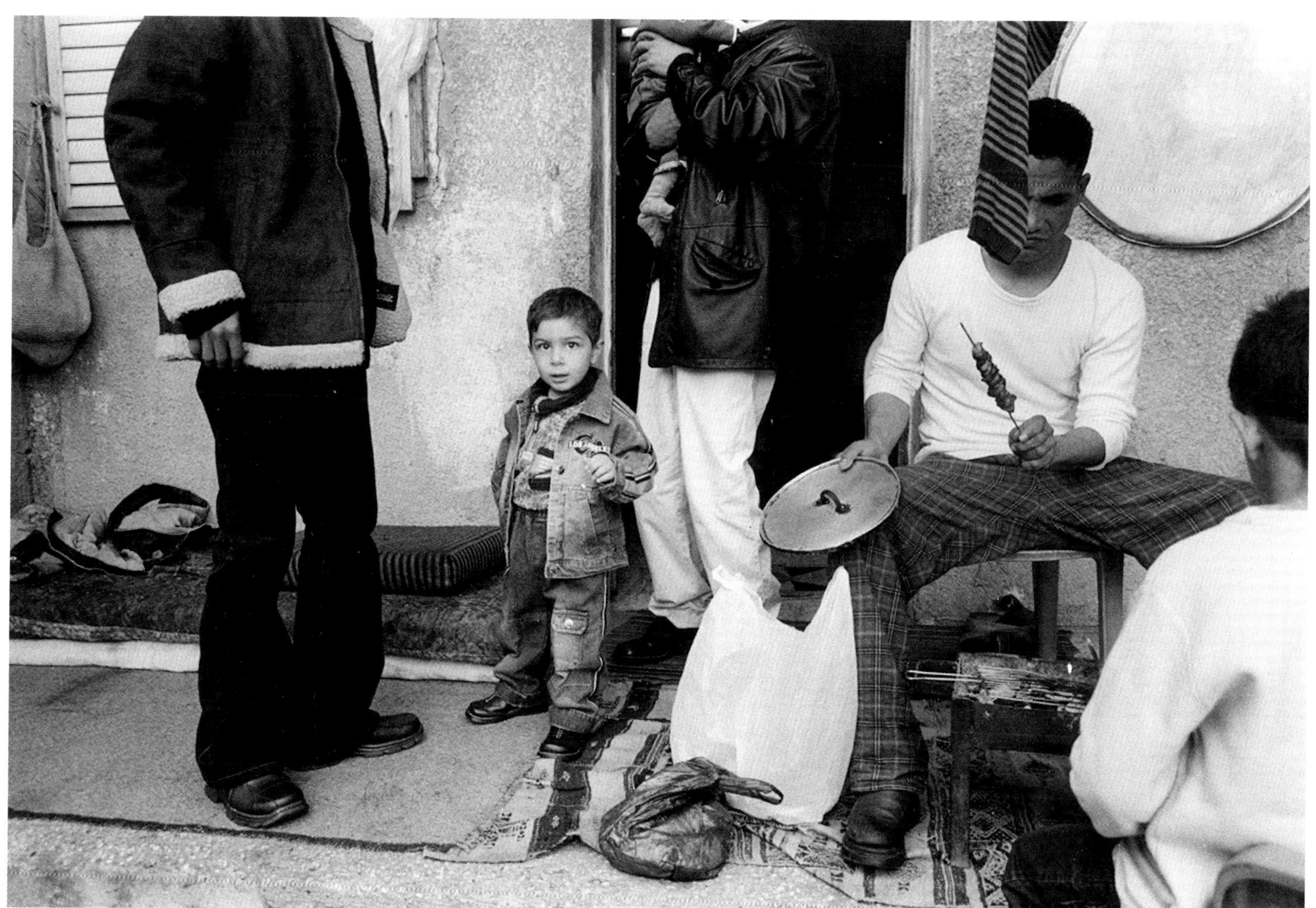

Eid barbecue at the Tanji family home in the Tulkarem refugee camp.

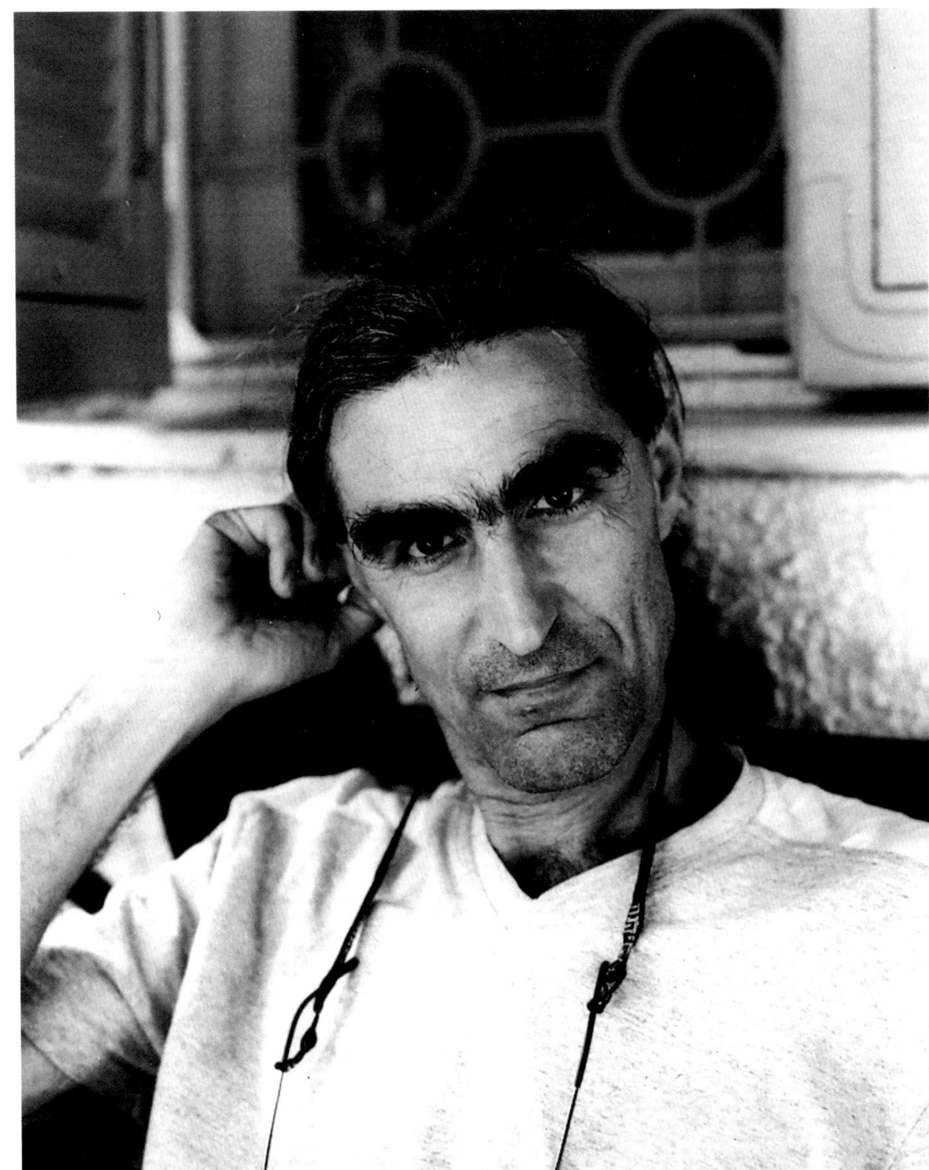

"When I started asking questions about what I saw in the Army, people didn't want to talk about it. They cut me off saying 'everybody sees this, it is war, shut the fuck up!'"

Amir, Rehovot
Jewish Israeli.

"There are no limits to my hope, I dream
for people to live together in peace,
democracy and justice not only in Palestine
and Israel, but the whole world living
in equality without borders."

Aziz Tanji, Tulkarem
Palestinian.

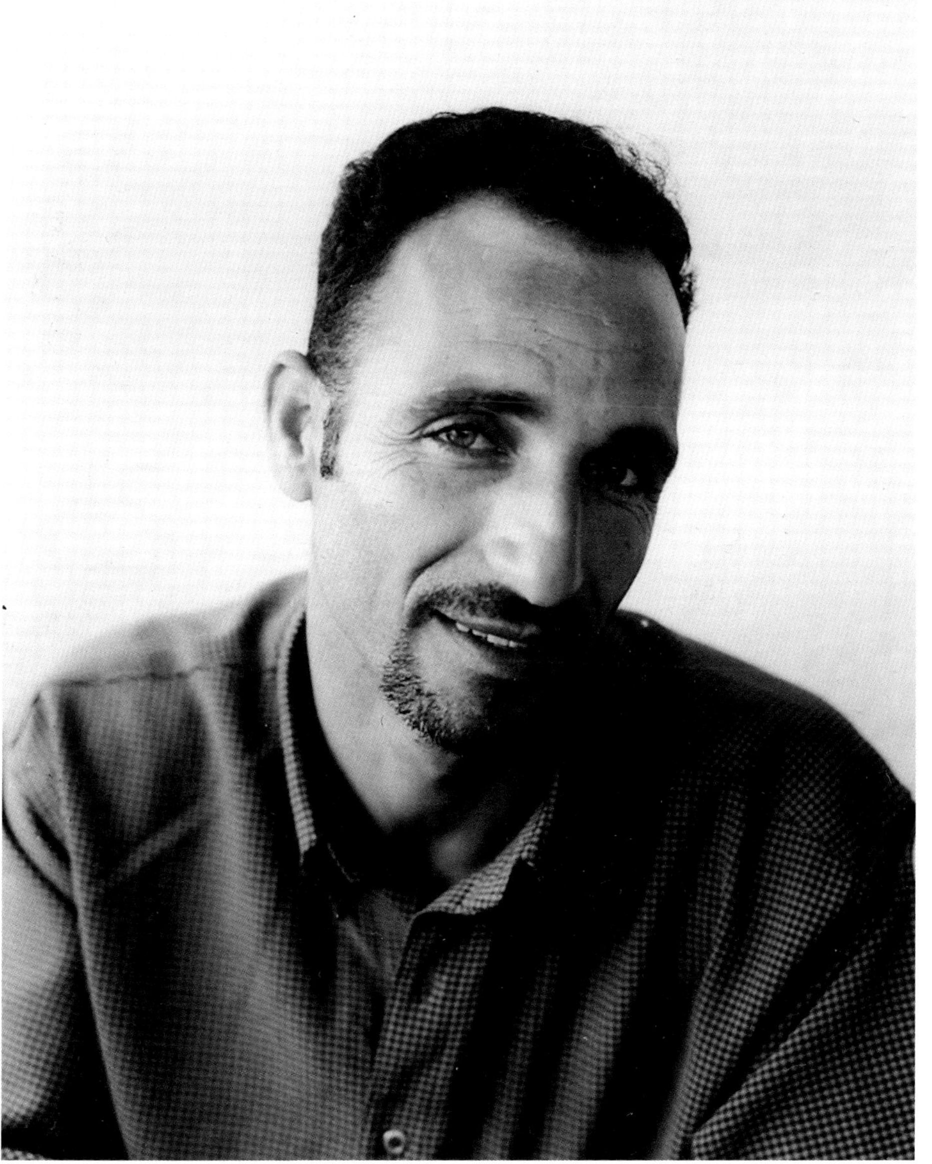

According to the Amnesty International report on house demolitions more than 3,000 Palestinian homes have been demolished by the Israeli Army since September 2000.[4]

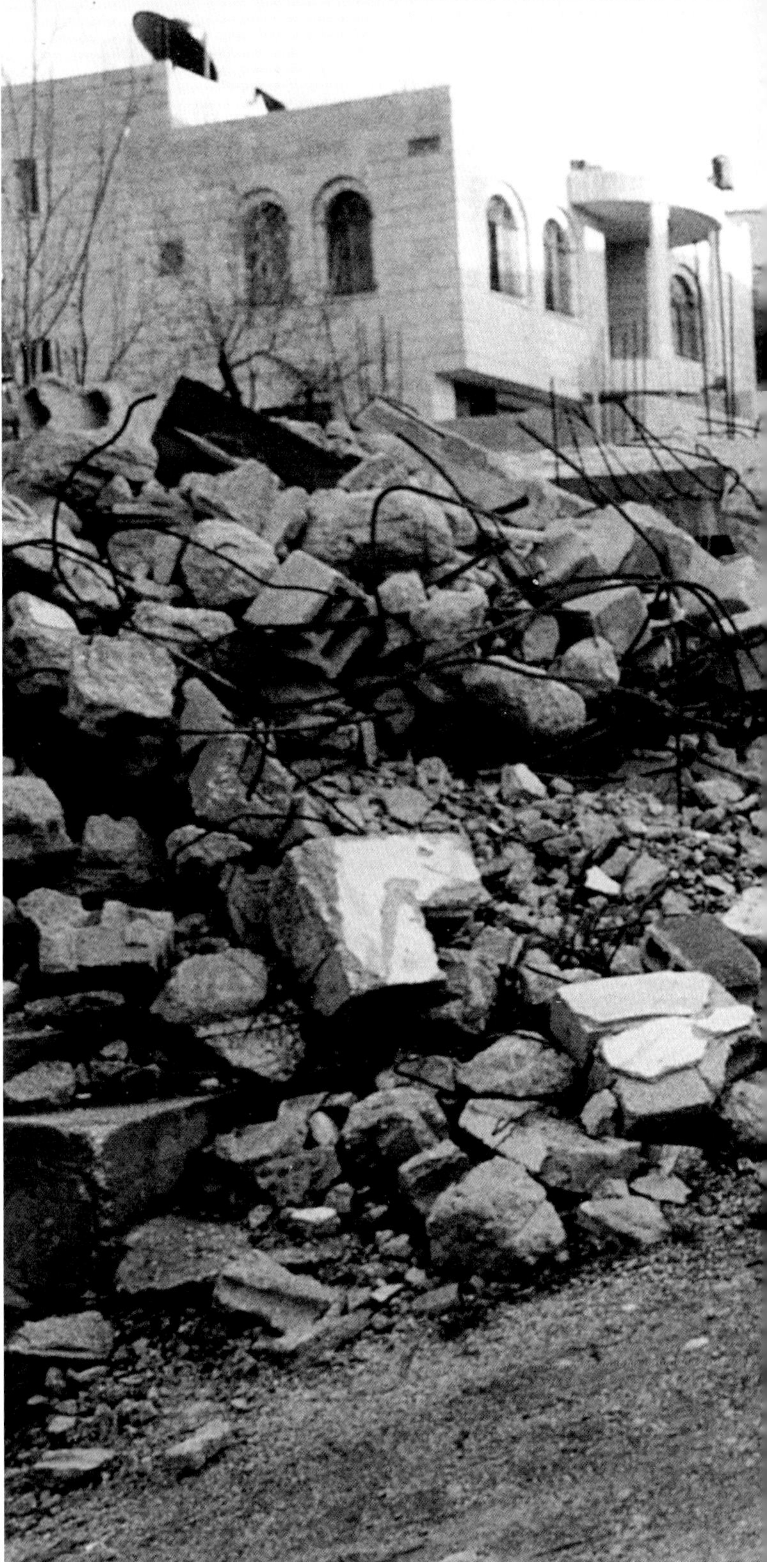

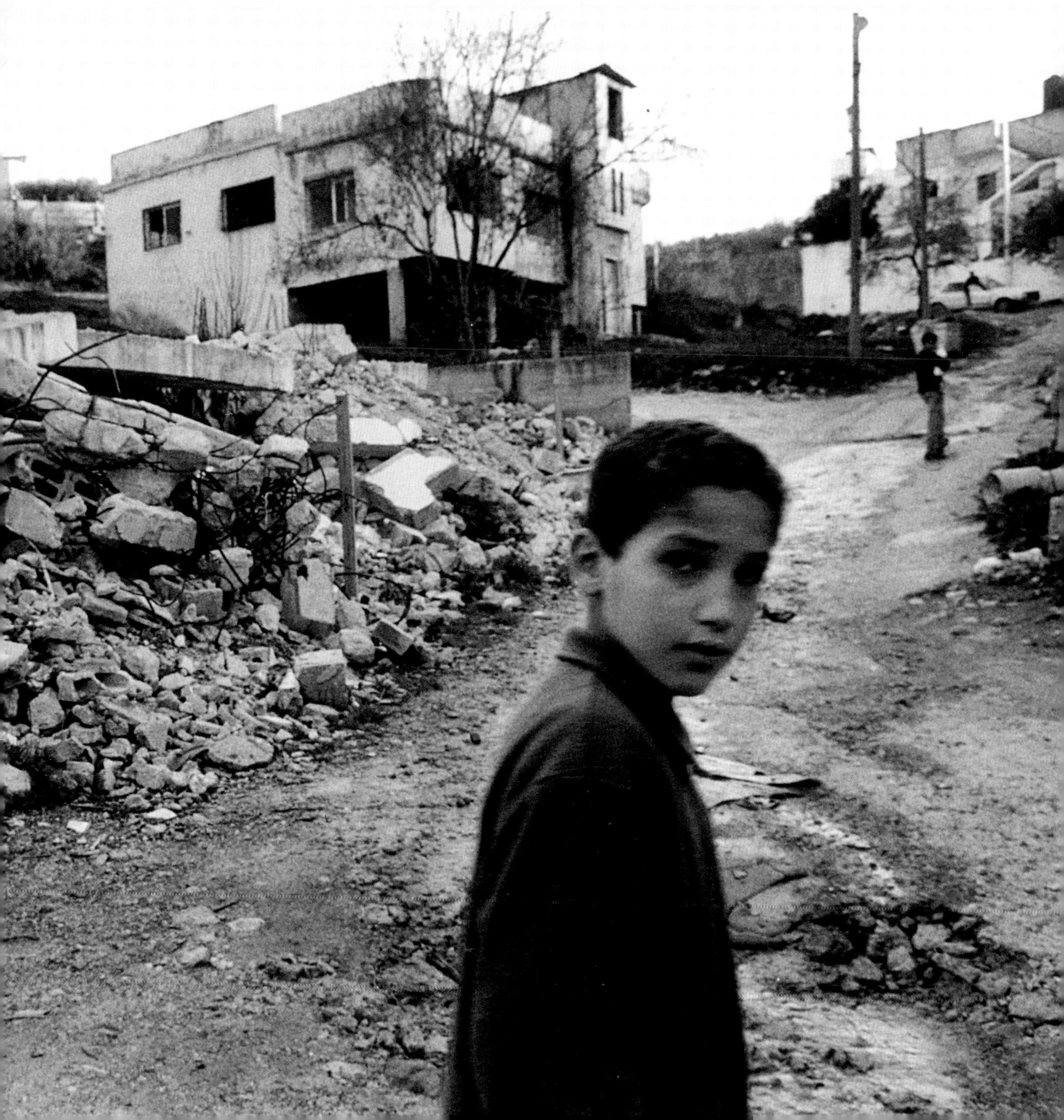

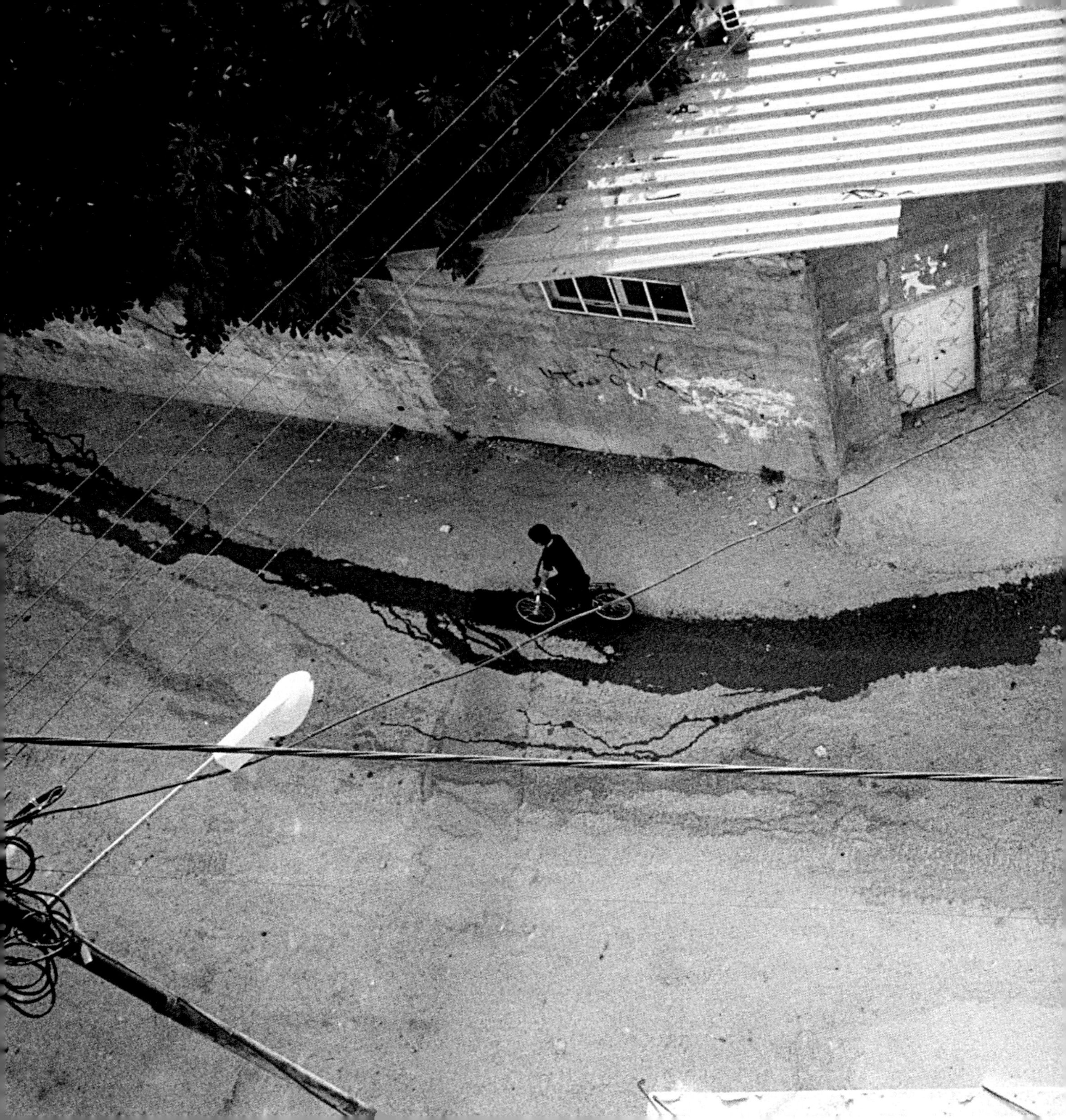

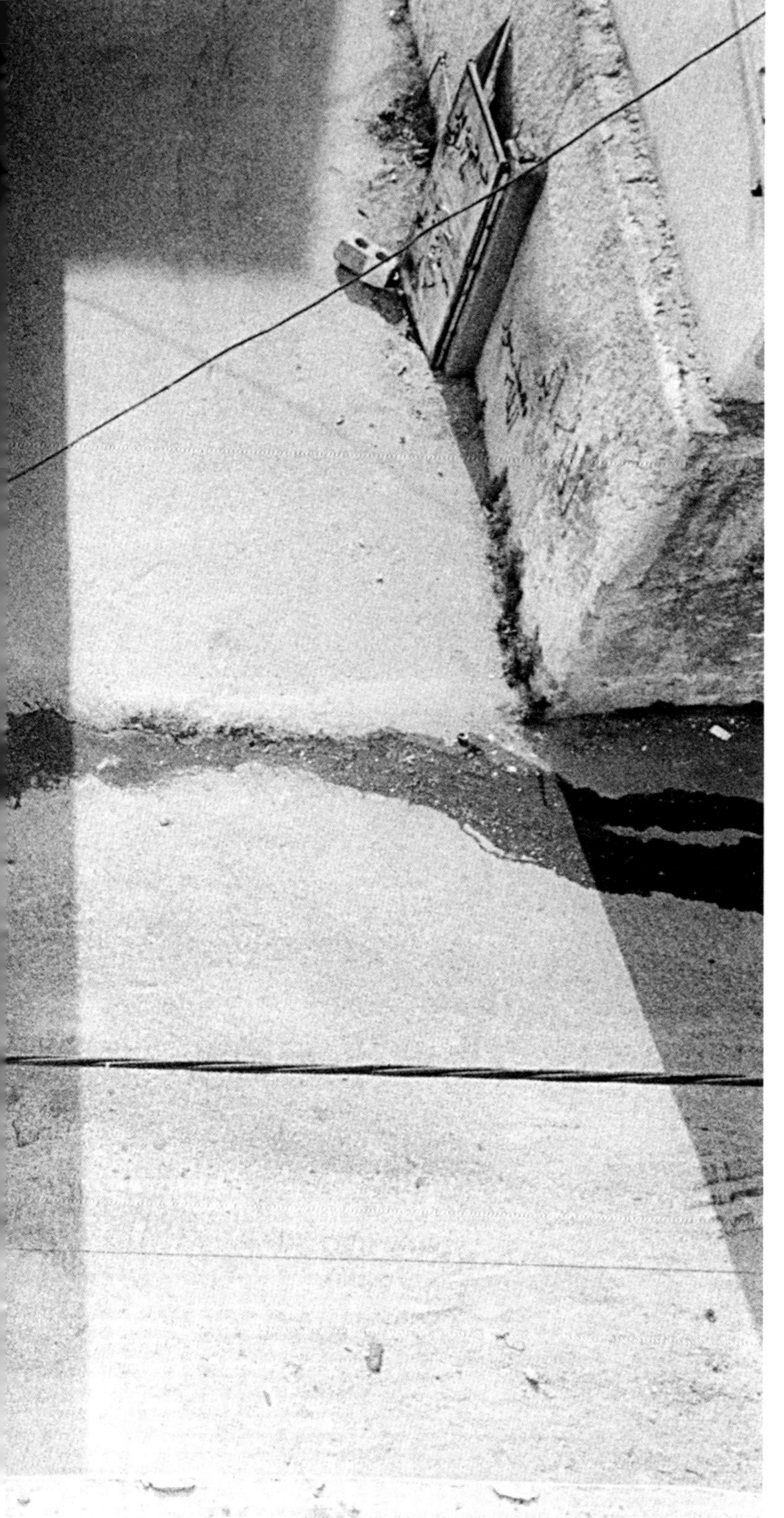

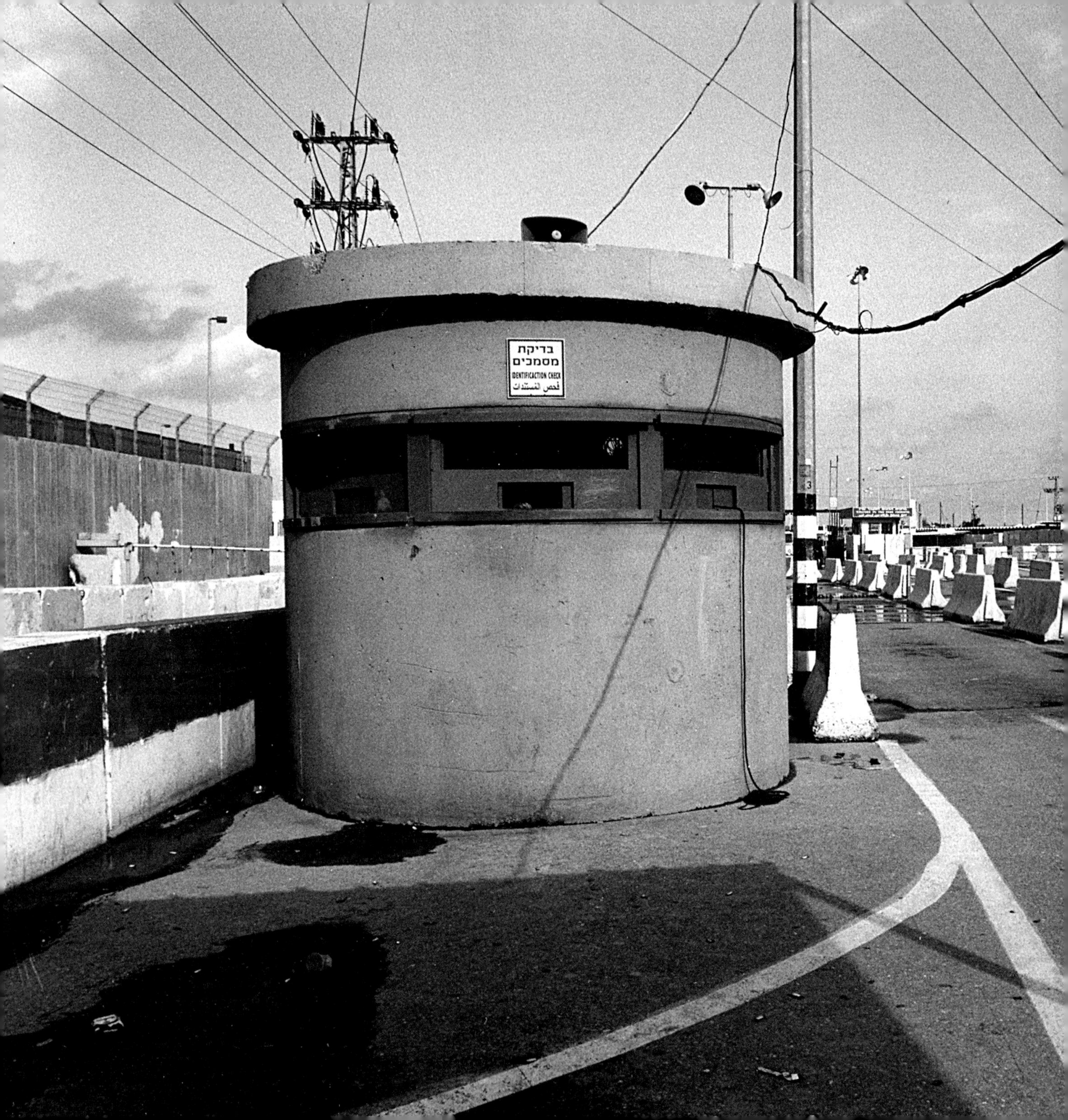
בדיקת
מסמכים
IDENTIFICACTION CHECK
فحص المستندات

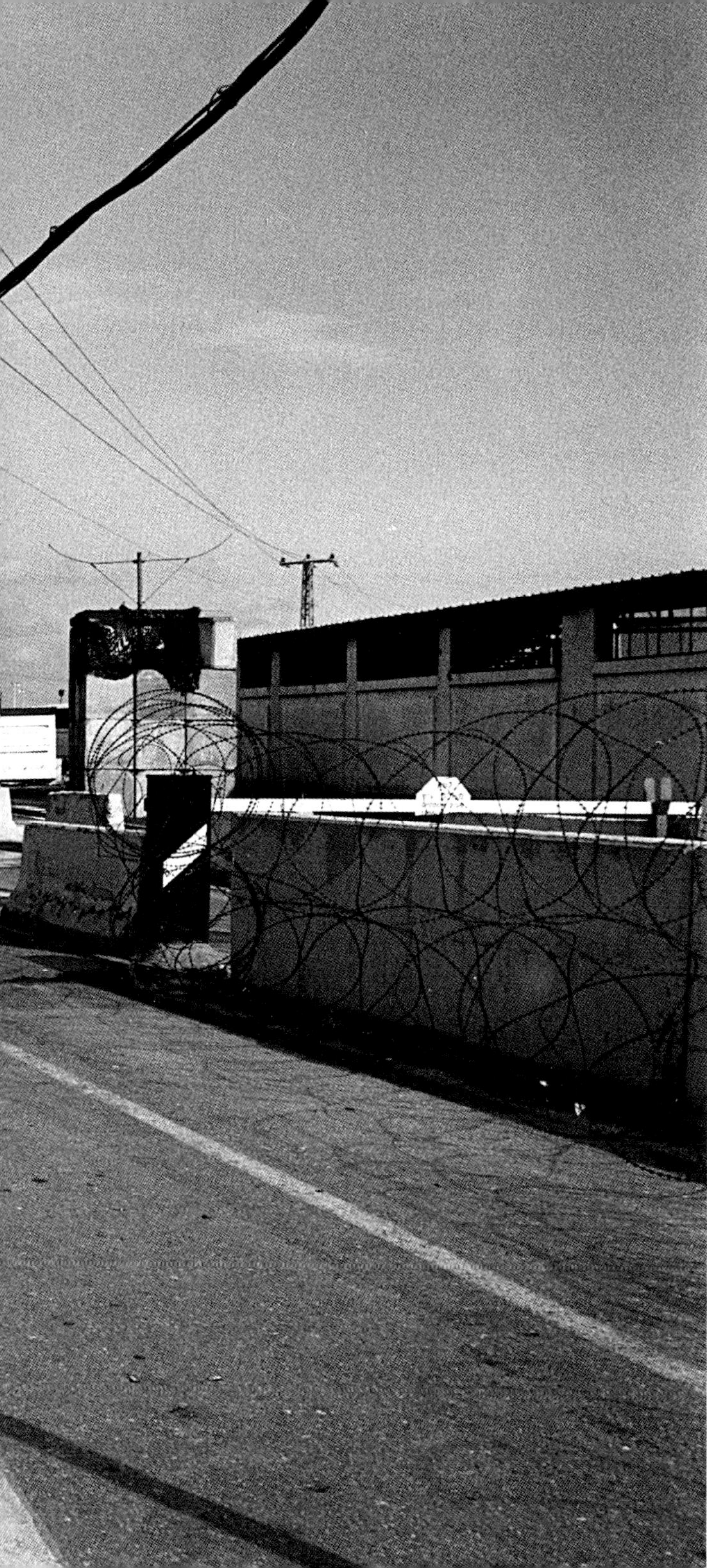

The first sight upon
re-entering Israel is this
concrete "pillbox"
checkpoint at the Erez
border crossing
between Israel and
the Gaza Strip.

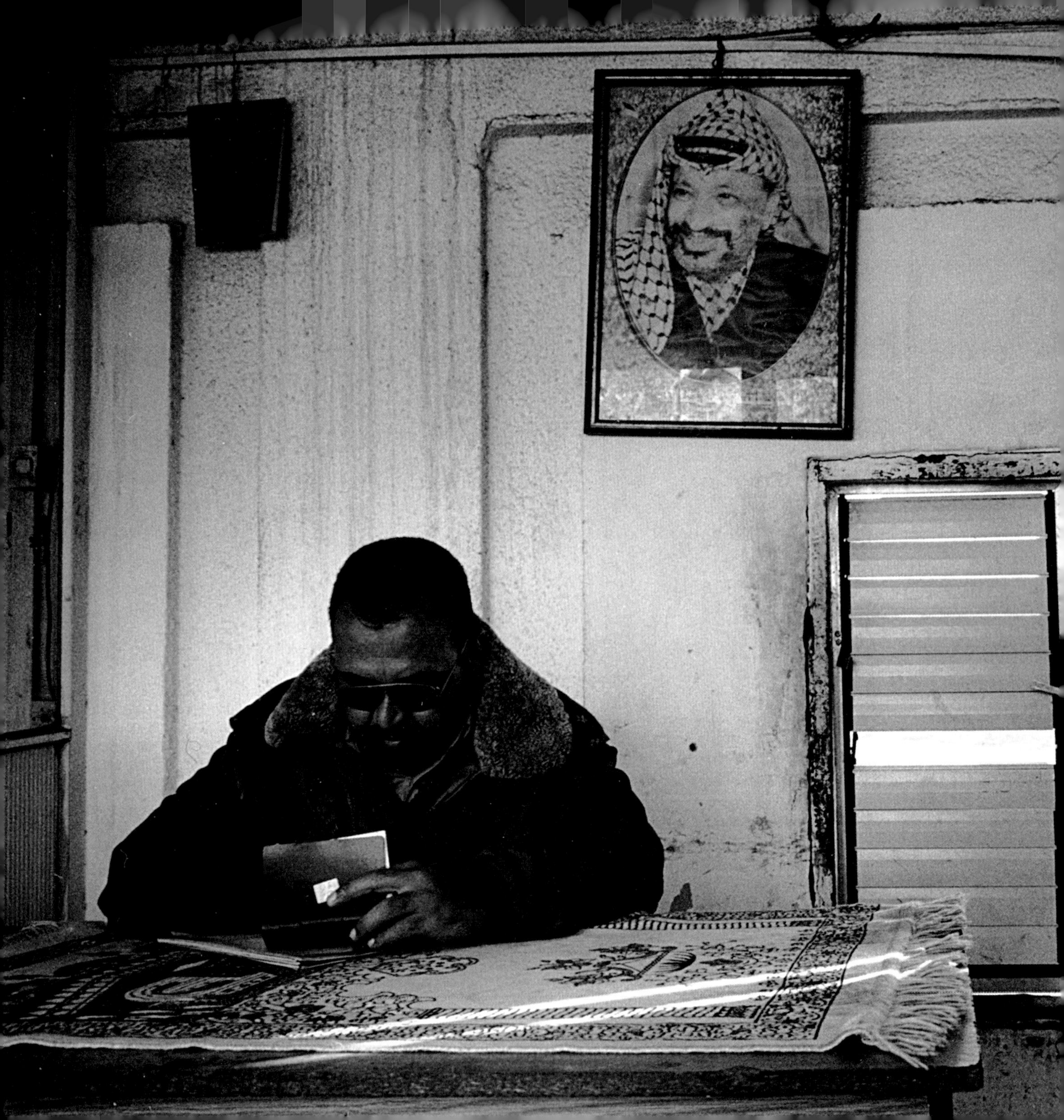

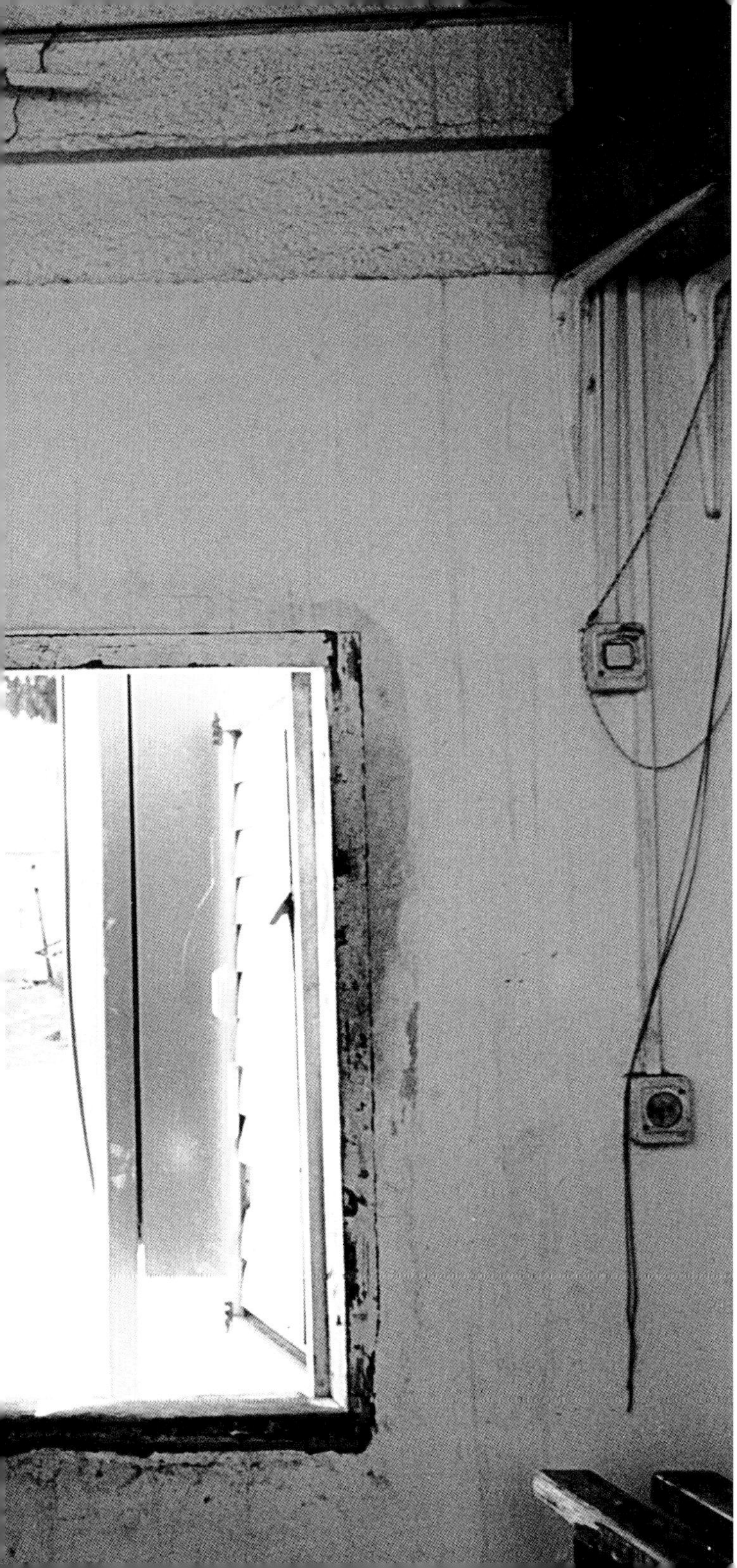

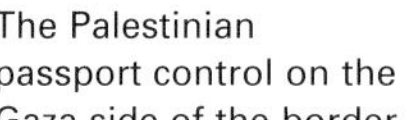

The Palestinian
passport control on the
Gaza side of the border.

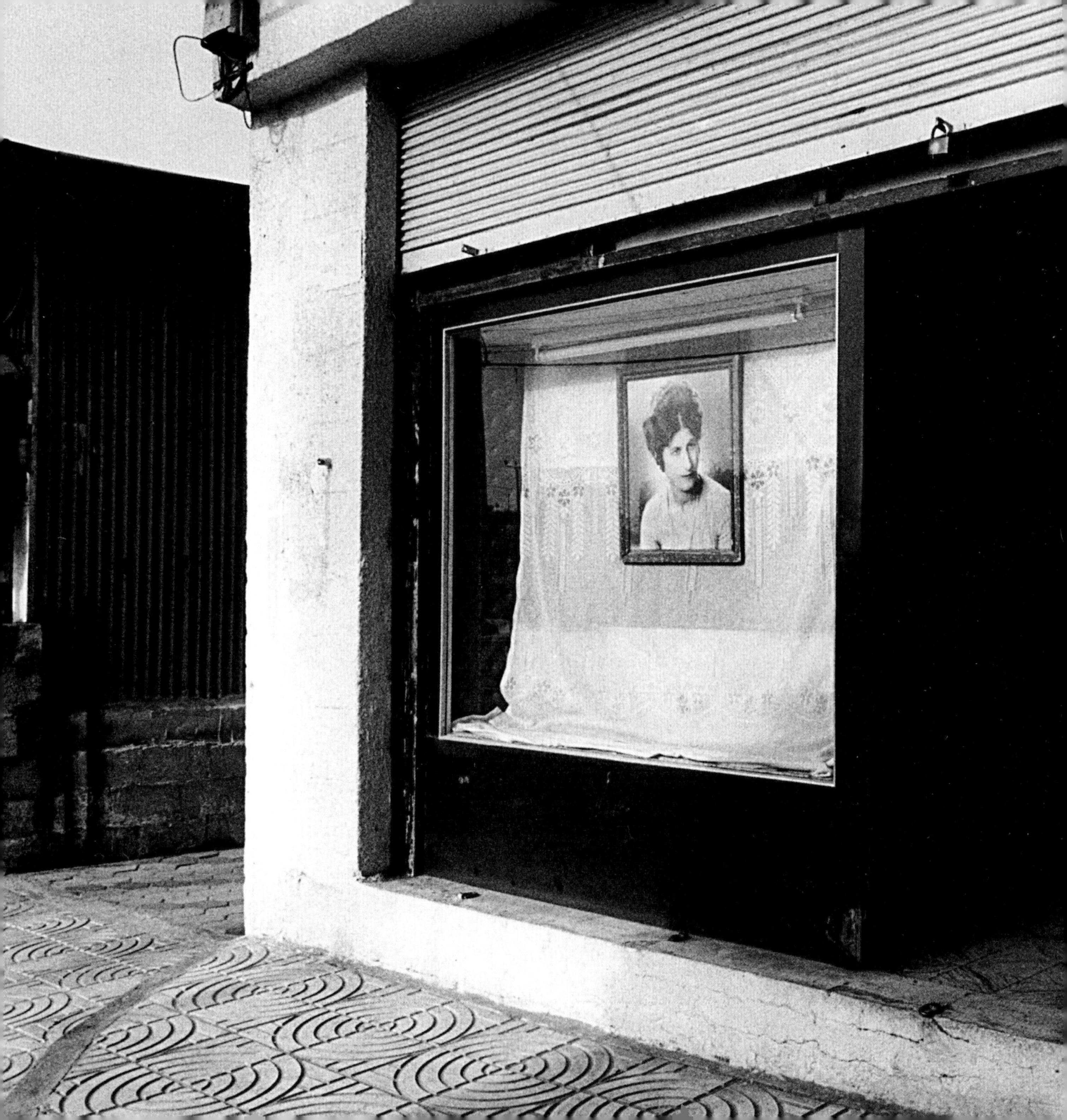

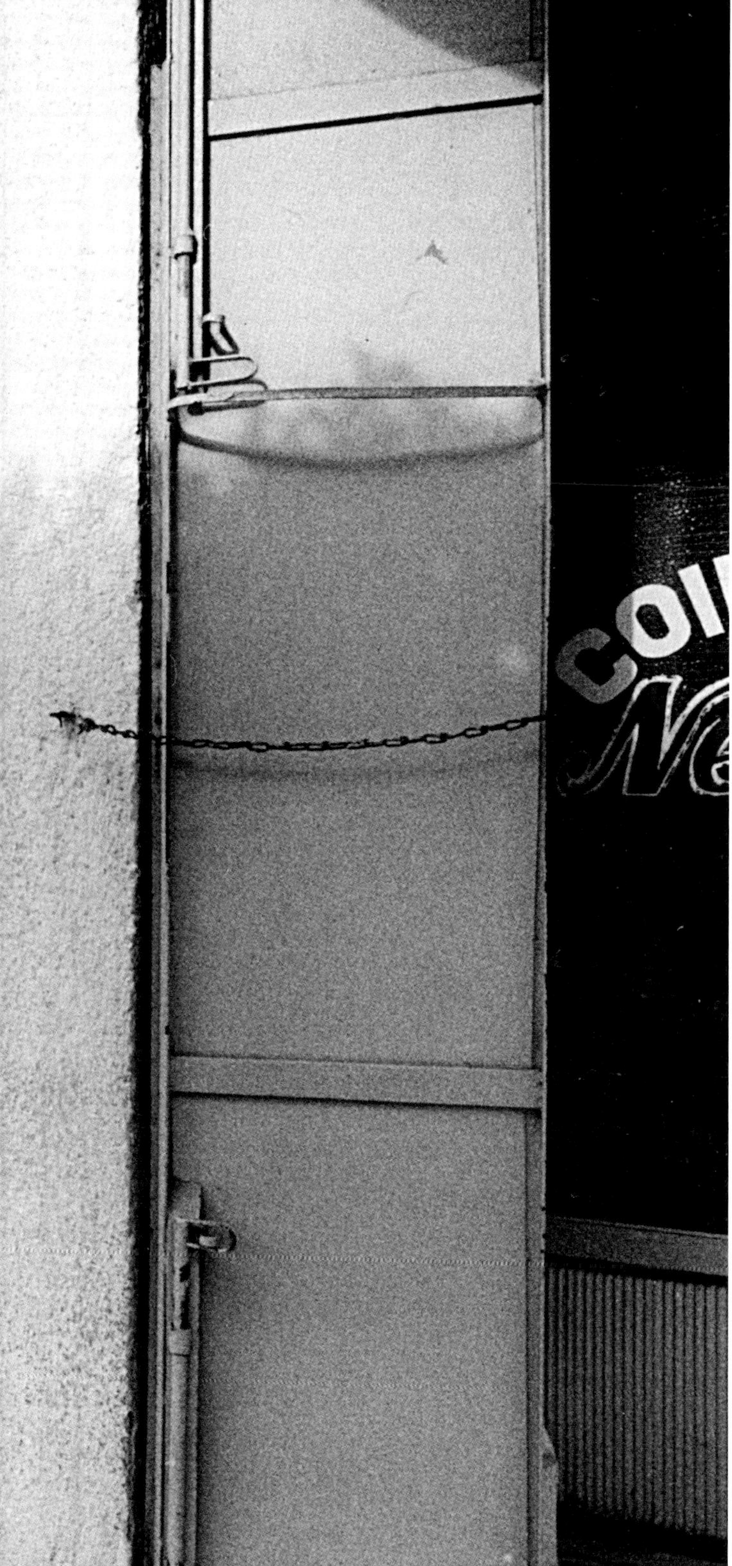

Photographer's studio,
Gaza City.

The Gaza Strip is one of the most densely populated areas in the world. Before the Israeli settlers were evacuated in 2005, there were 1.4 million Palestinians and 8,000 settlers living in a total area of 365 square kilometers (220 square miles).[5]

The six meter (20 ft.)
high wall separating
between Baqa Al
Sharqia (Baqa East)
and Baqa Al Gharbia
(Baqa West).

In April 2002 the Israeli government decided to construct the "Security Barrier". The authorities described the Barrier as "a defensive measure, designed to block the passage of terrorists, weapons and explosives into the State of Israel…" The total length of the Barrier is said to be more than 670 kilometers (420 miles), the average width is between 80–100 meters (260–330 ft.) occupied by barbed wire, ditches, large trace paths, and tank patrol lanes on both sides of the Barrier.

Overleaf. A view of the Barrier near the northern West Bank village of Atil. The Barrier has caused thousands of Palestinian farmers to be separated from their farmland. The house in the center photograph is located on the west side, the "Israeli side", of the Barrier, causing this family to be isolated from their village — including their market, their schools, and their health services. The current route of the Barrier cuts off 400,000 Palestinians from their sources of livelihood by encircling them in isolated enclaves or by stranding them outside the Barrier with no connection to the West Bank.[6]

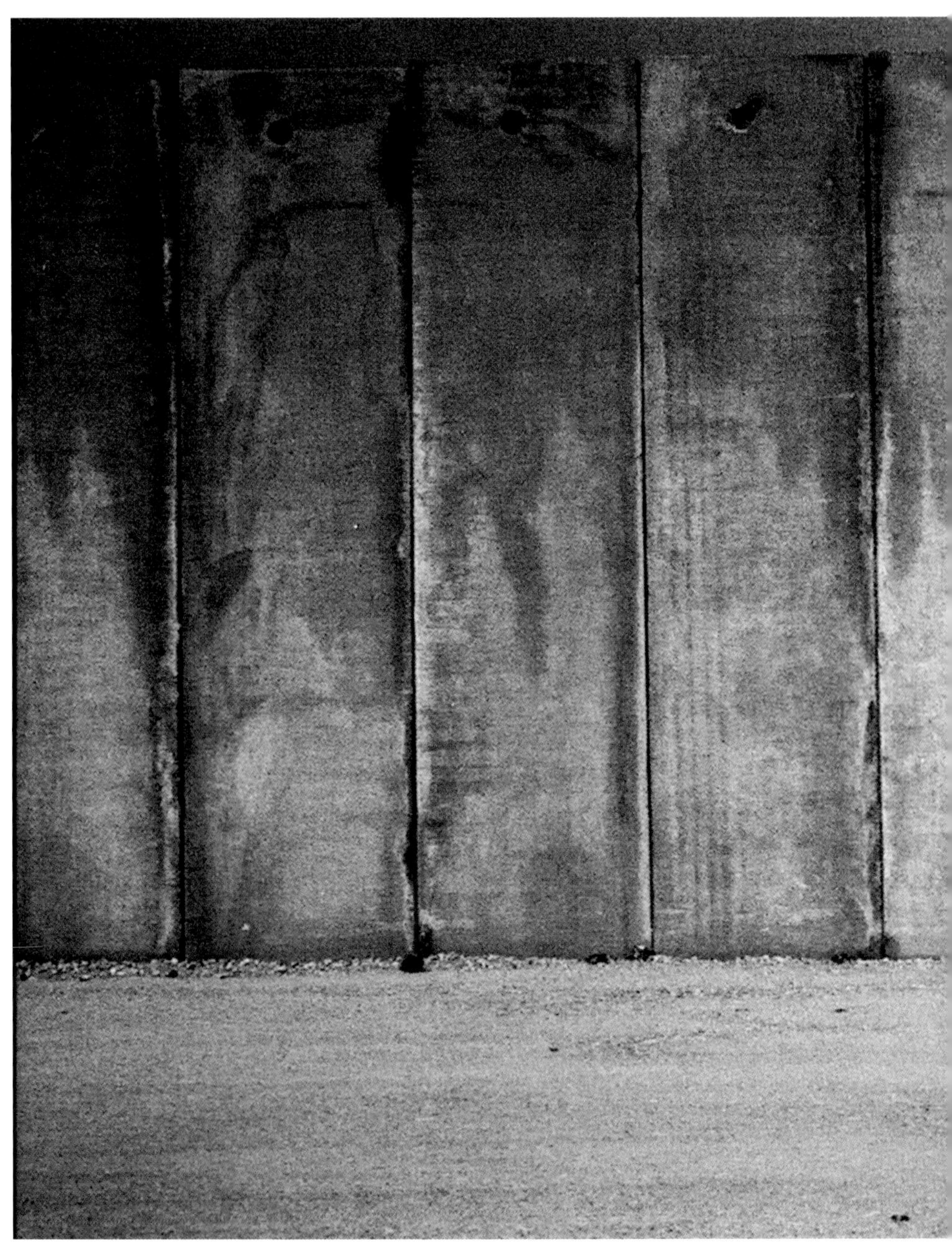

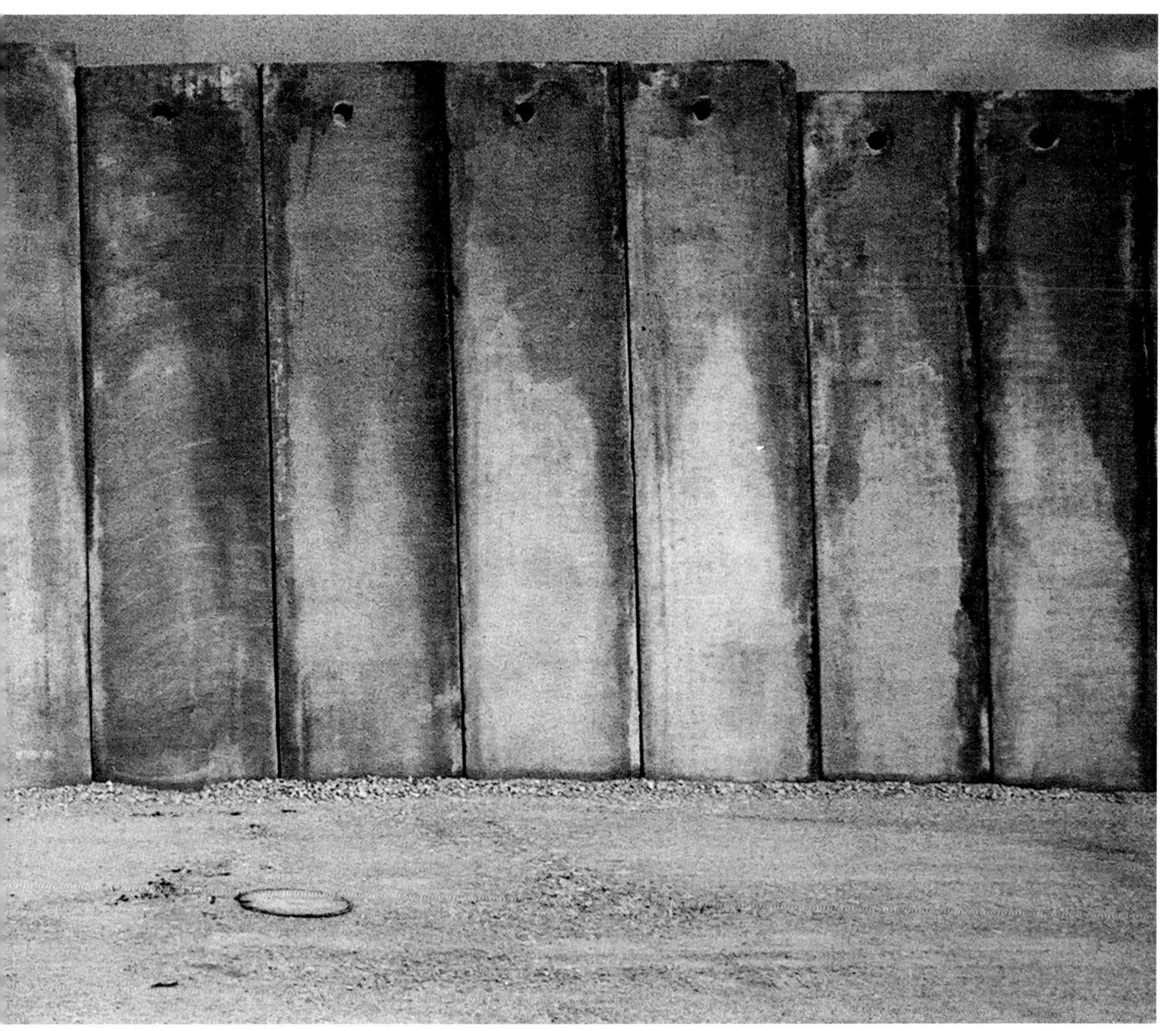

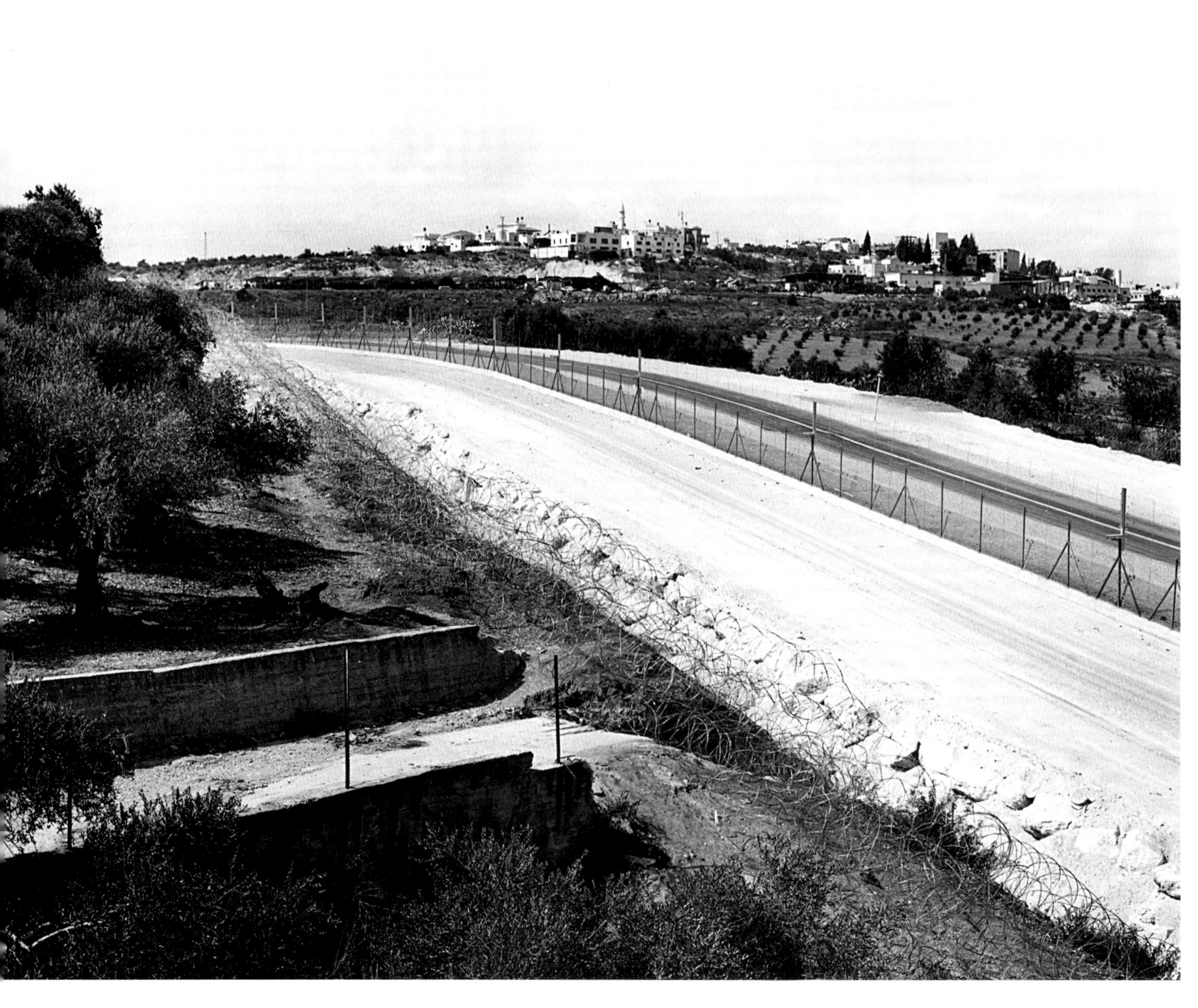

Due to the construction of the Barrier these two farmers from the West Bank village of Zeita are no longer able to reach their land. Rather than locating the Barrier on "the Green Line", the internationally recognized border between Israel and the West Bank, the Israeli government has built 90% of the Barrier on Palestinian land, often well inside the West Bank.

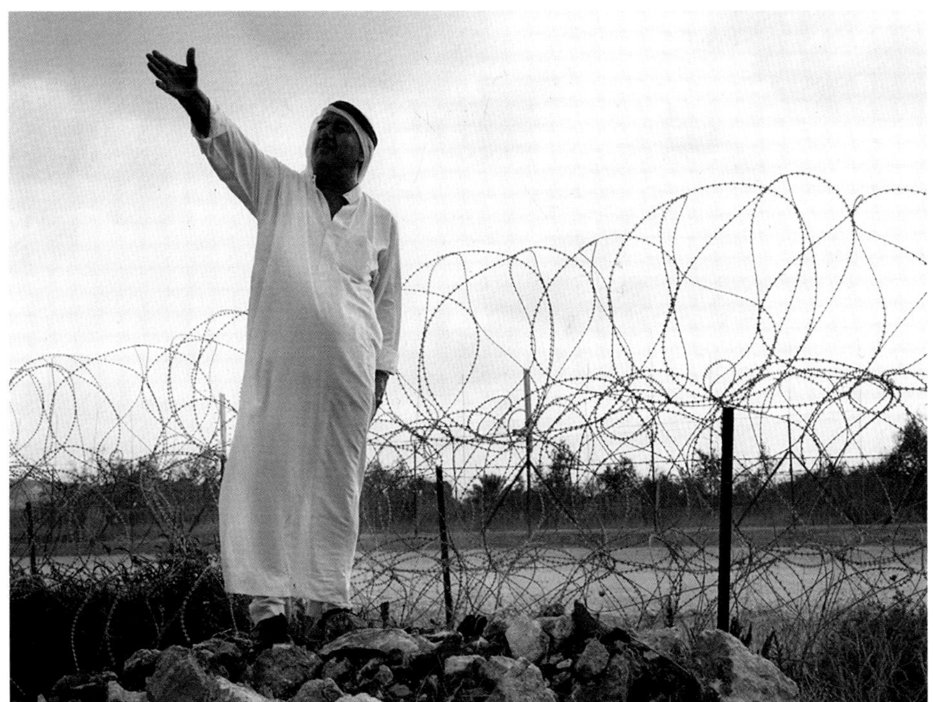

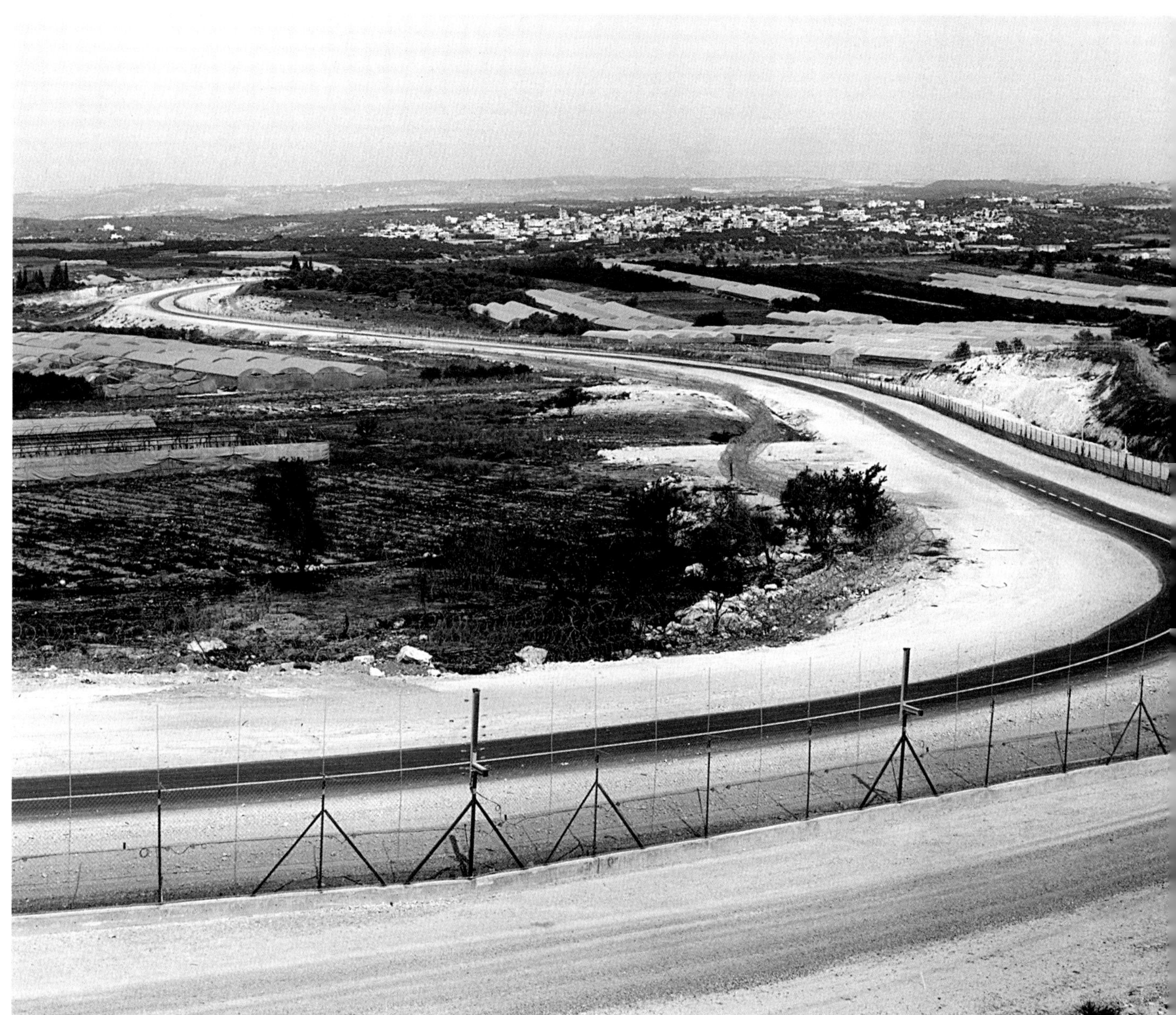

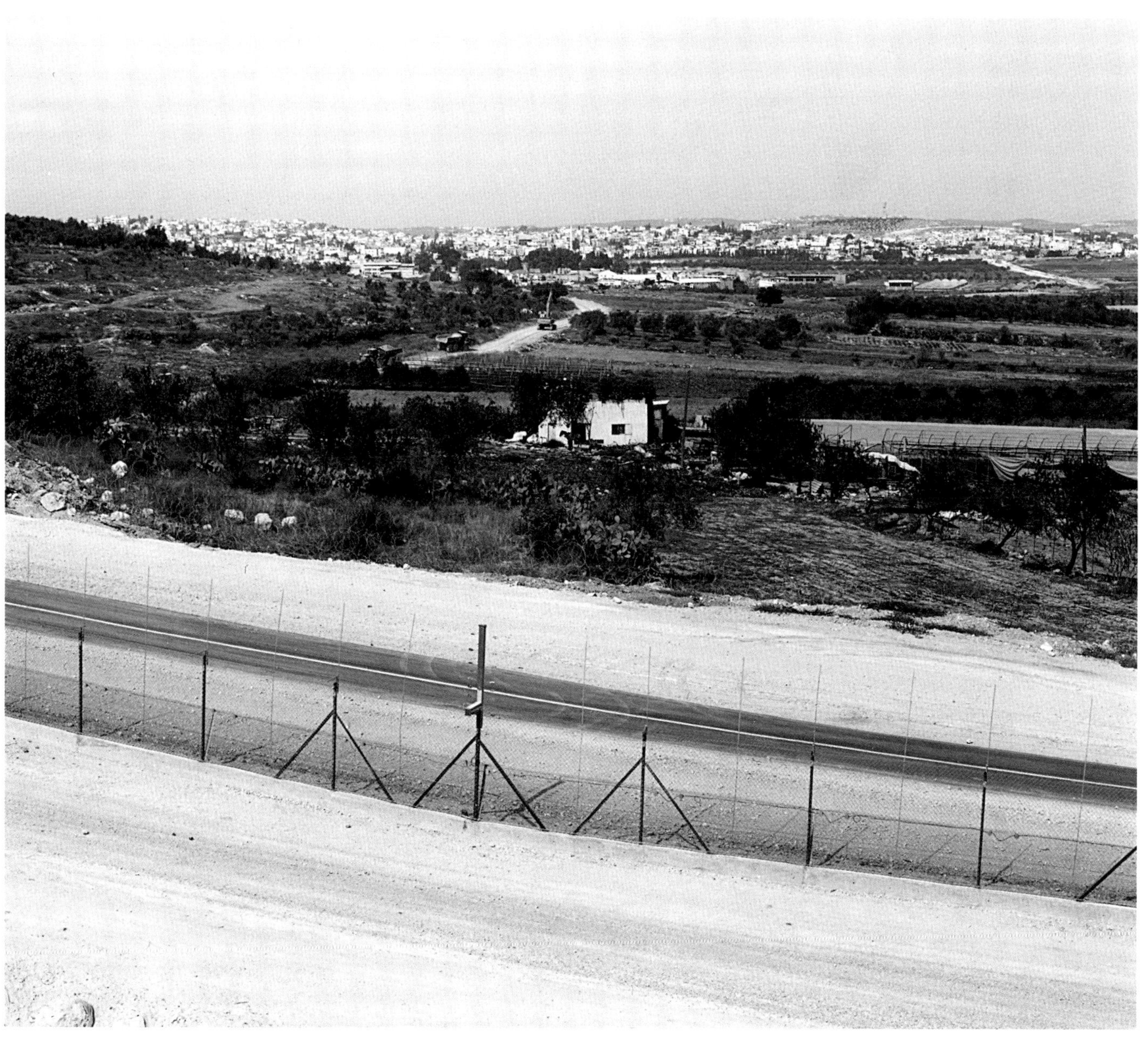

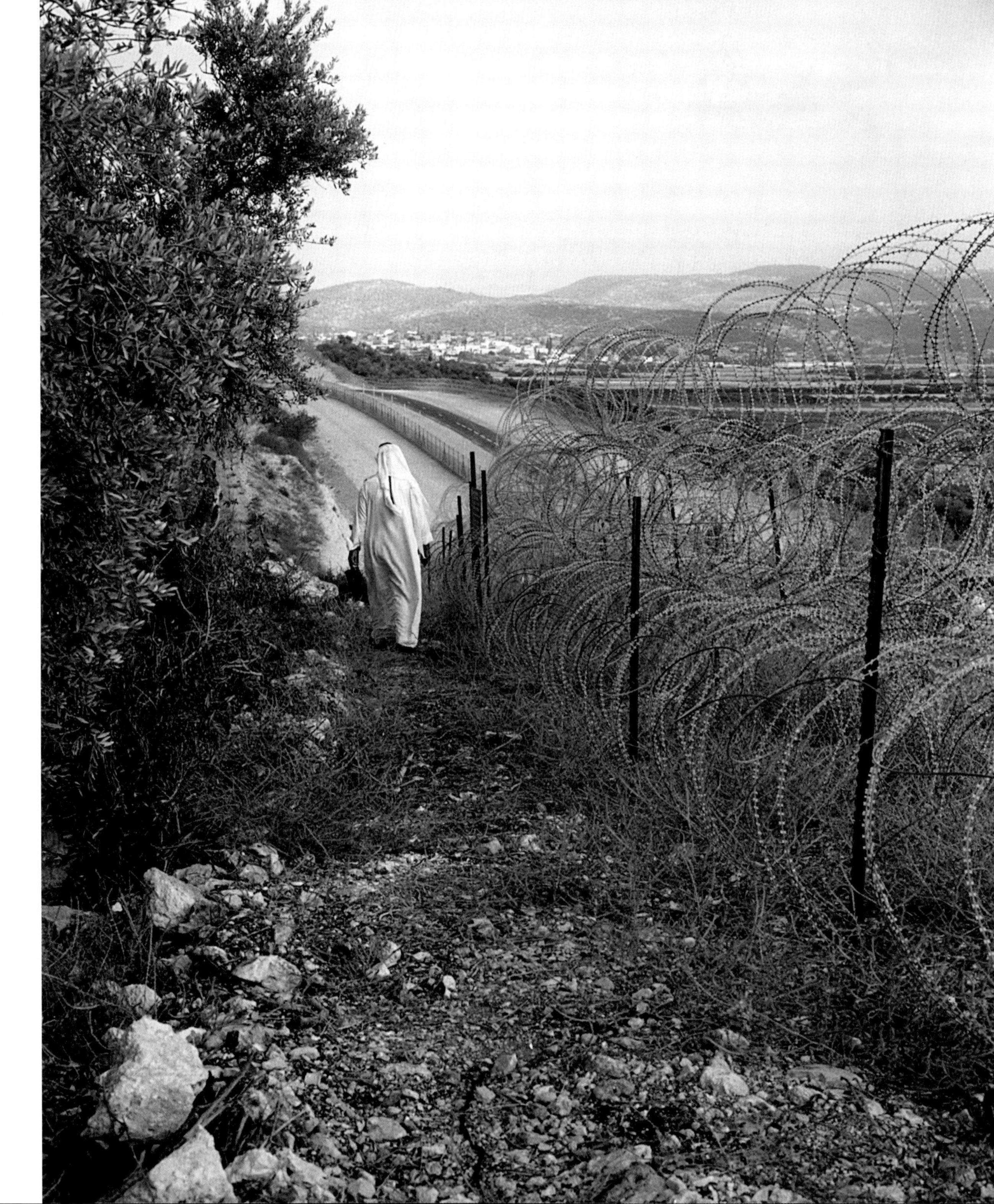

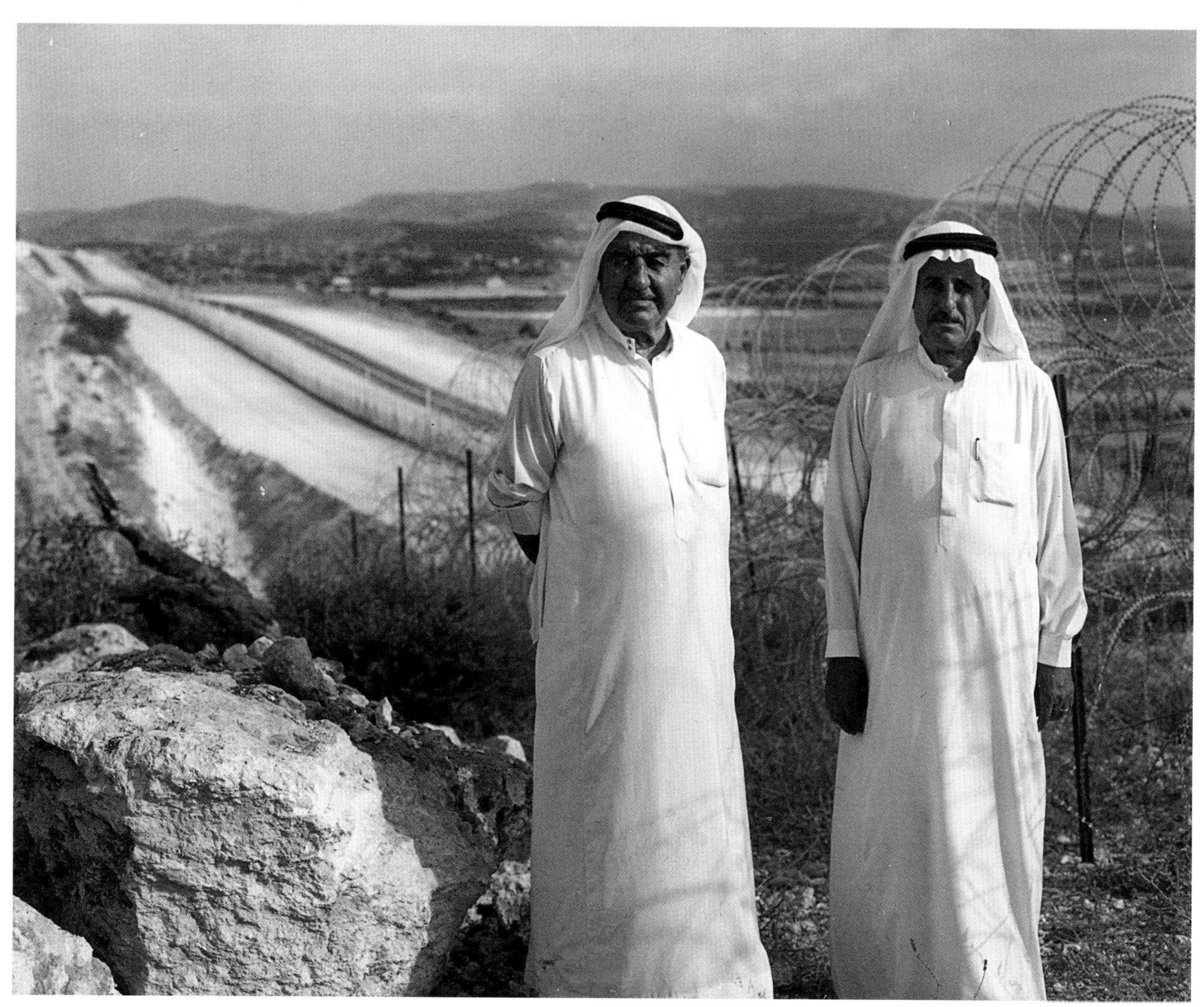

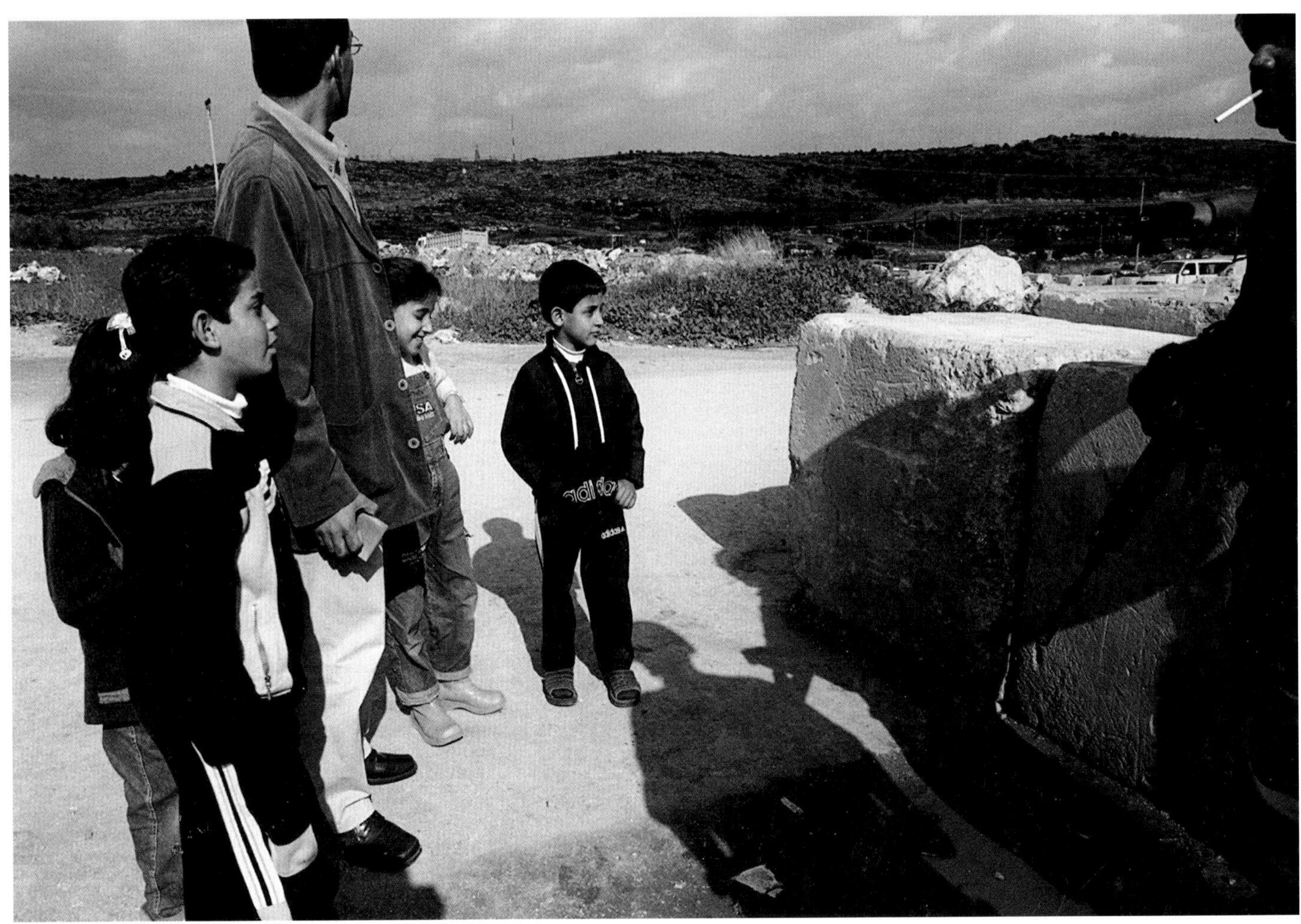

A Palestinian family
waiting at the Qalqiliya
checkpoint guarded
by Israeli soldiers.

The Palestinian city of Qalqiliya (38,000 residents) has
been encircled on all sides by the Barrier since its com-
pletion in 2003. This checkpoint is the only entrance
and exit that connects Qalqiliya with the West Bank.

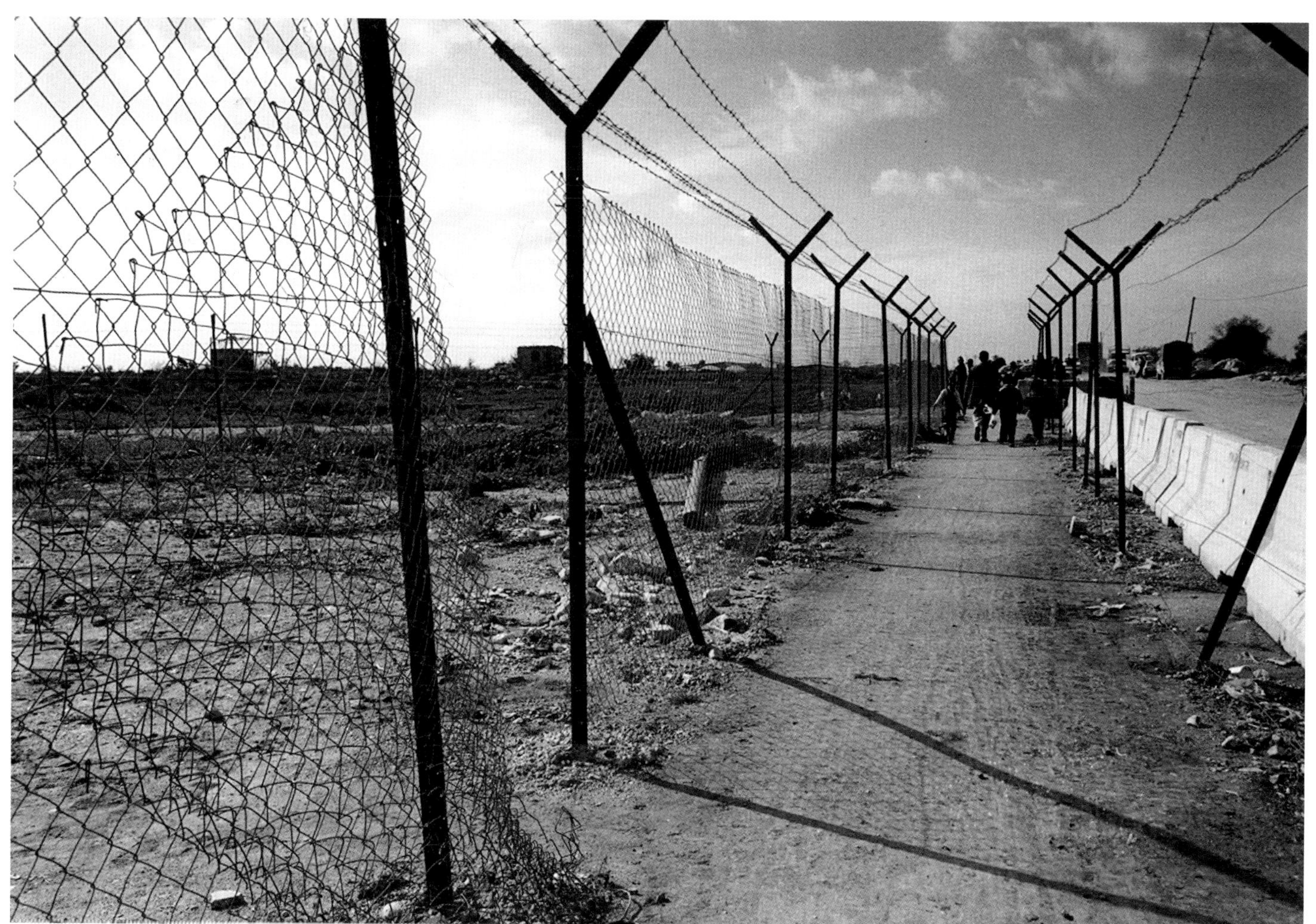

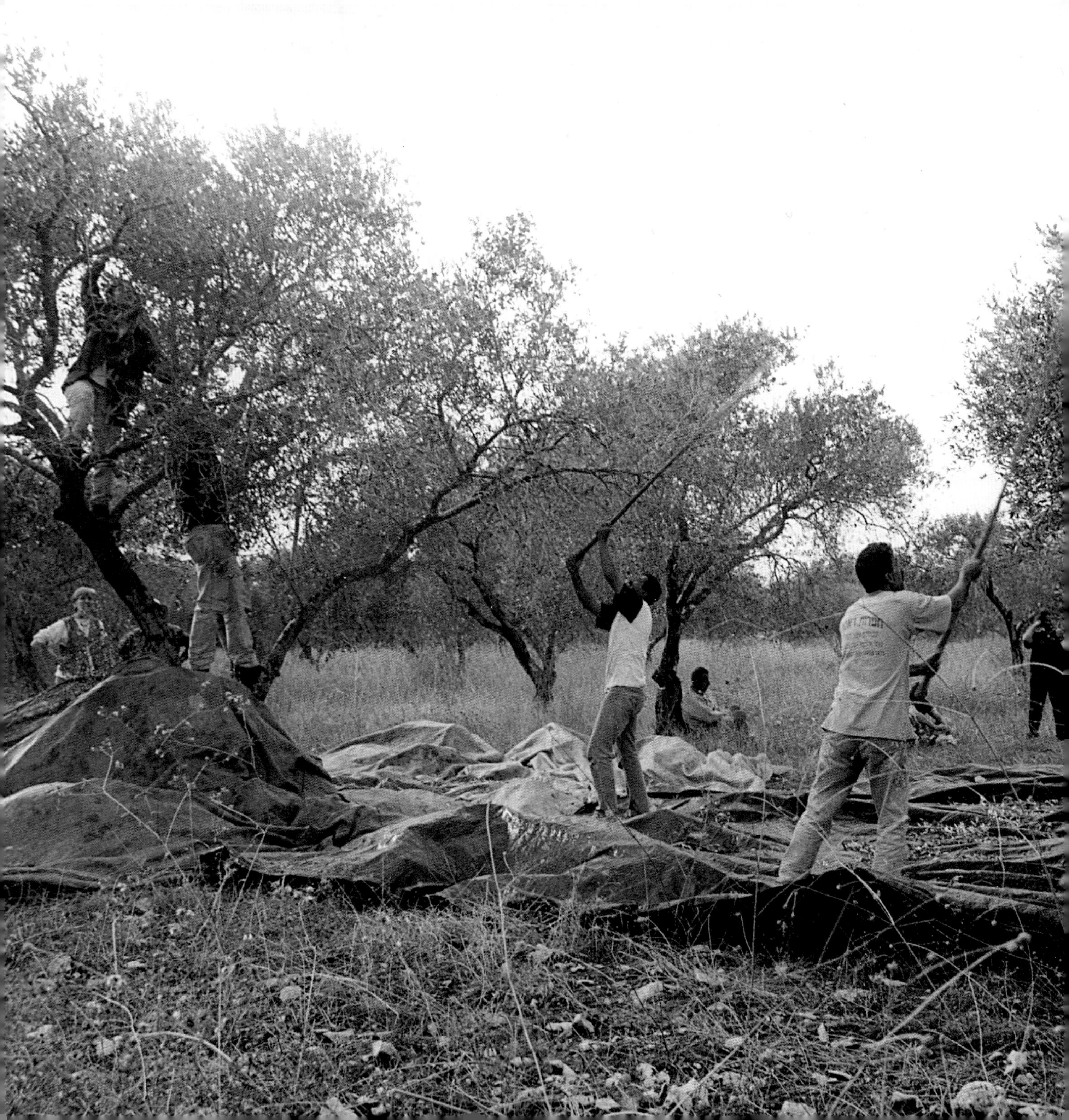

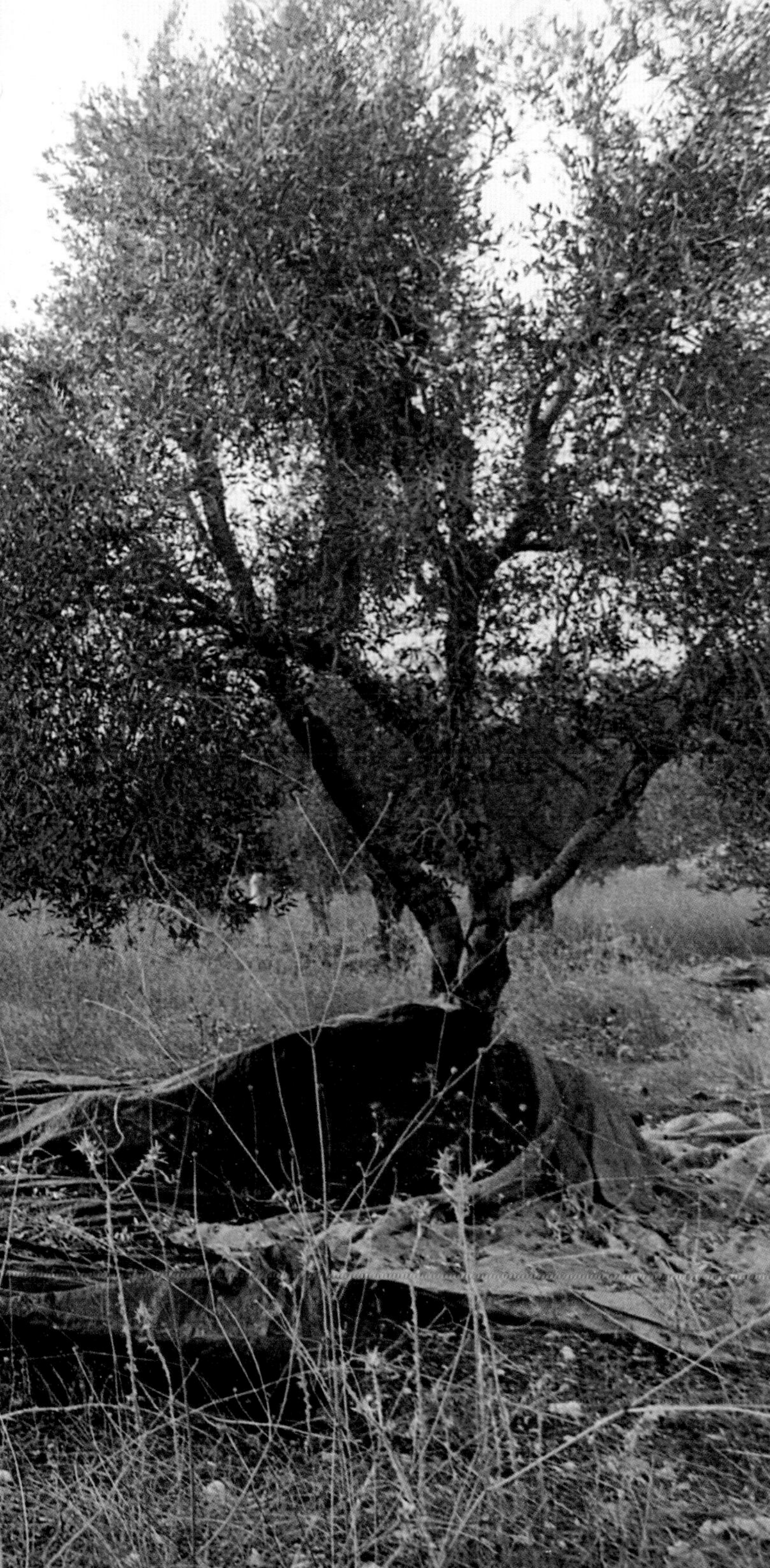

Israeli and Palestinian
activists from the
organization Ta'ayush
(Arab-Jewish
Partnership) work
together to harvest
olives near the
northern West Bank
village of Arabeh near
Jenin.

Ta'ayush activists taking a rest in the olive grove situated between the Israeli settlement of Mevo Dotan and the Palestinian village of Arabeh.

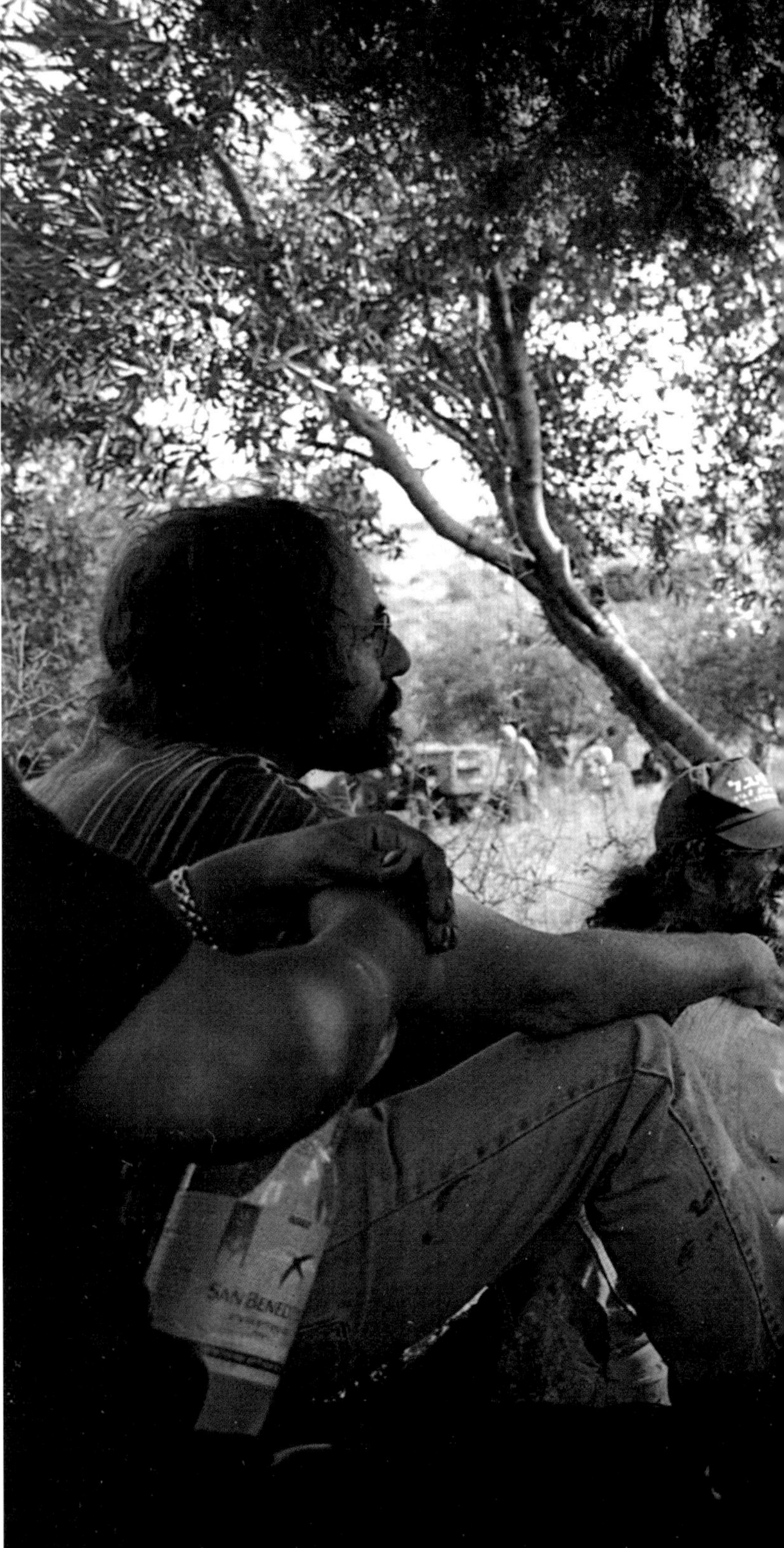

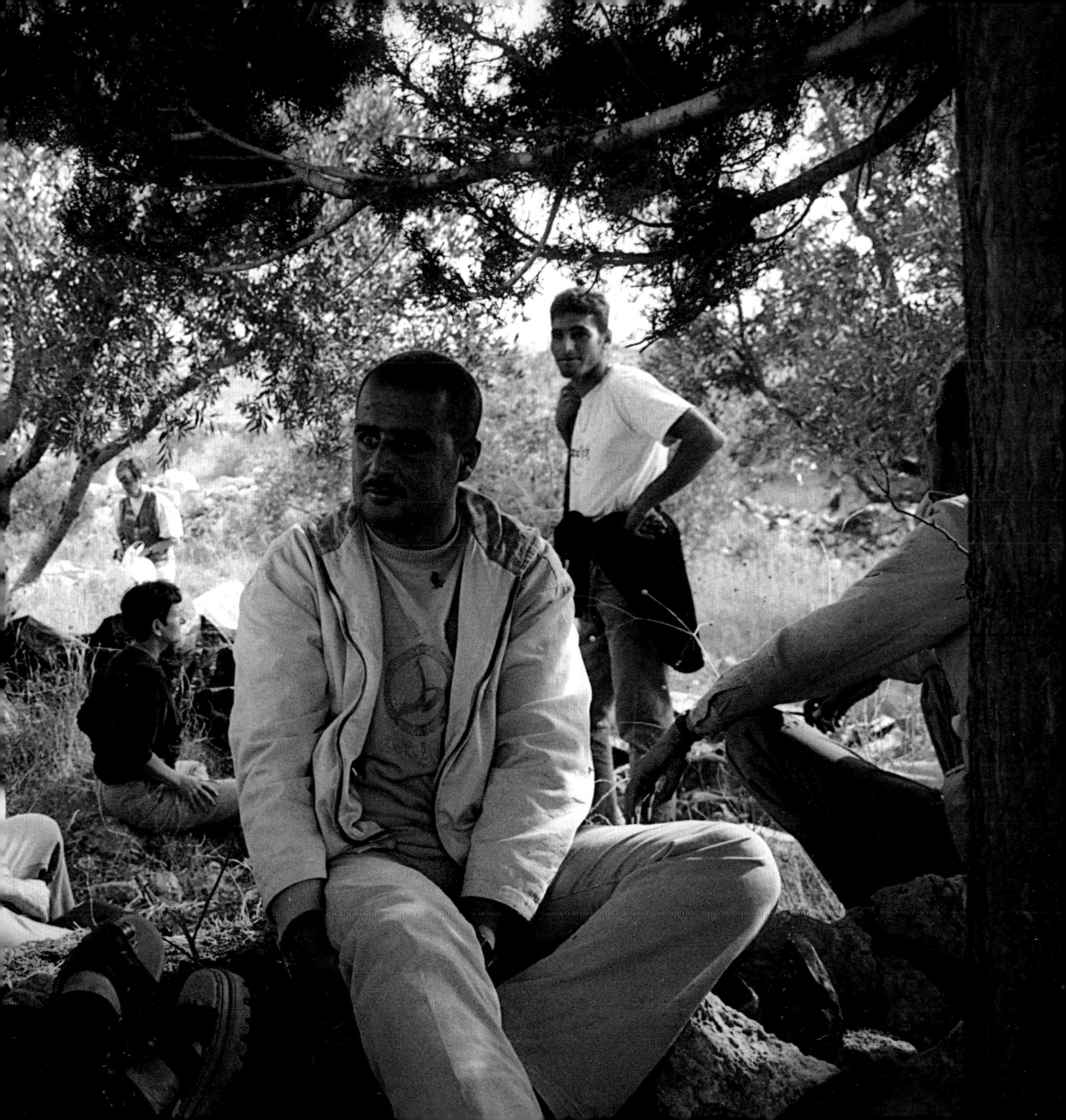

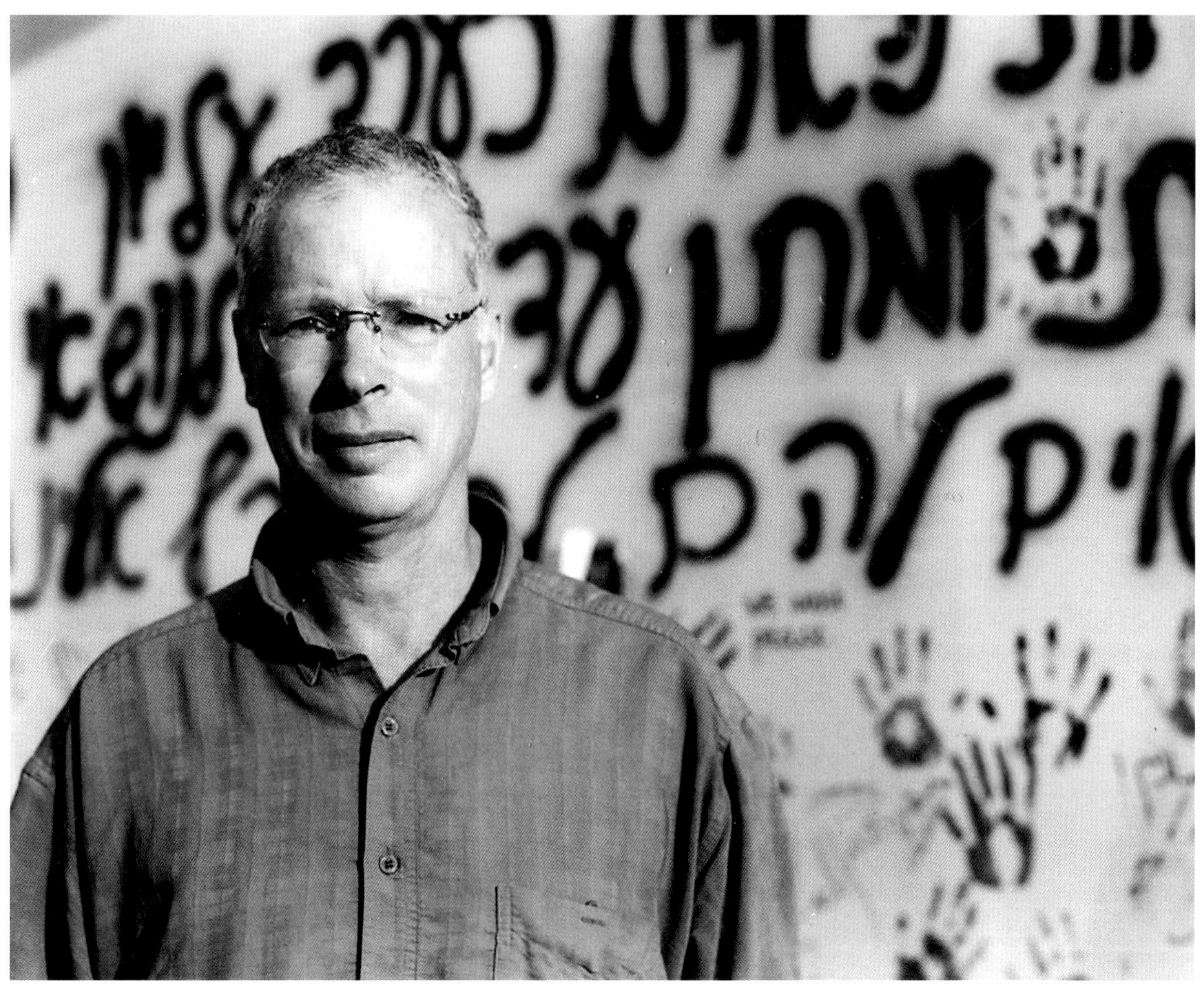

"I believe that our souls have become so dark that ultimately this country will implode due to this darkness. It is as though we have been sleeping on a corpse for fifty years and nobody wants to talk about it."

David Nir, Rehovot
Jewish Israeli.

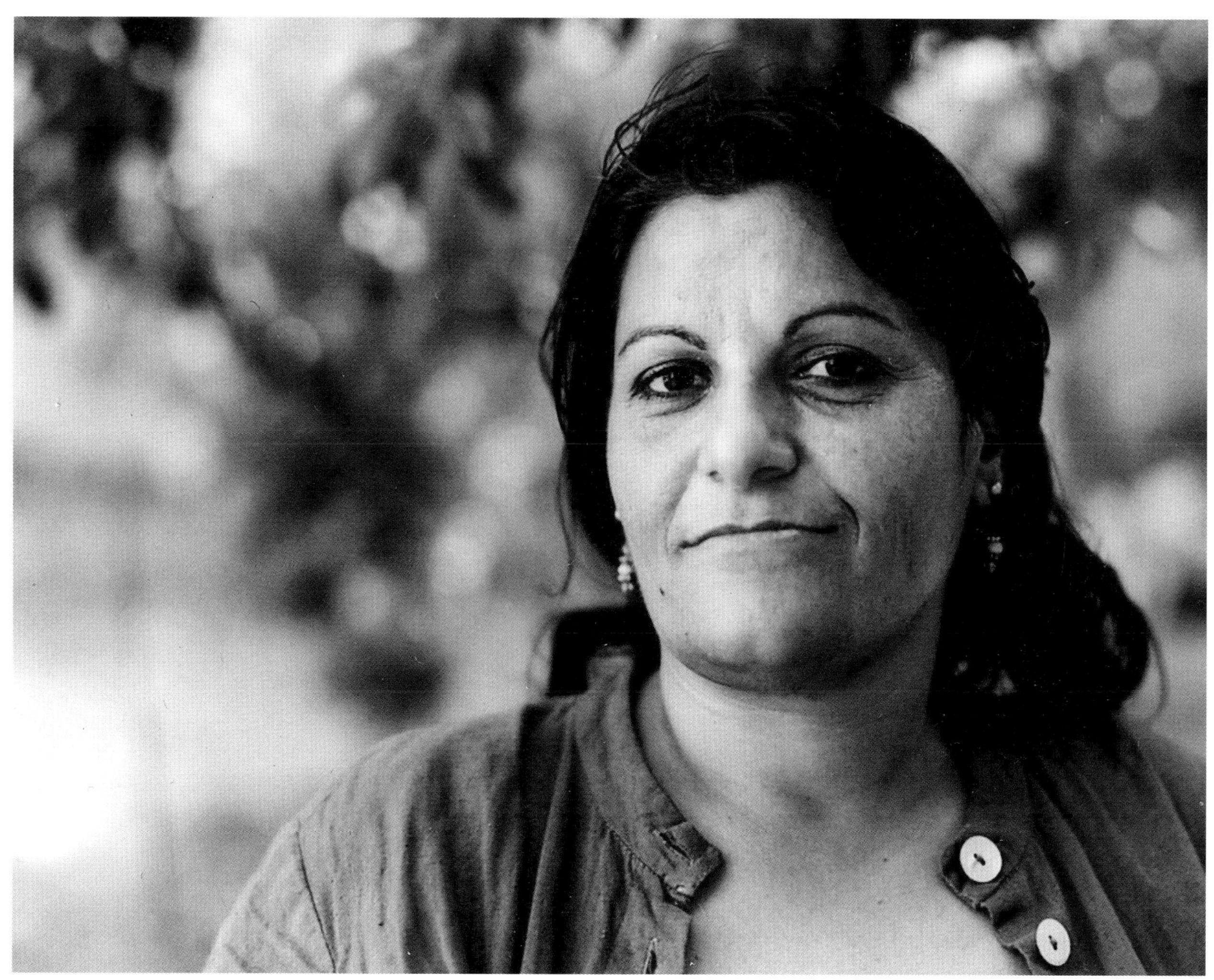

"My dream is to live here in Israel, in a true
democratic country next to our Arab and
Palestinian neighbors, without the army,
checkpoints, walls or bombings. My fear is
if Israel becomes a country exclusively for
Jews, then there will be no hope for peace.
We will live only in a big Jewish ghetto."

Yafit, Rishon Letzion
Syrian-born Jewish Israeli.

Yafit visits the
international house
established in Yanun
and speaks with the
newly arrived French
activists.

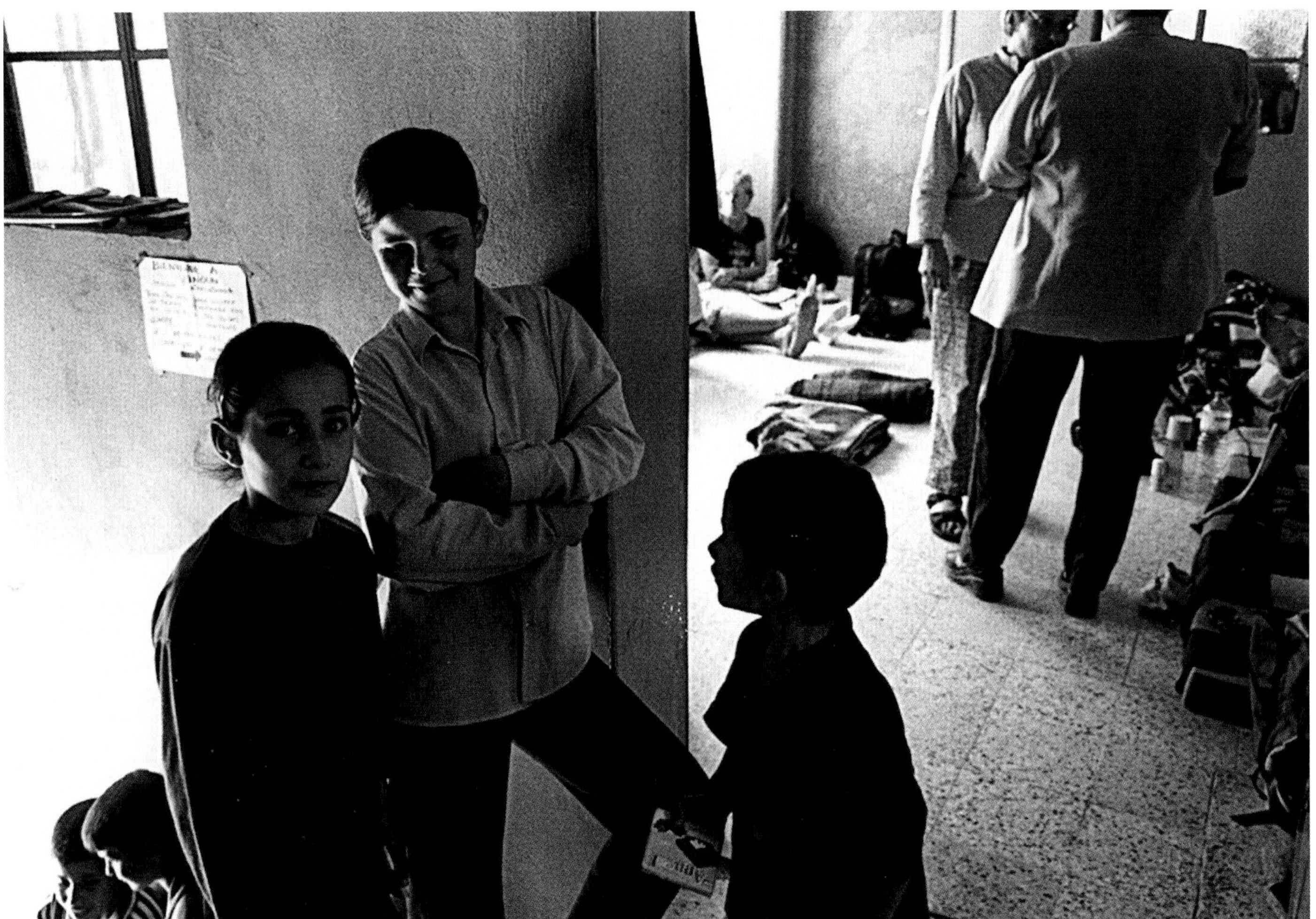

All of the villagers in Yanun were forced to leave the small agricultural village due to the repeated attacks by the Israeli settlers of Itamar in 2002. This is the one family who was determined to remain and called on Israeli and International NGOs (non-governmental organizations) to help protect them. There is now an international house in Yanun with rotating Israeli and International activists to keep a constant presence in the village, in order to deter the militant settlers of Itamar. The villagers have now returned.

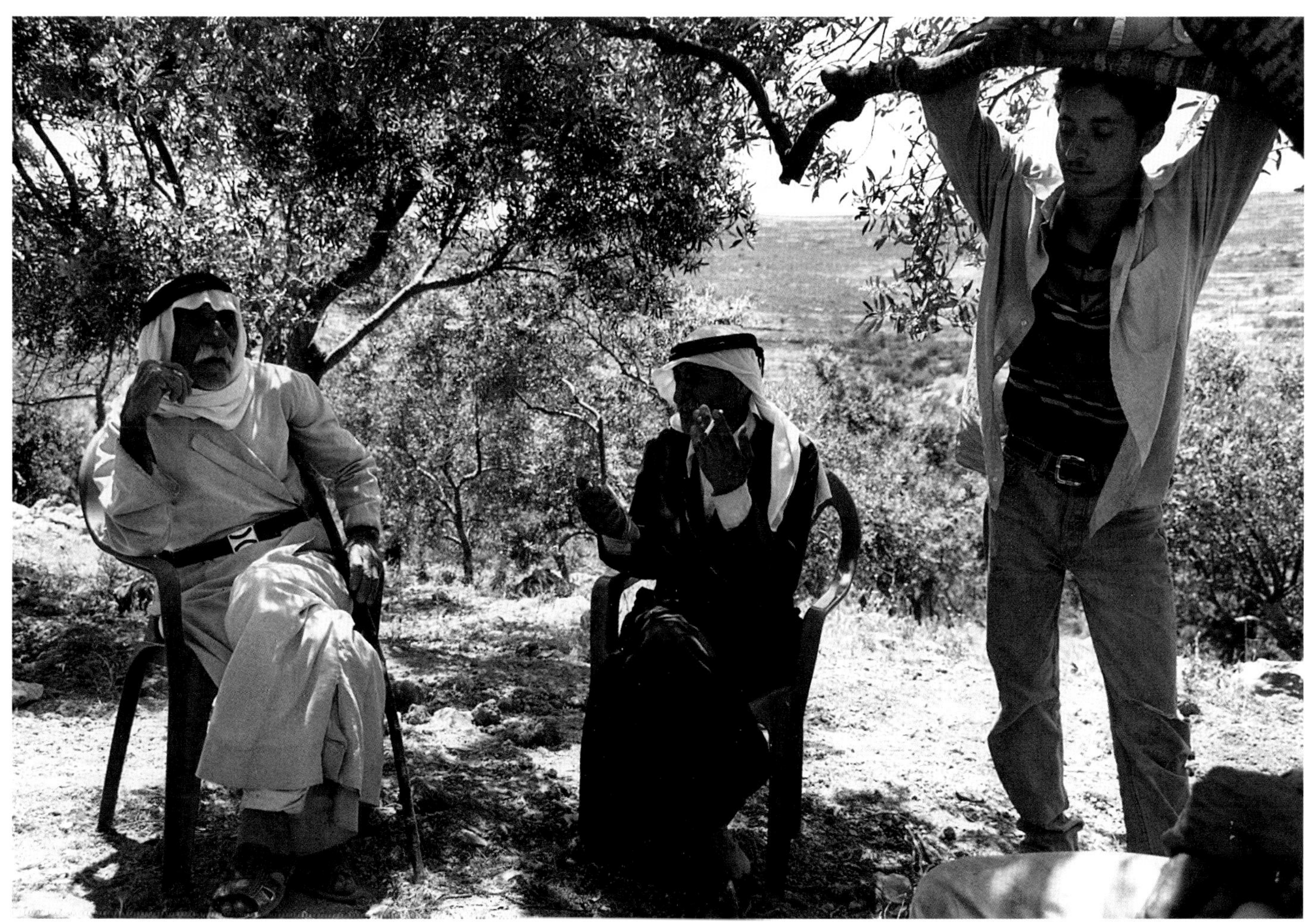

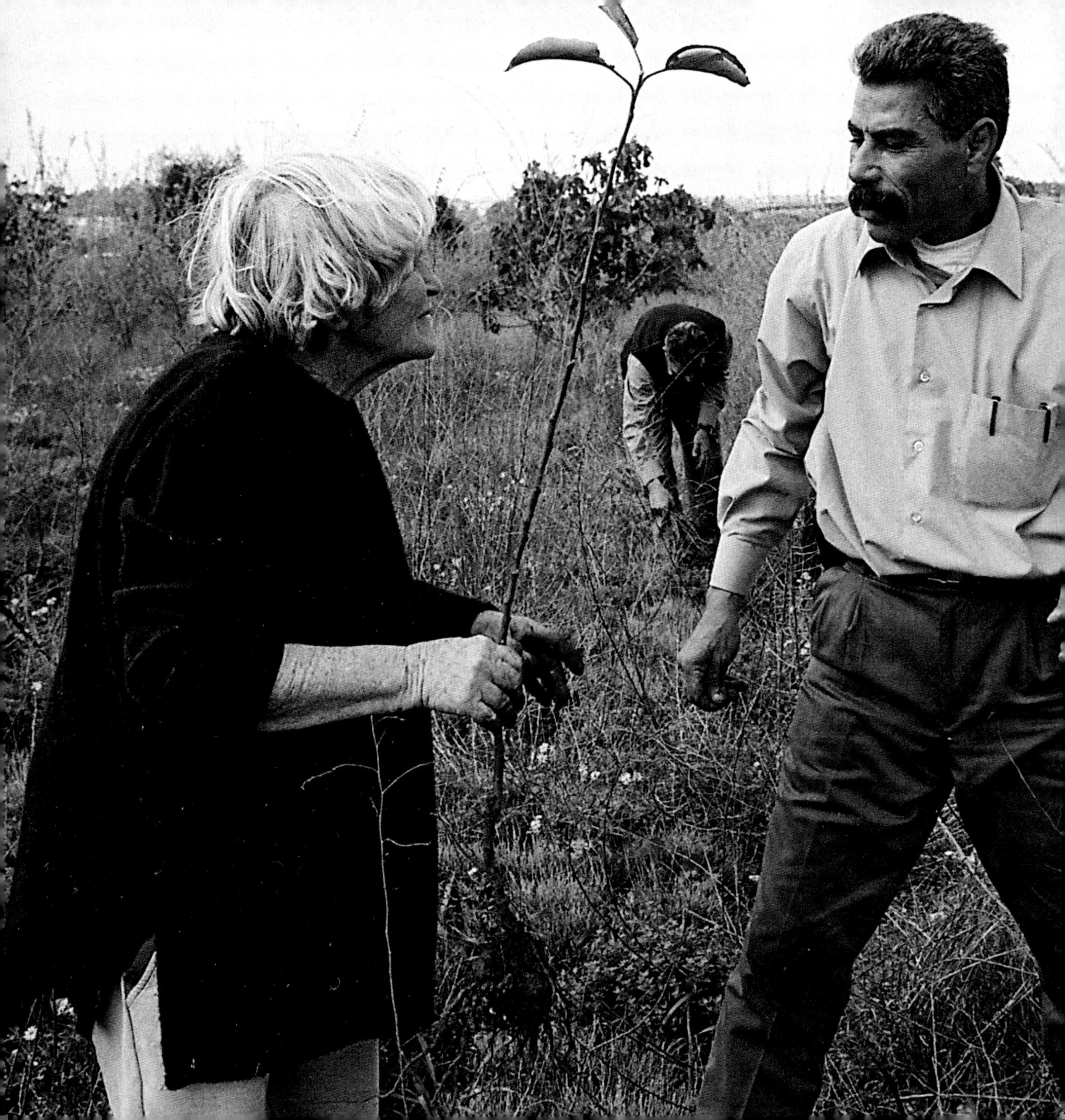

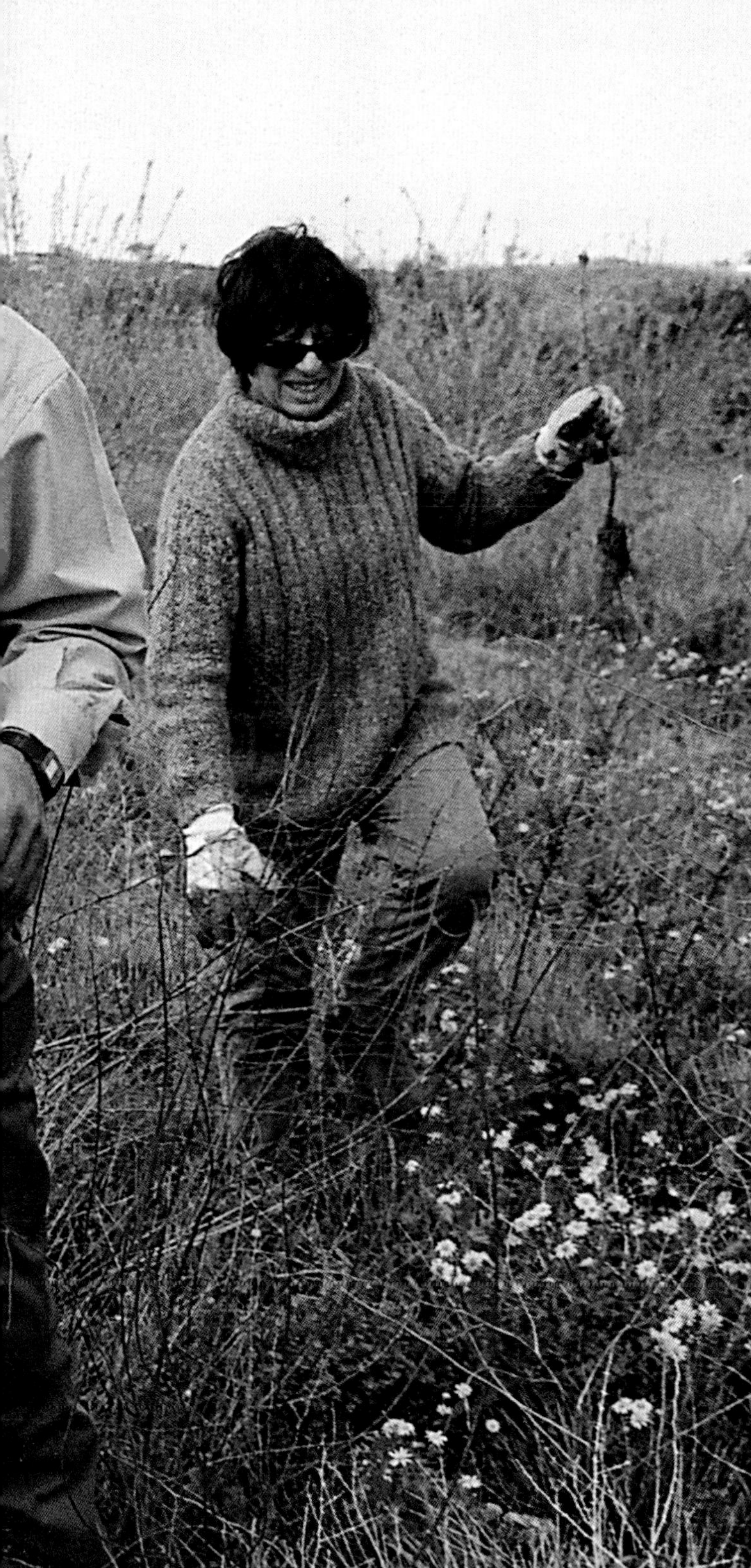

Veteran peace activists Chava Keller and Susanne Moses work with representatives from the P.A.R.C. (Palestinian Agricultural Relief Committees) to plant trees on Abu Za'hee's land near the village of Far'un, in the Tulkarem district. This event was organized by the Rabbis for Human Rights organization based in Jerusalem.

"Women build peace not Walls!" Israeli and Palestinian women protest together at the Tulkarem checkpoint.

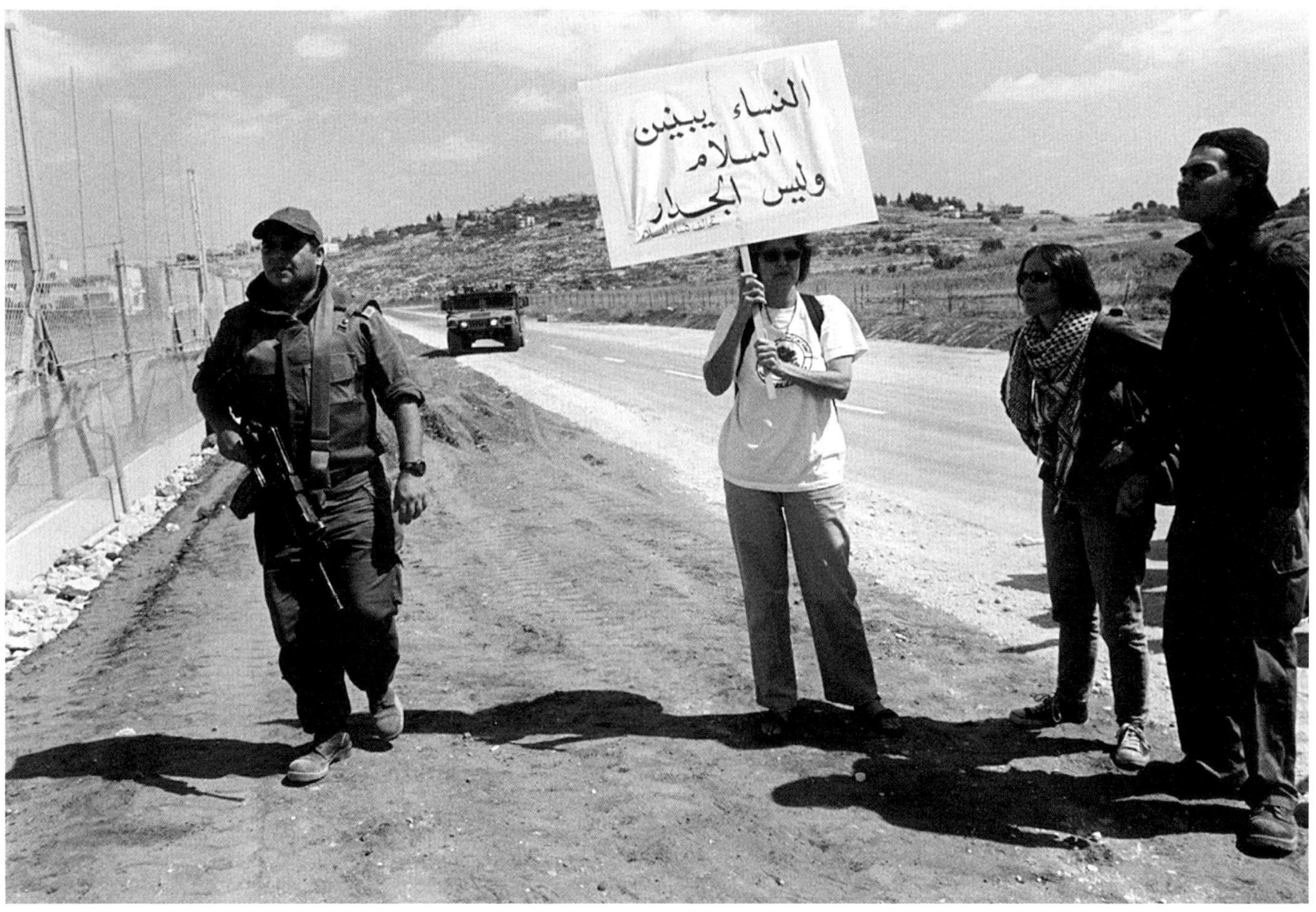

Israeli and Palestinian
peace activists are able
to meet briefly inside
the Tulkarem
checkpoint.

Overleaf. Palestinian
teenagers play soccer
on the farmland leveled
by the Israeli Army to
build the Barrier on the
outskirts of Ma'asha,
a village in the West
Bank.

According to Israeli Authorities, more than 63,000 olive trees have been uprooted to make way for the Barrier. The Authorities claim that many trees have been replanted, however it was not specified if they were replanted on Palestinian land or in Israel.

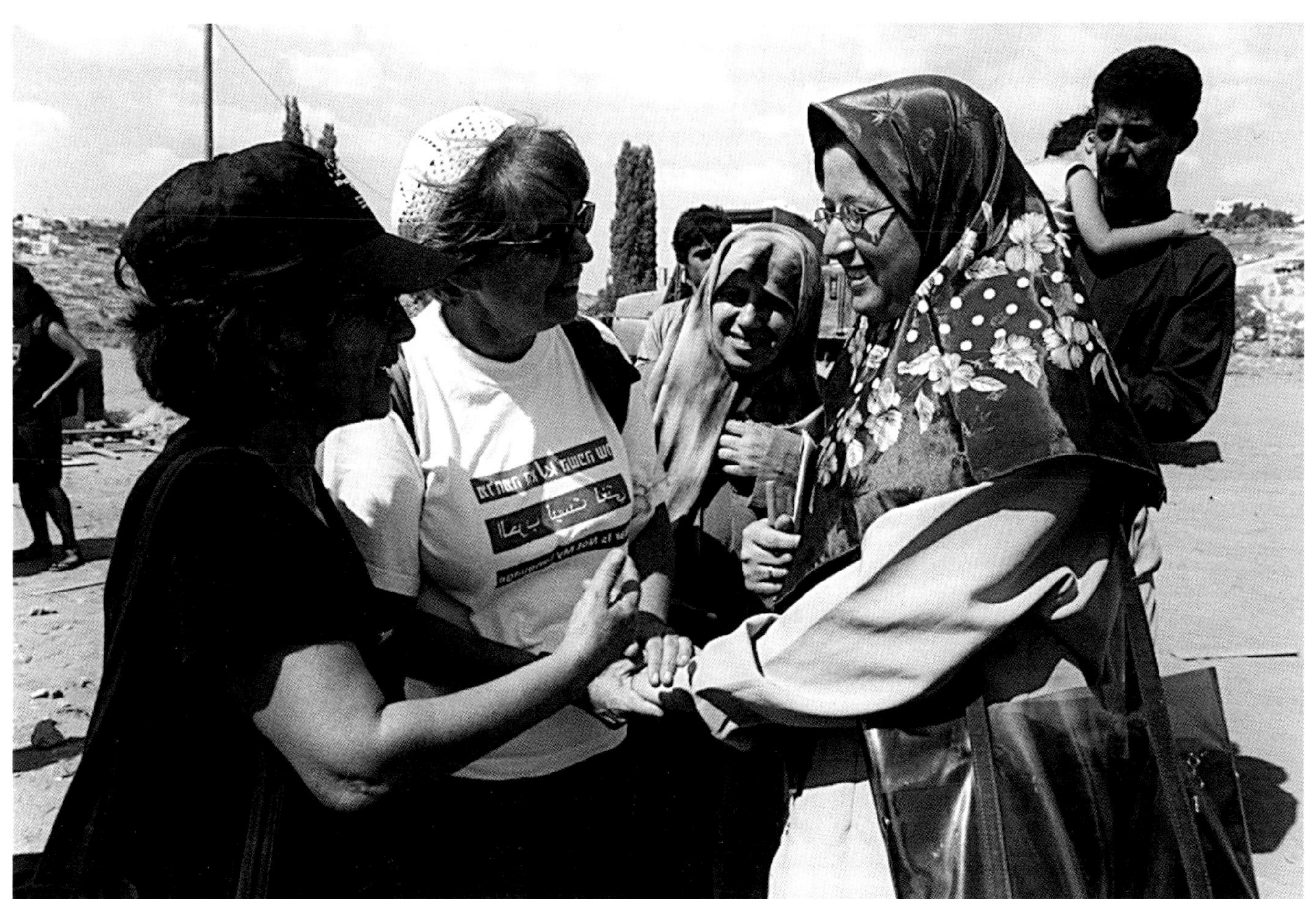

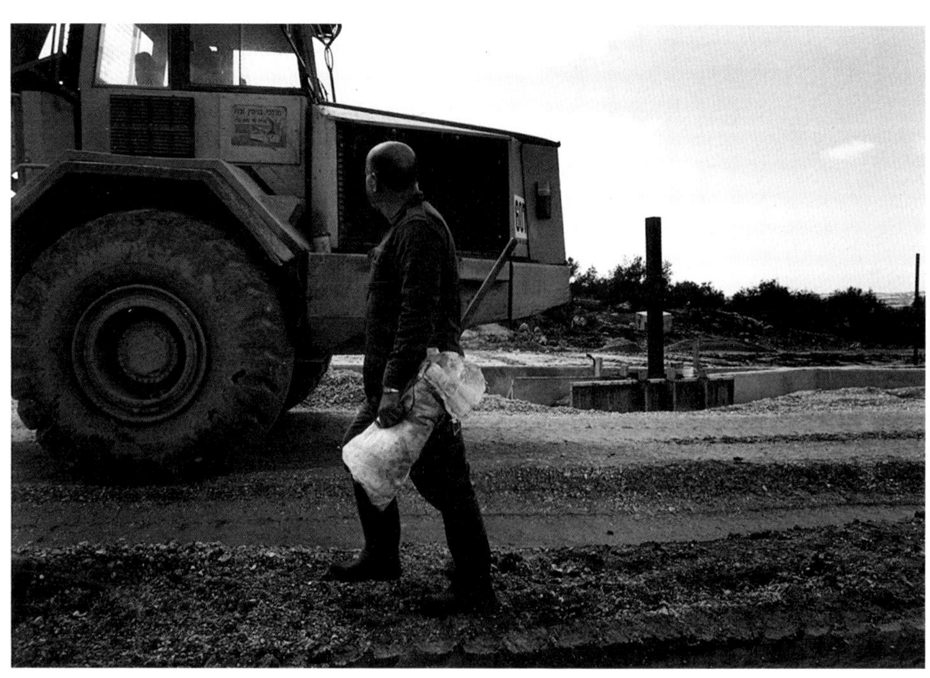

Abu Za'hee, the farmer from the small agricultural village of Far'un, points out the foundation for the Barrier that was built between the village and his farmland in January 2003.

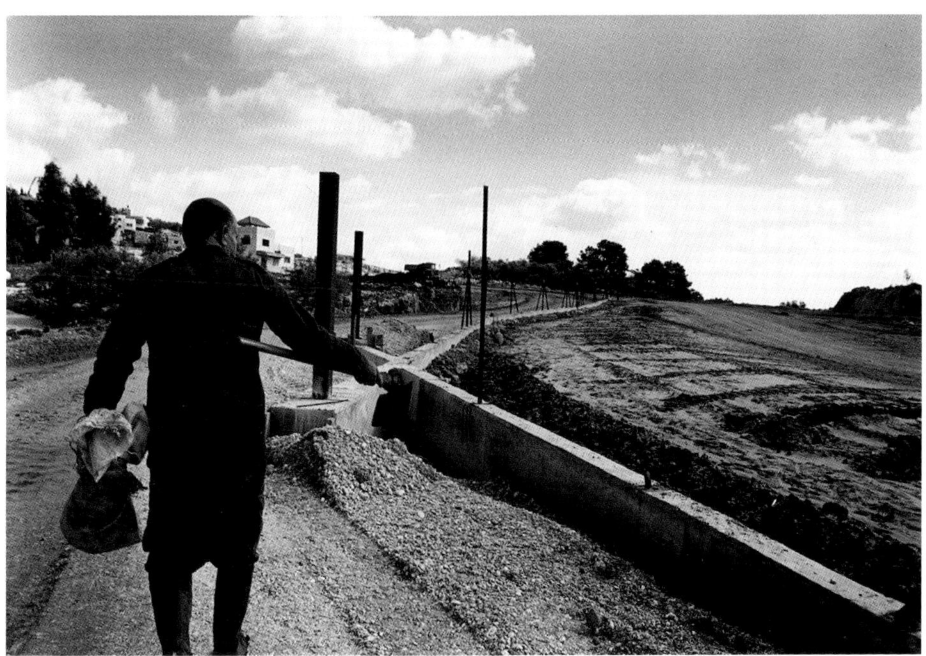

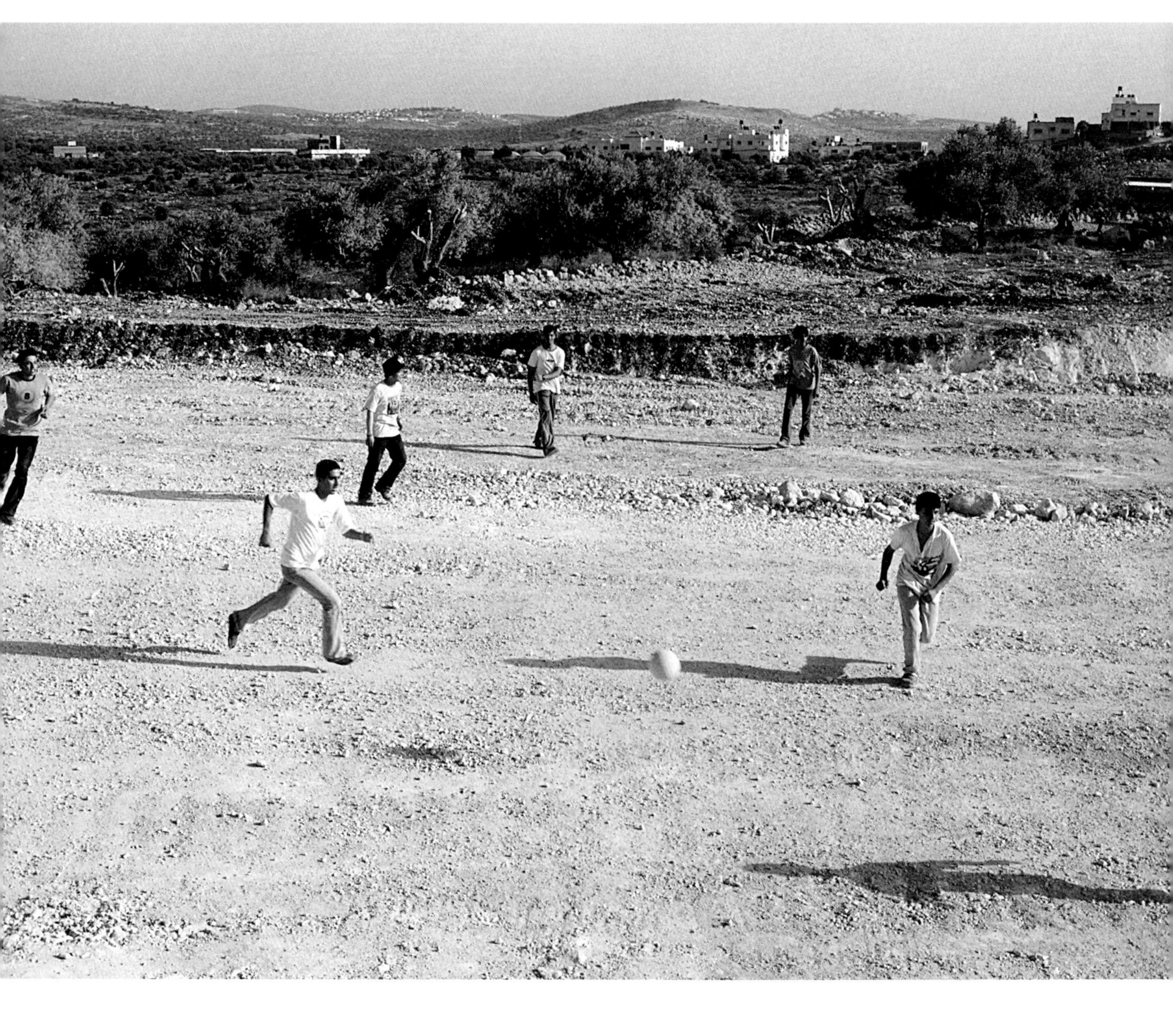

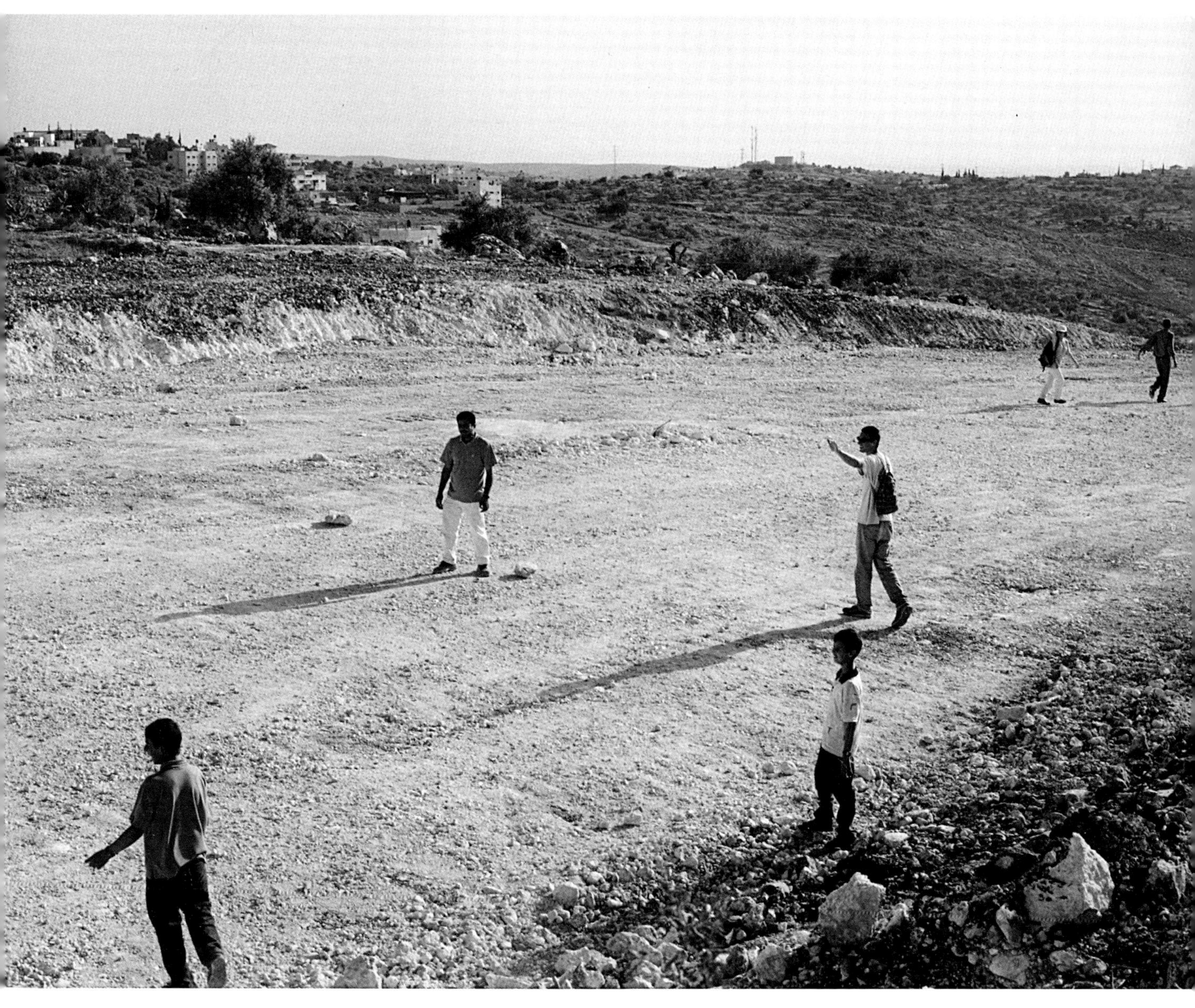

Abu Za'hee's youngest
son with the photo
from my previous trip.

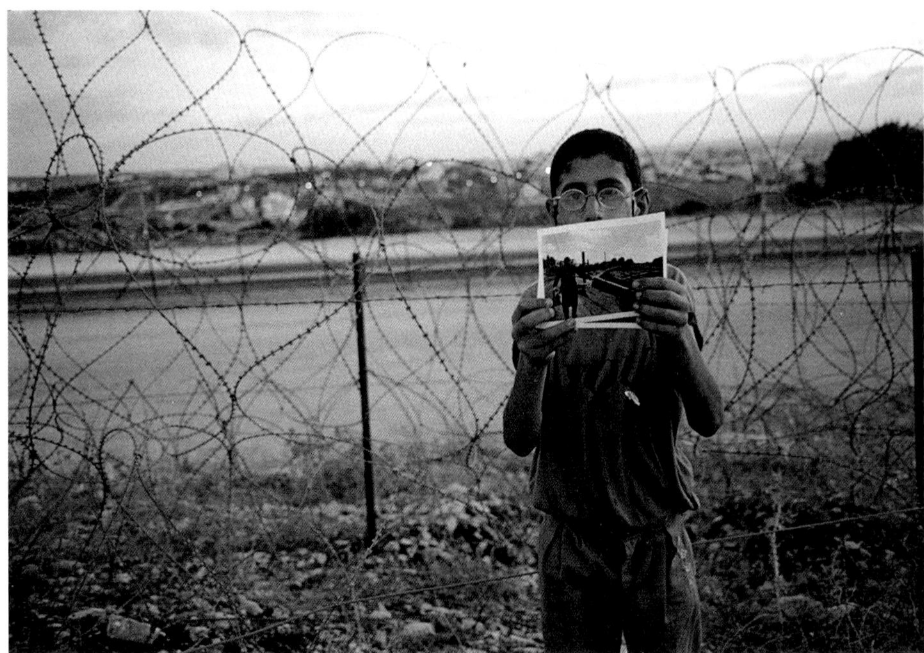

I returned to visit Abu Za'hee in September 2003 to find the Barrier completed and to learn that even though the Israeli Army had built gates in the fence to allow farmers to reach their land, Abu Za'hee had not been able to harvest because these gates have remained locked[7].

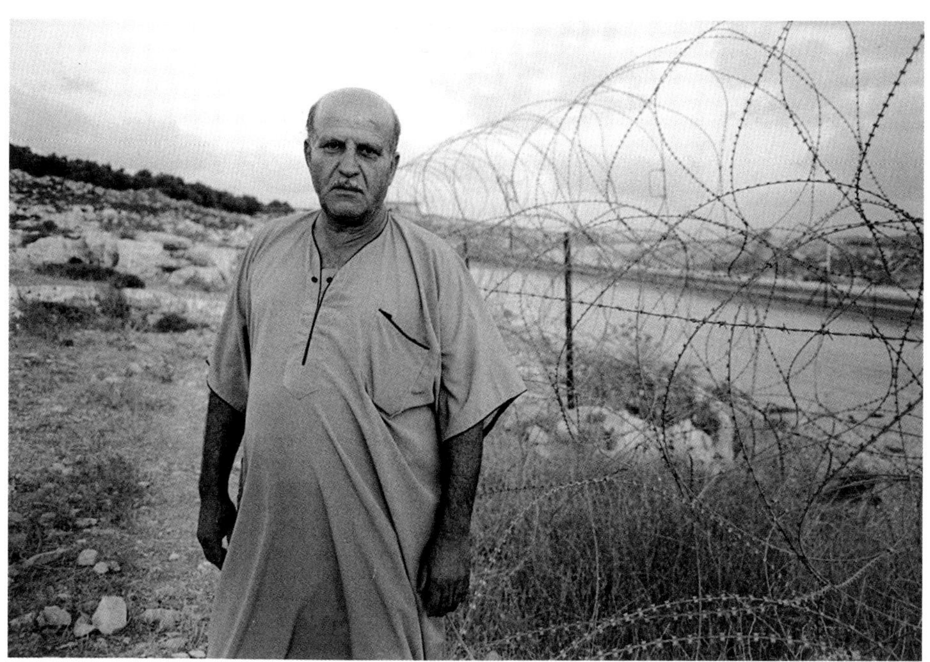

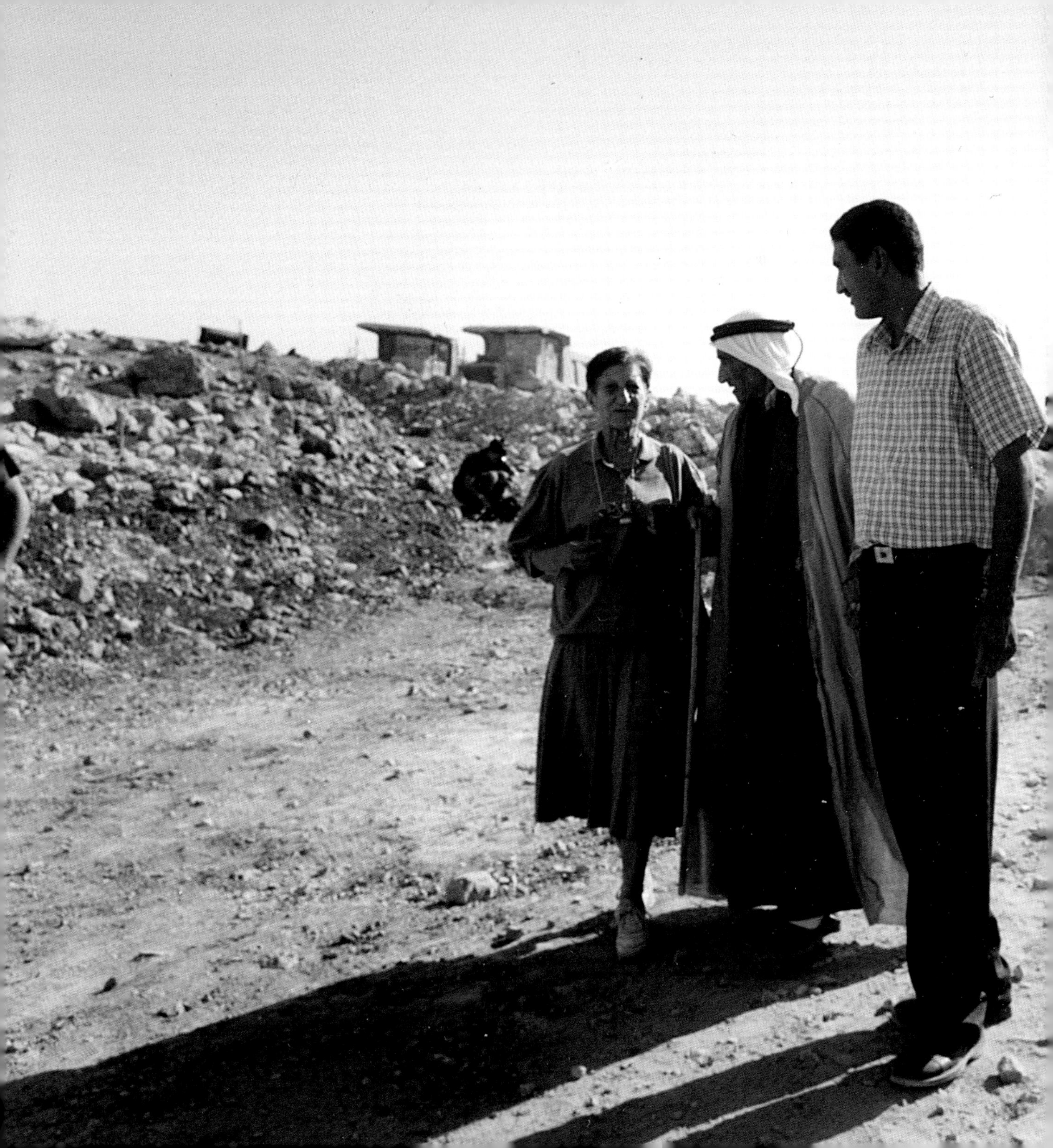

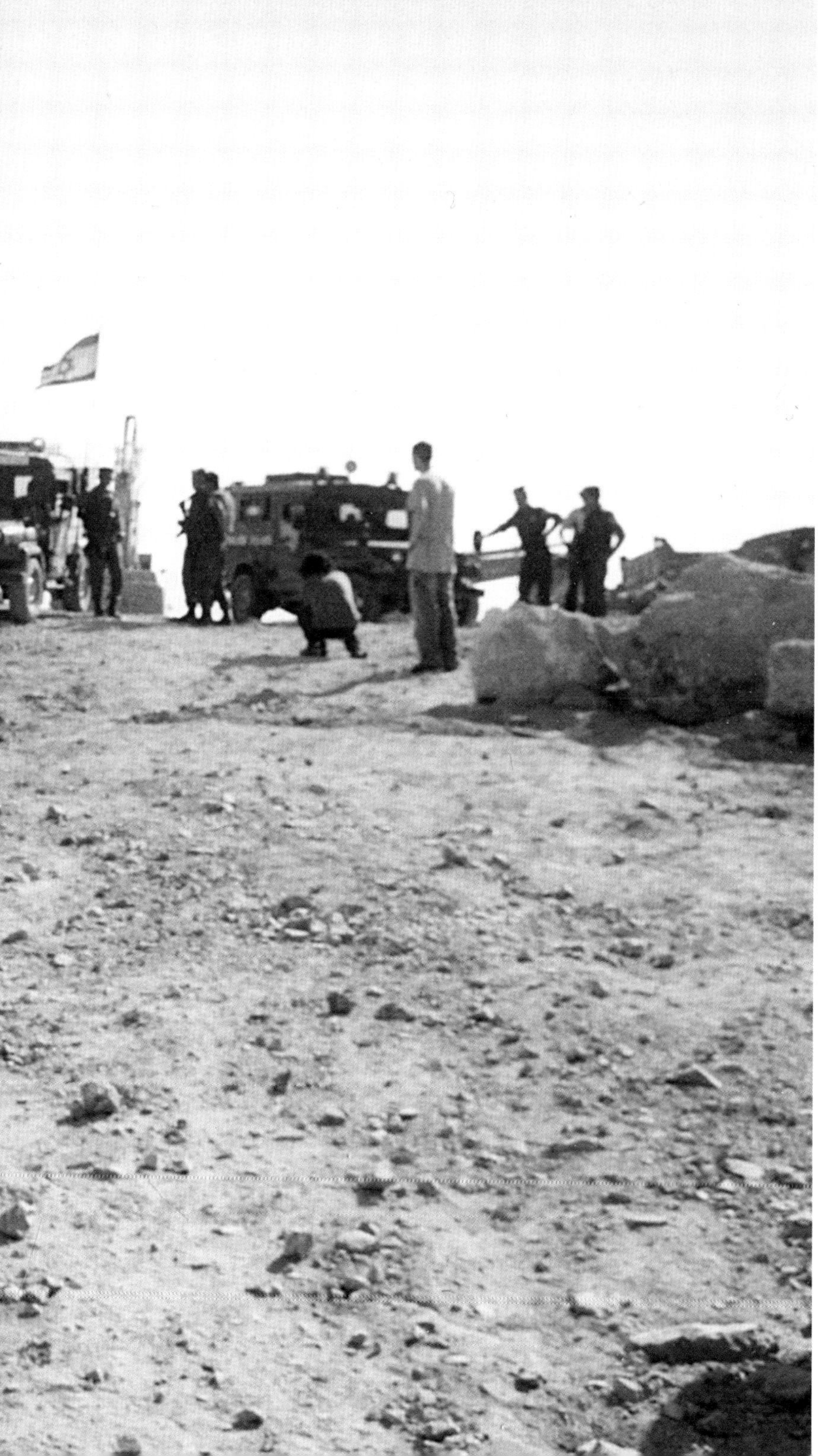

Local Palestinians speak with an Israeli activist about how the construction of the Barrier will affect their lives in Abu Dis, near Jerusalem, the West Bank.

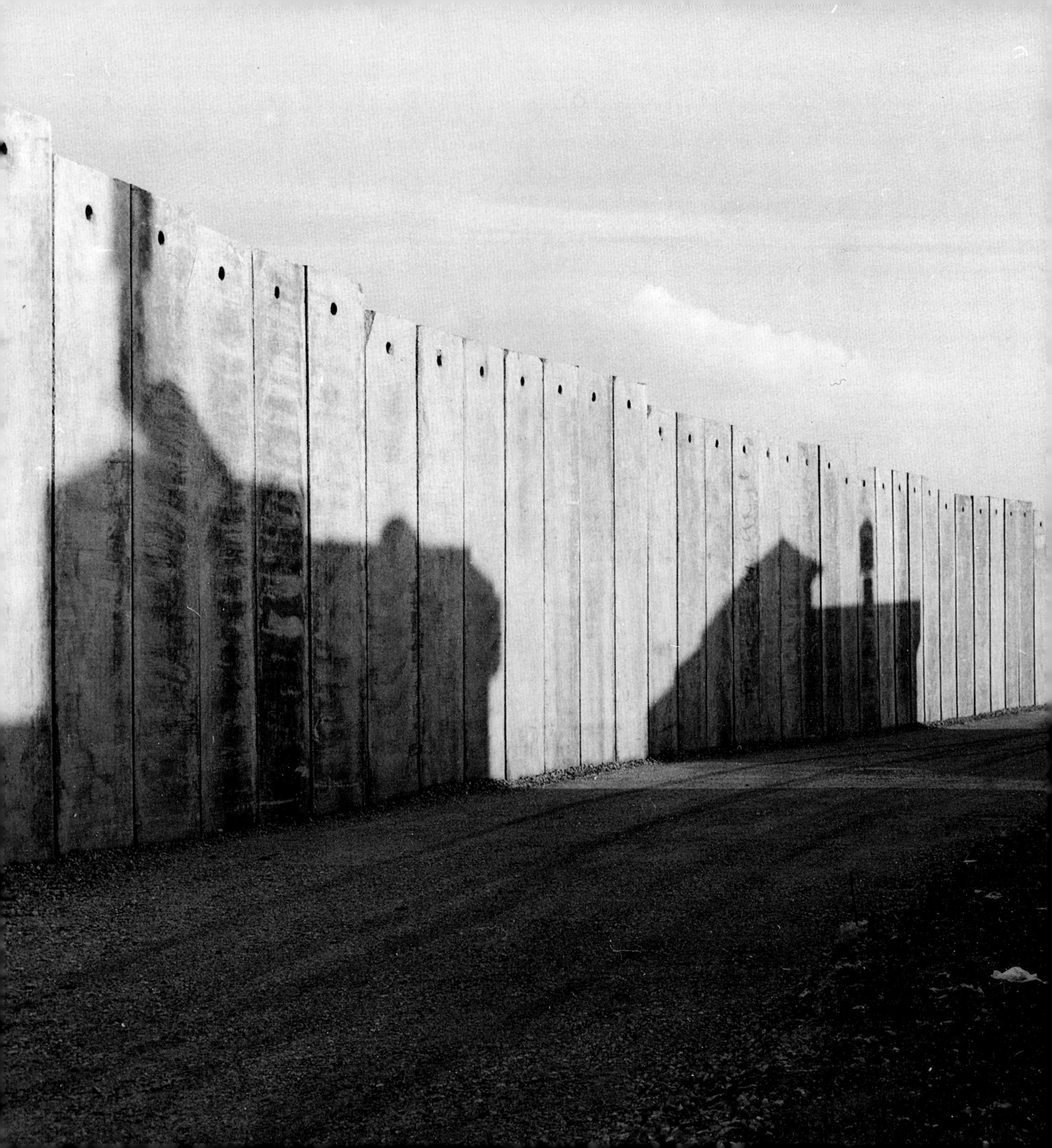

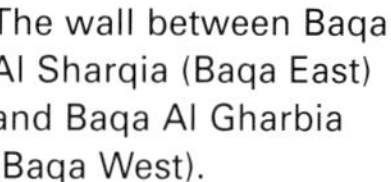

The wall between Baqa
Al Sharqia (Baqa East)
and Baqa Al Gharbia
(Baqa West).

Walls

"We'll build a wall"
they say.

"They" being those who know.
The generals
who first declared
we'd have to live together
side by side,
and trust the others
to behave like us.
Or like we'd like to be, that is.

And now "They" say
it's better to build walls
that separate
and keep us out of range
of rage unbridled
and the lust for blood
set free.

But no one listens now
because we've learned
that walls cannot contain
the fury
any more than words can
realize
the dream.

Ricky Friesem
November 2001

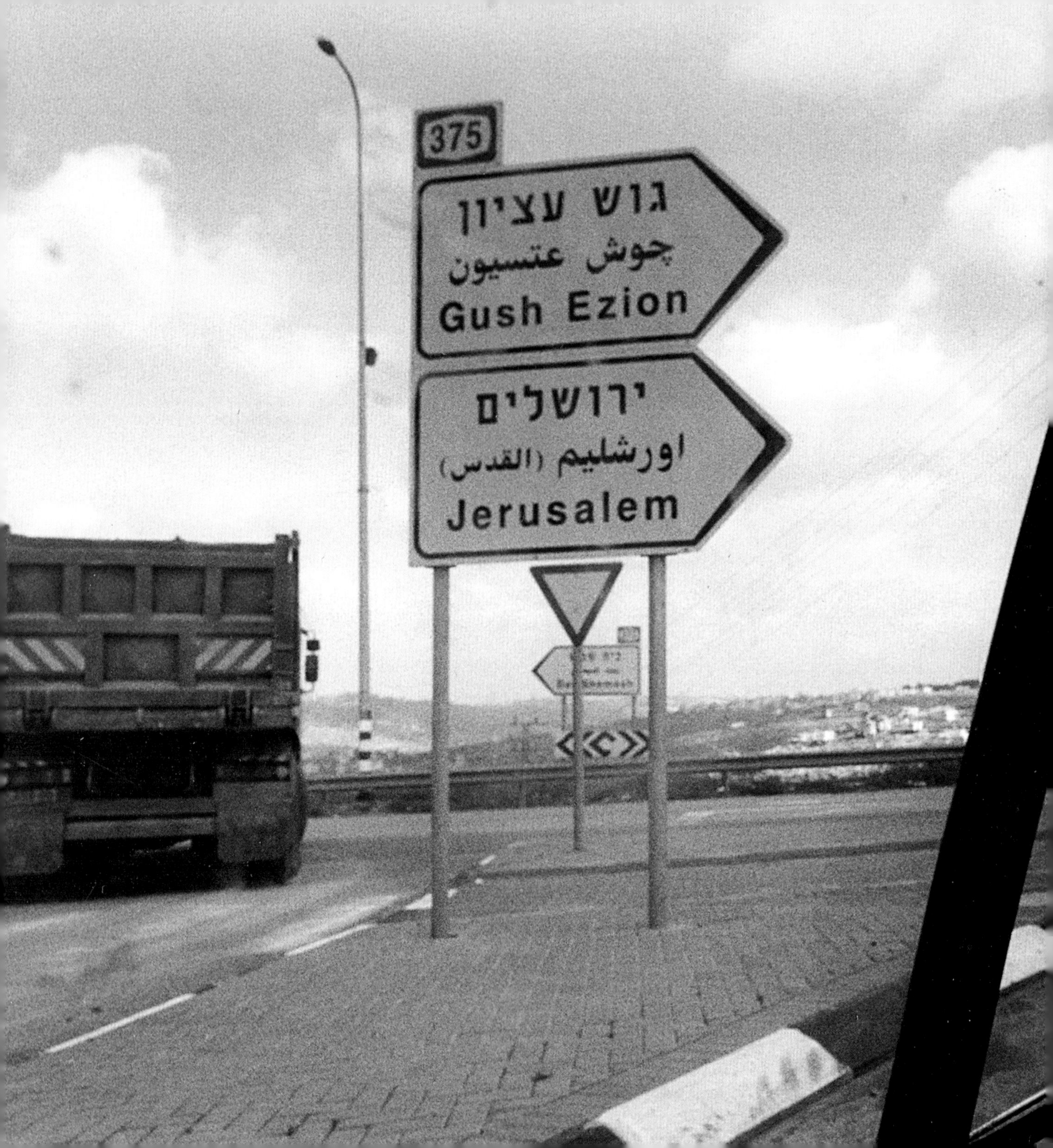
375
גוש עציון
جوش عتسيون
Gush Ezion
ירושלים
اورشليم (القدس)
Jerusalem

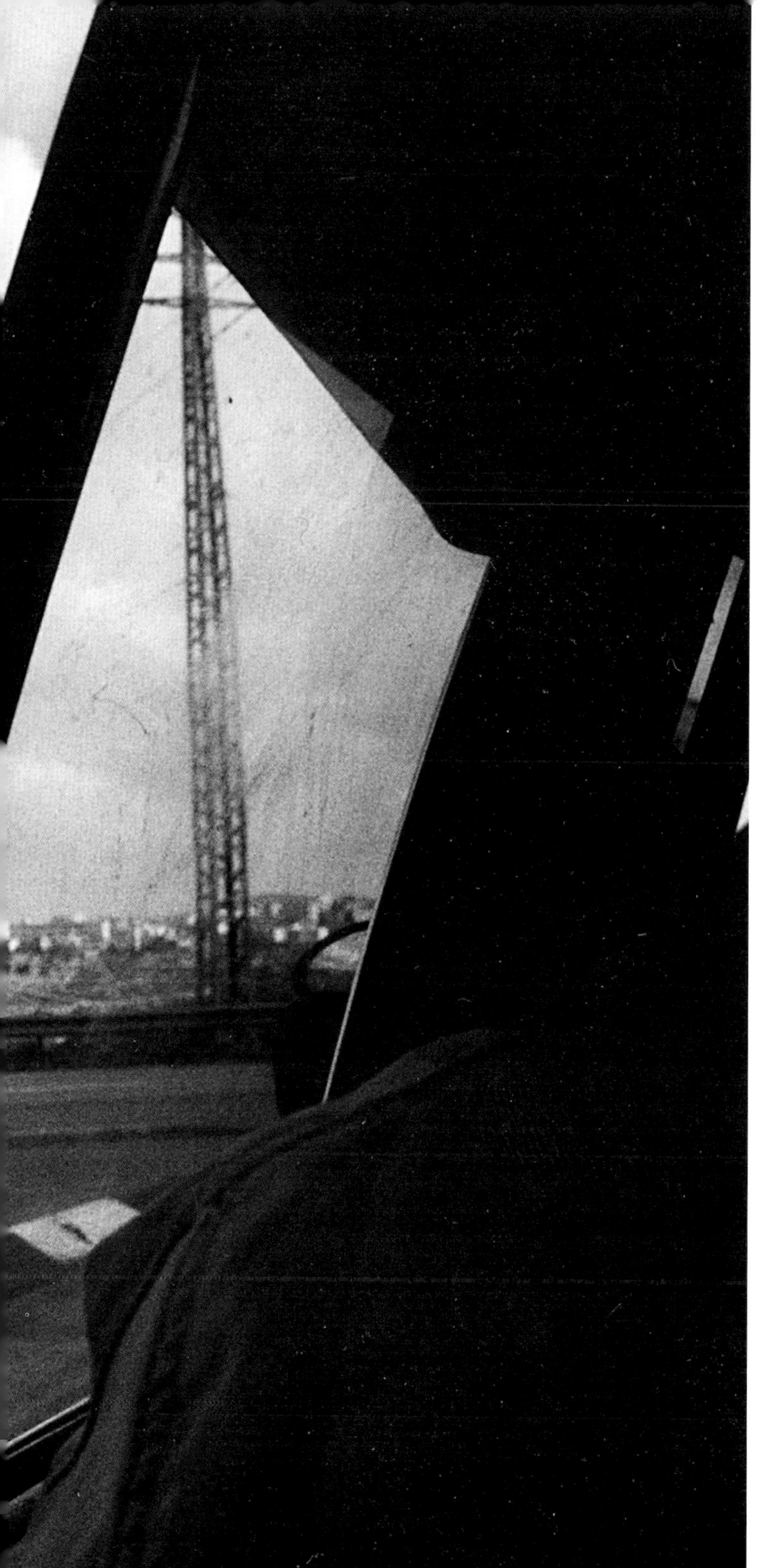

The bypass roads between Jerusalem and the Ezion bloc of Israeli settlements to the south in the West Bank. Palestinians are forbidden from using these roads.

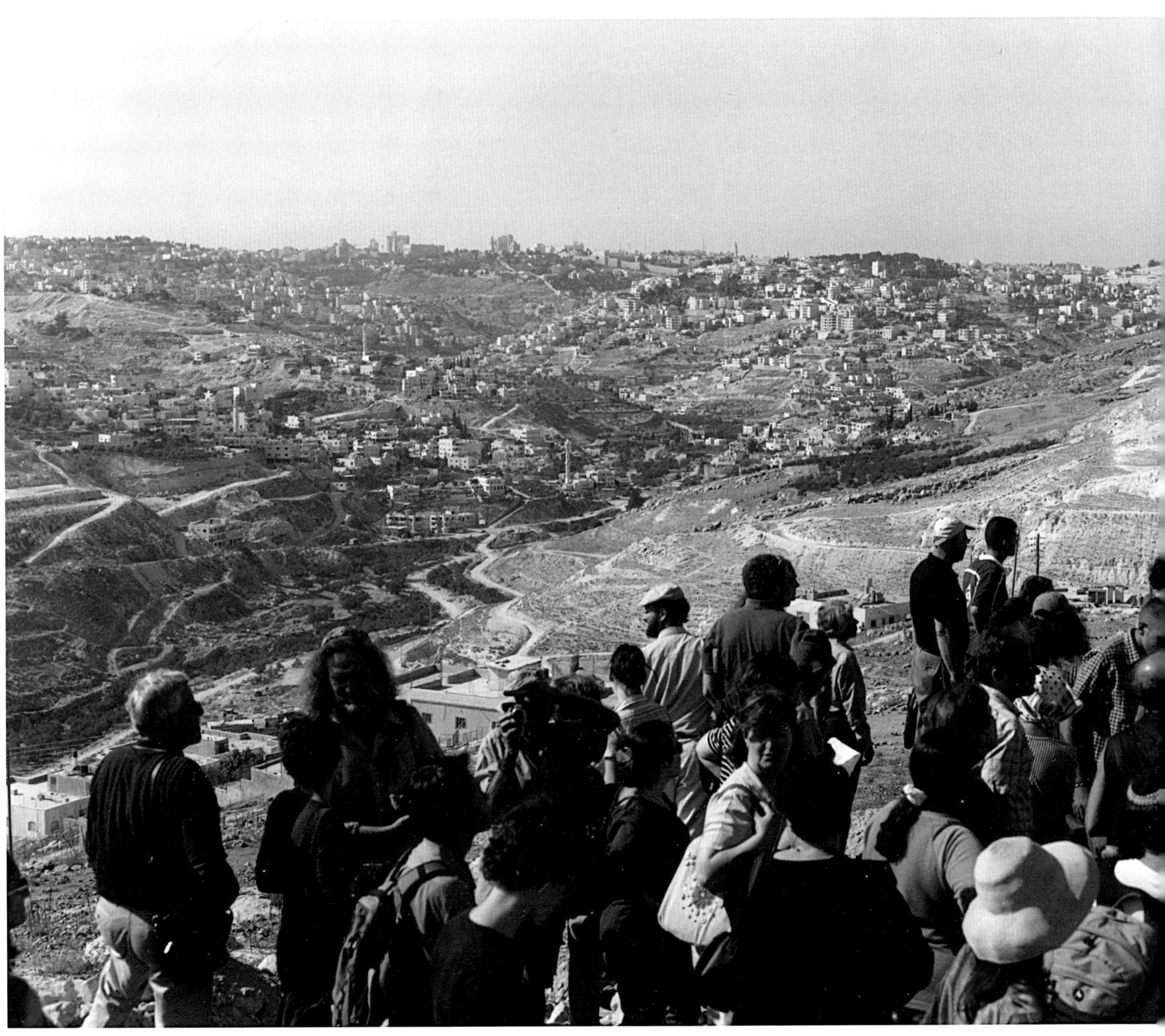

Overleaf. Palestinians living in close proximity to where the Barrier will be built in Abu Dis giving their testimonies to a crowd of Israeli peace activists. The construction of the Barrier will gravely restrict the Palestinians' freedom of movement, often separating them from their families, land, schools, and universities. The ancient walls of Jerusalem's Old City are visible in the distance in the left image and the Al Quds University is in the far right image.

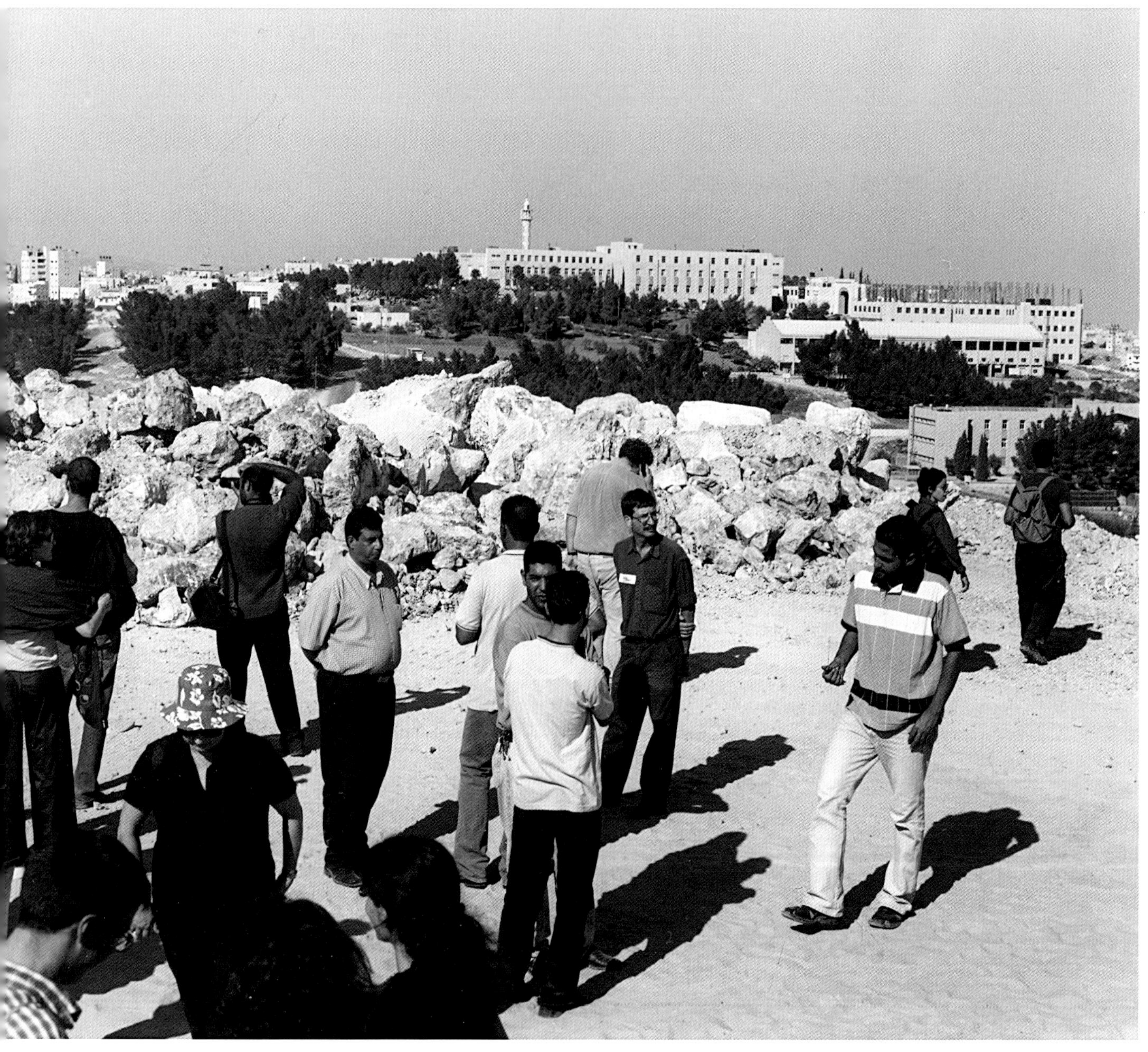

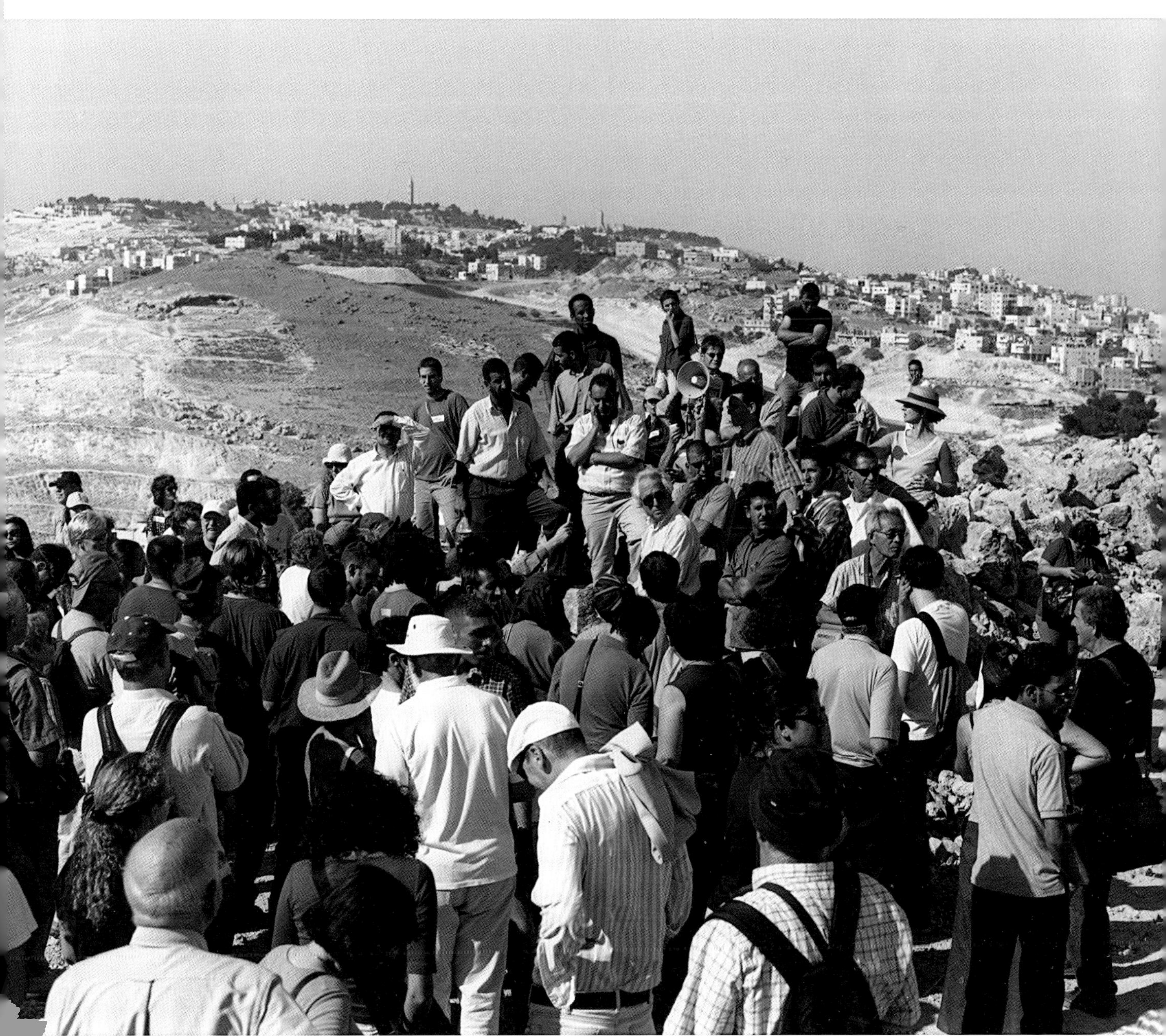

A new section of Betar
Illit, an Israeli
settlement that was
founded in 1990. It is
one of the fastest
growing settlements
in the West Bank:
presently there are
30,000 residents and
construction continues.

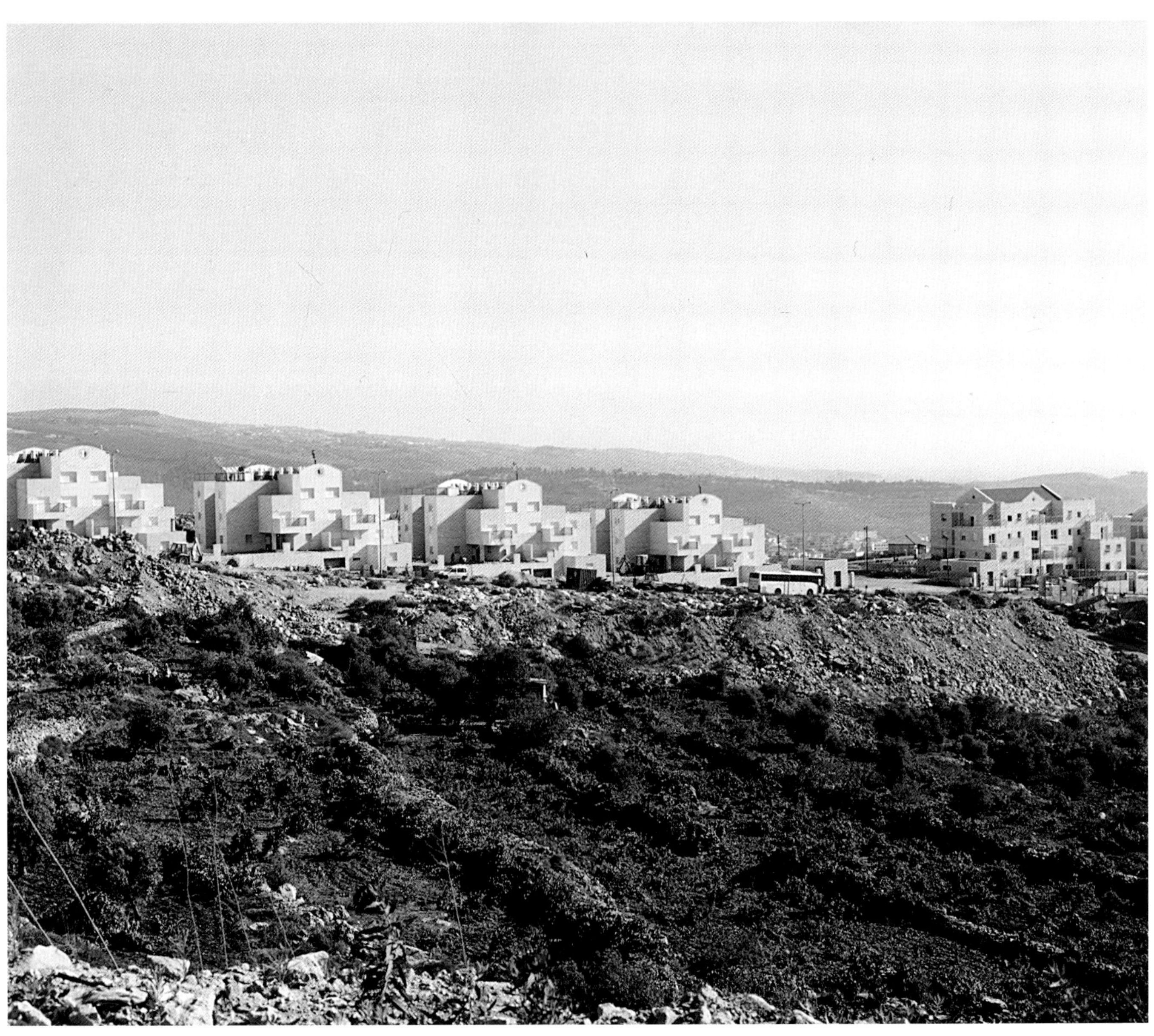

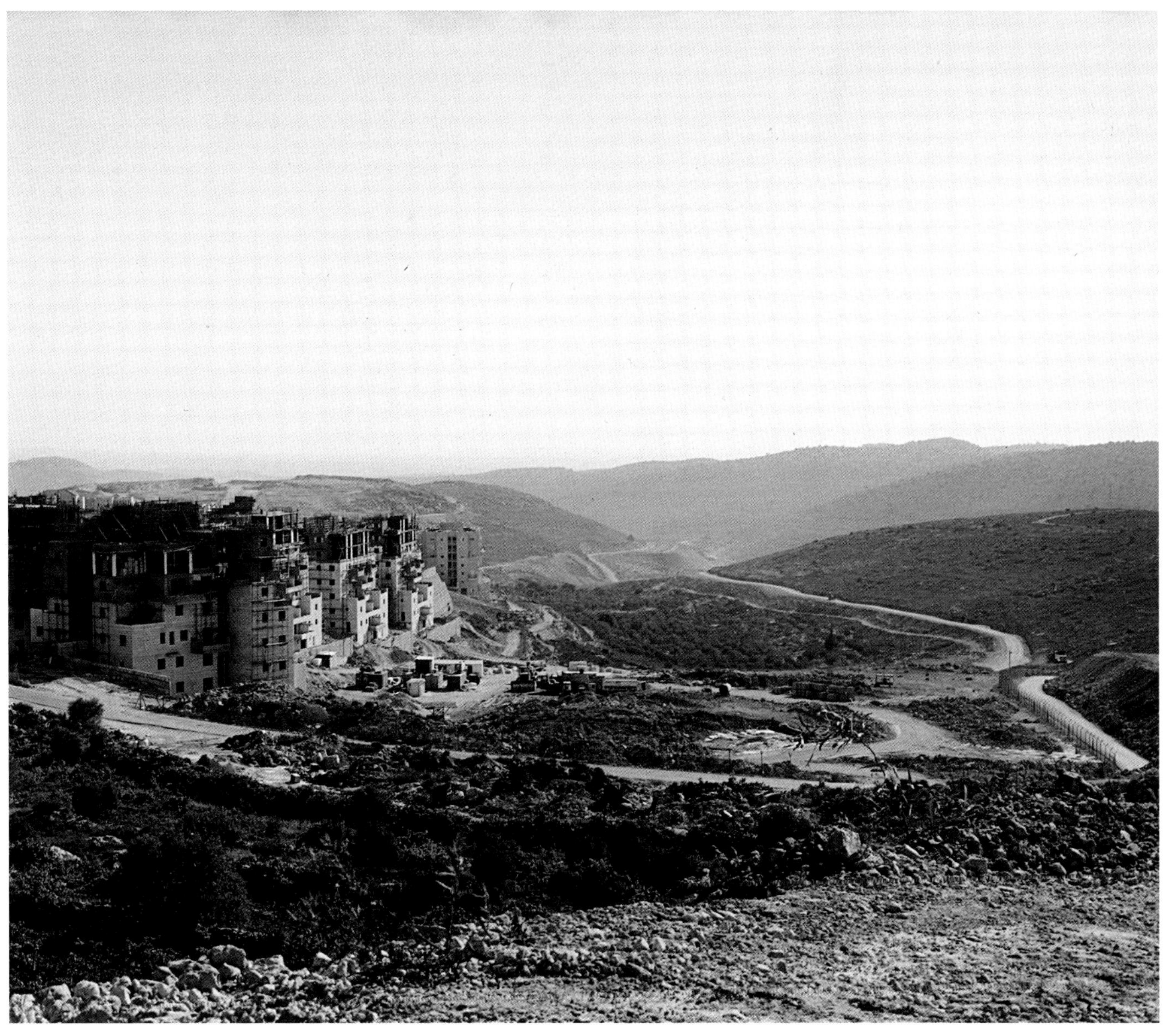

Wadi Fukin,
Palestinian village.

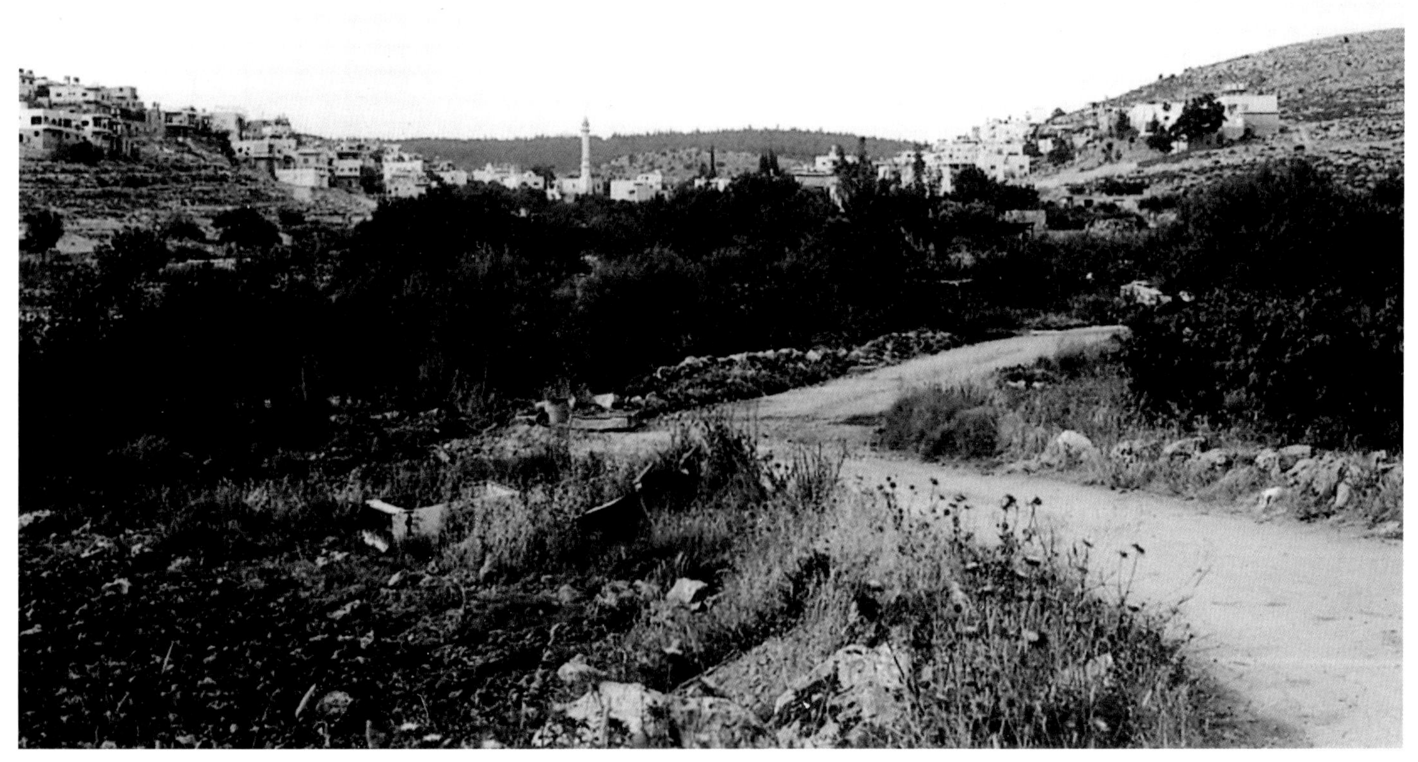

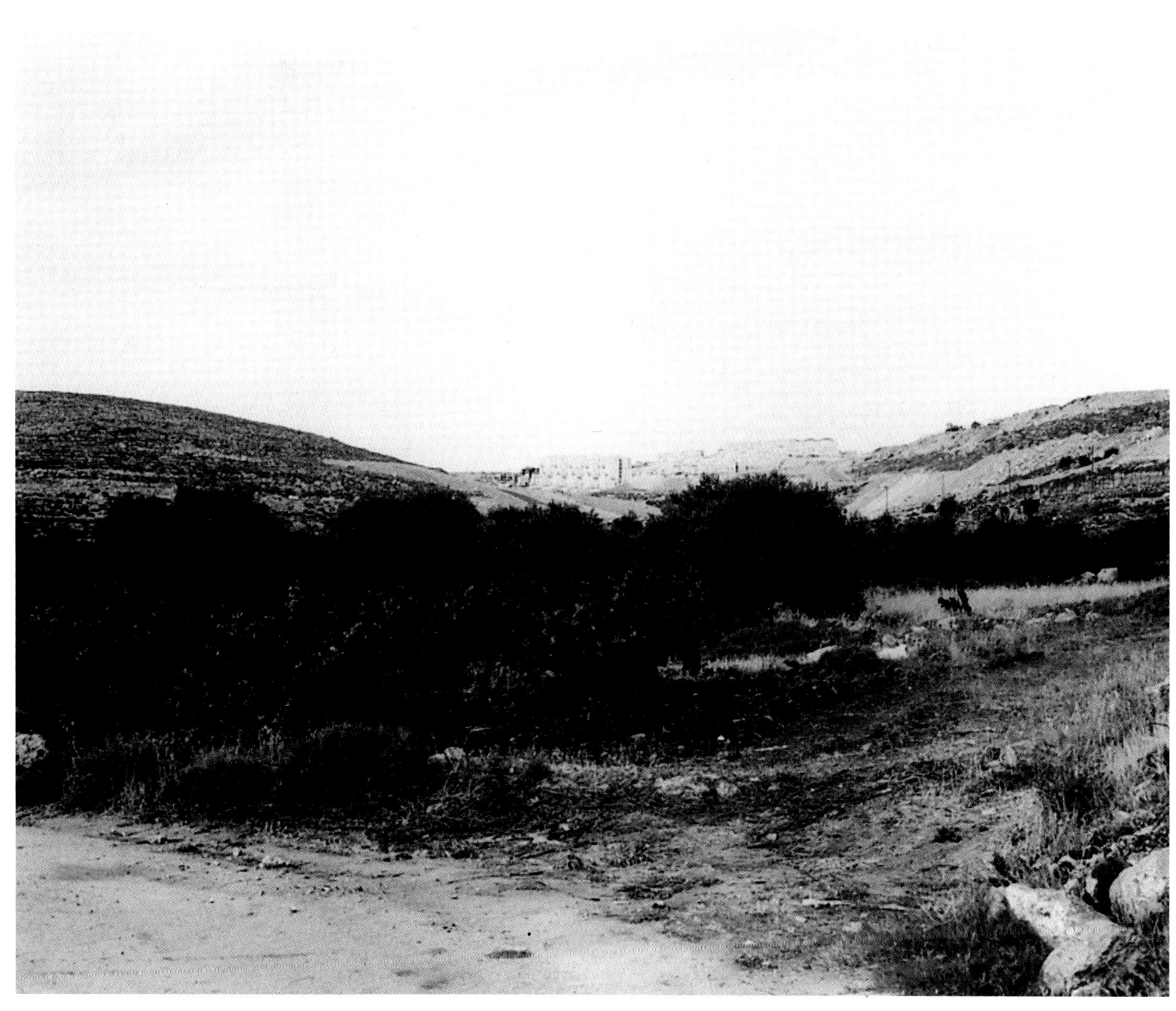

Betar Illit,
Israeli settlement.

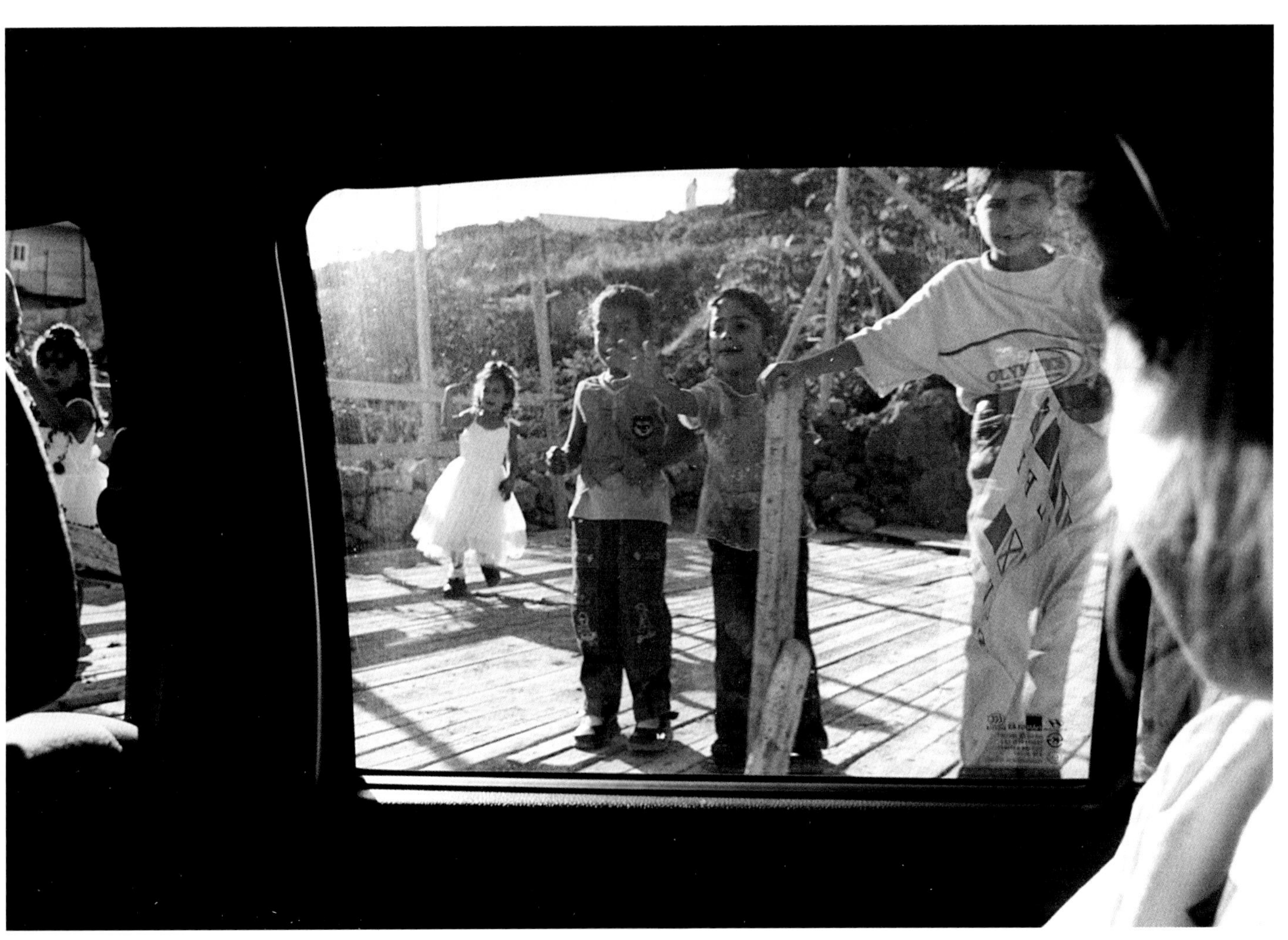

Israeli members of the joint Palestinian–Israeli organization, Windows, are welcomed by Palestinian children as they enter the small village of Wadi Fukin to meet with their Palestinian counterparts.

Wadi Fukin is in a fertile valley 16 kilometers (10 miles) west of Bethlehem, situated between the "Green Line" and Betar Illit settlement. The name of Wadi Fukin comes from ancient Aramaic meaning "the valley of thorns". It has a unique bittersweet story in that its residents were made refugees in 1948 and lived in refugee camps. But then after 24 years of exile some were able to return to their lands. Israeli writer David Grossman interviewed Wadi Fukin residents and titled his book *The Yellow Wind* after their story.[8] In 1972, the villagers received a notice from the Israeli military government that they could return to Wadi Fukin on the condition that they built a house within one month. After living in the refugee camps for more than two decades, many of the former villagers were not able to afford the cost of building a house and thus were not able to leave the camp. Today the construction of the ever-growing Betar Illit settlement is encroaching on and destroying the fertile lands of Wadi Fukin. The Barrier has not yet arrived in its area, but it is slated to be built to the east of Wadi Fukin in order to annex Betar Illit to Israel. The villagers of Wadi Fukin live in fear of being uprooted and forced into exile yet again from their beautiful valley.

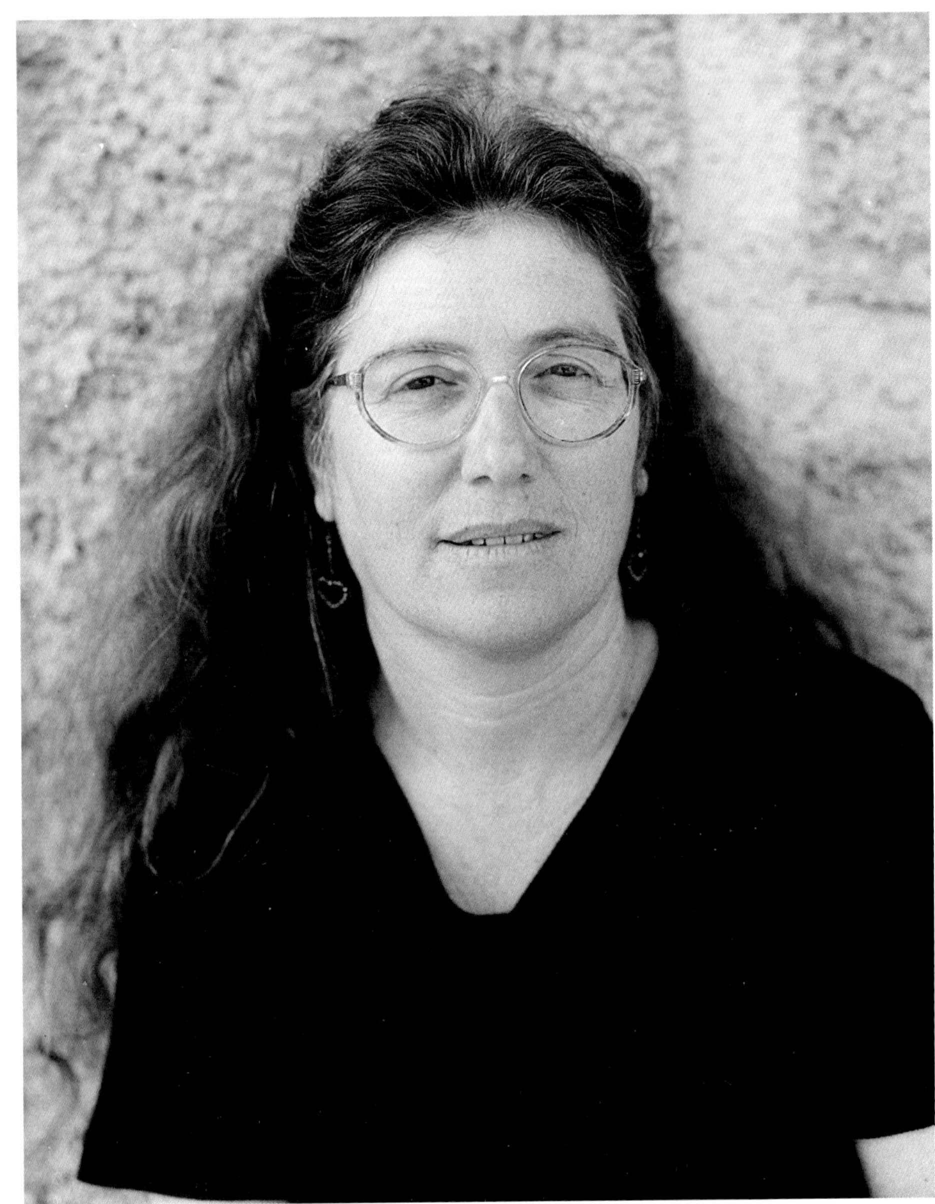

"My hope is that people and governments will choose talking and listening to solve problems instead of violence."

Rutie, Tel Aviv
Jewish Israeli.

"My hope is to have the freedom to move,
to work and to earn a living."

Fahmi, Wadi Fukin
Palestinian.

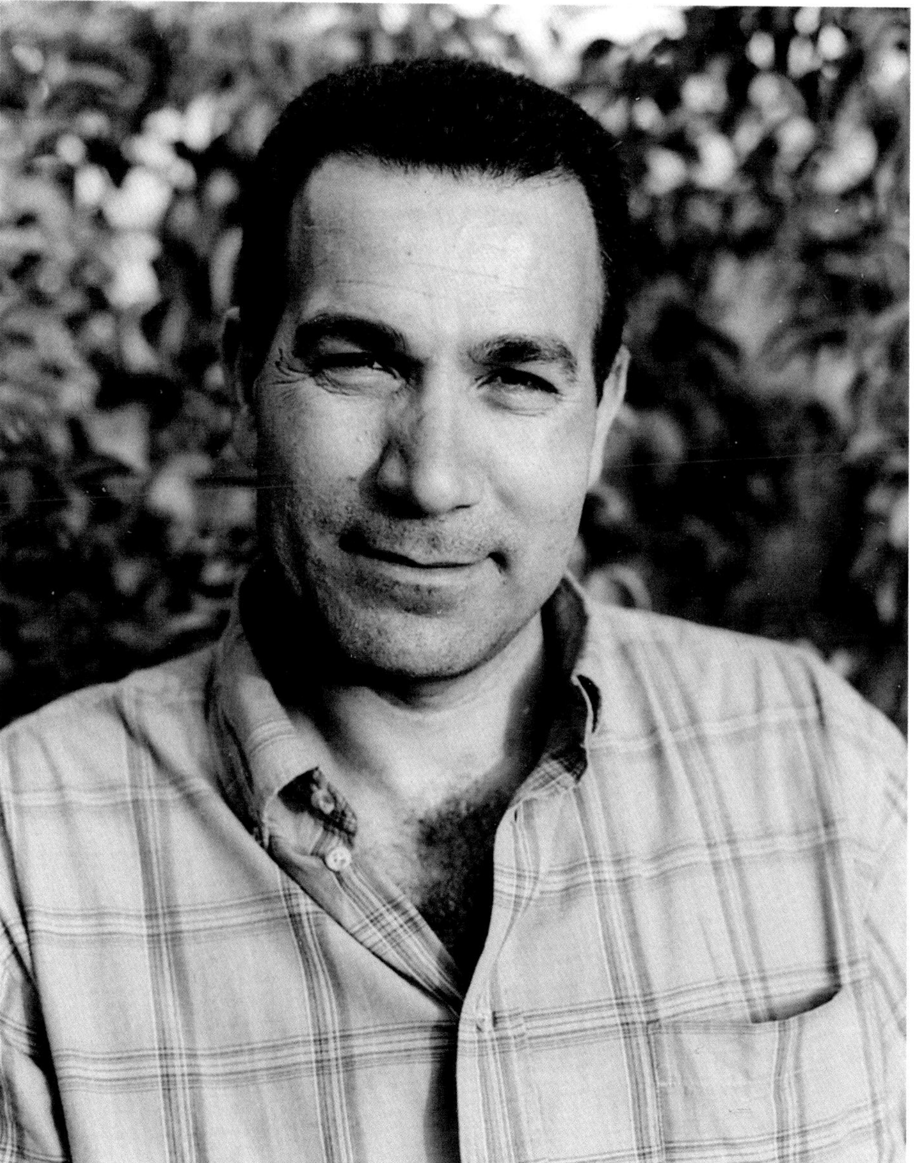

Agriculture in the fertile
valley of Wadi Fukin
has become the only
source of income for
the villagers, the
majority of whom had
permits to work in
Israel before the
Intifada.

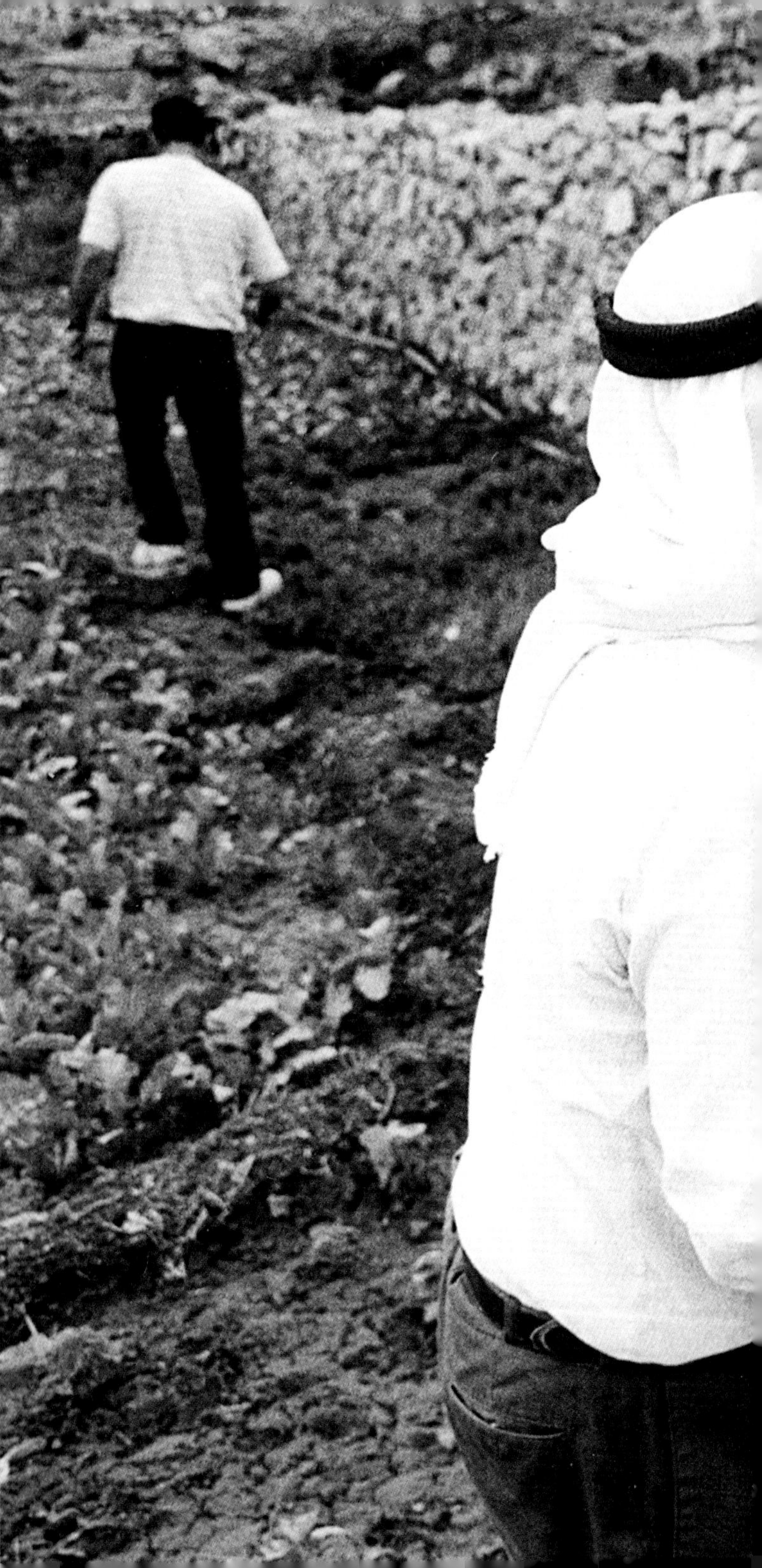

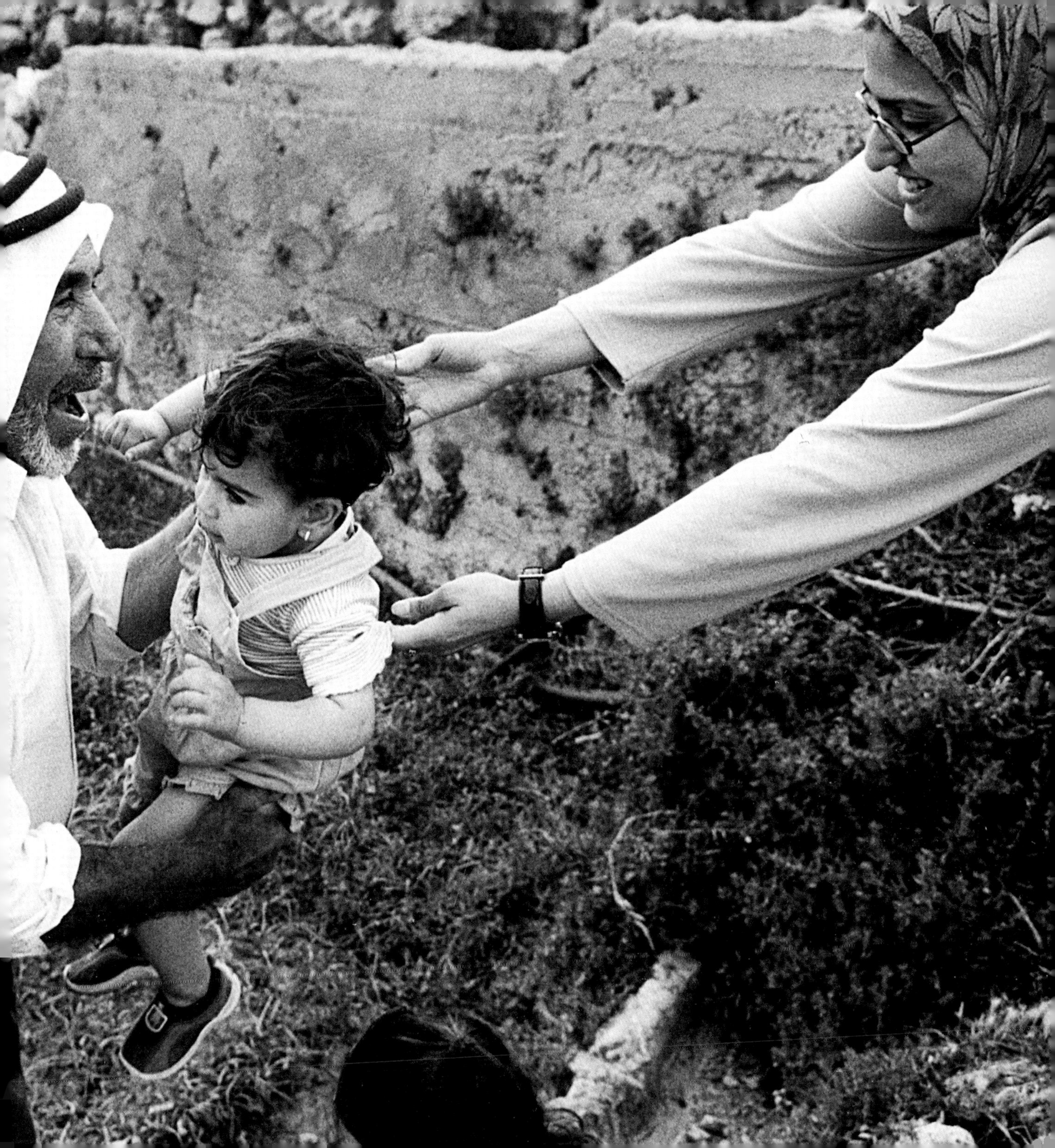

Bypass road used by
Israeli settlers who live
south of Jerusalem in
the West Bank.

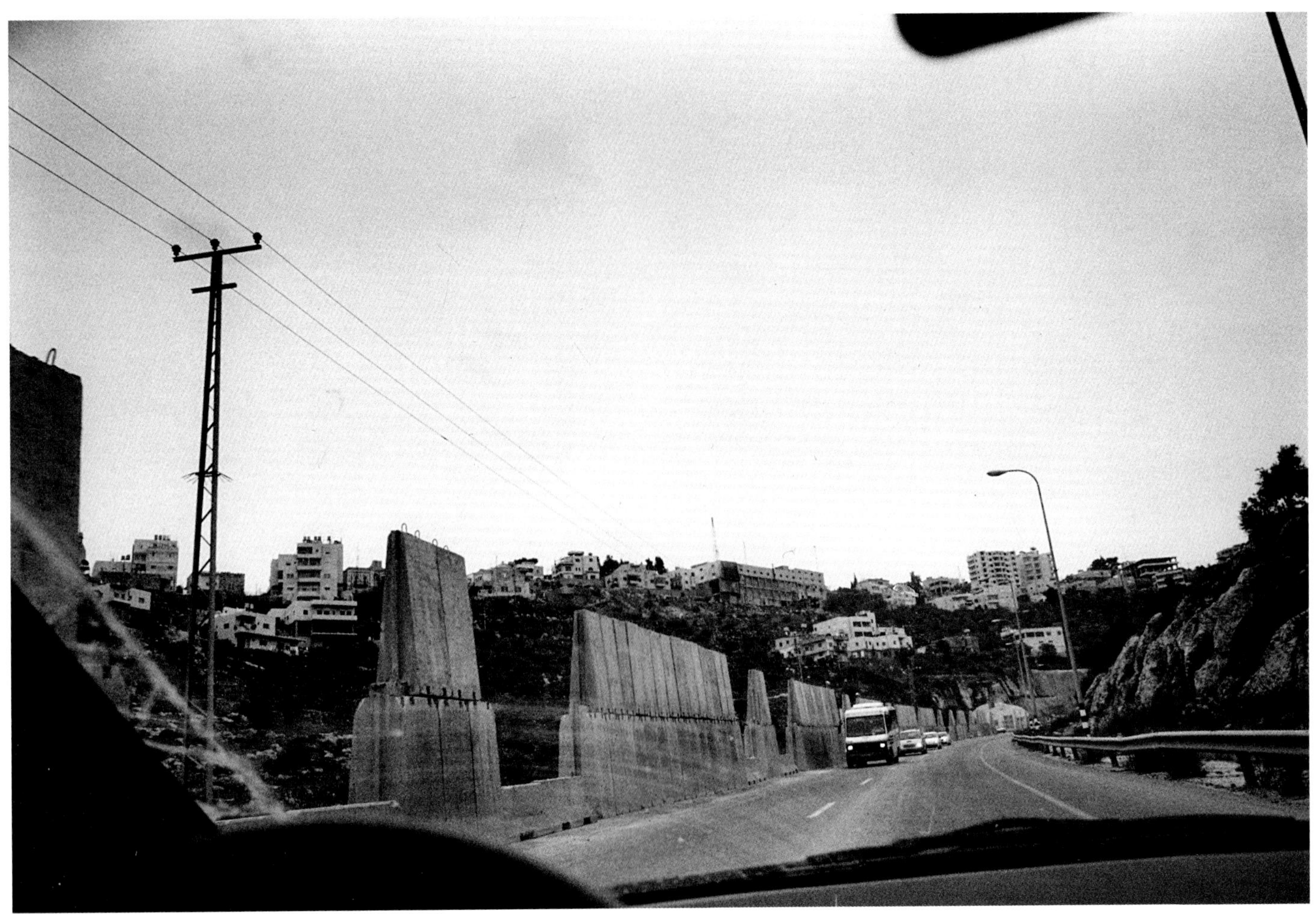

Many of the Palestinian
roads have been
blocked off with
obstacles allowing for
passage only by foot,
such as this one which
serves as a main road
to Beit Jala and
Bethlehem.

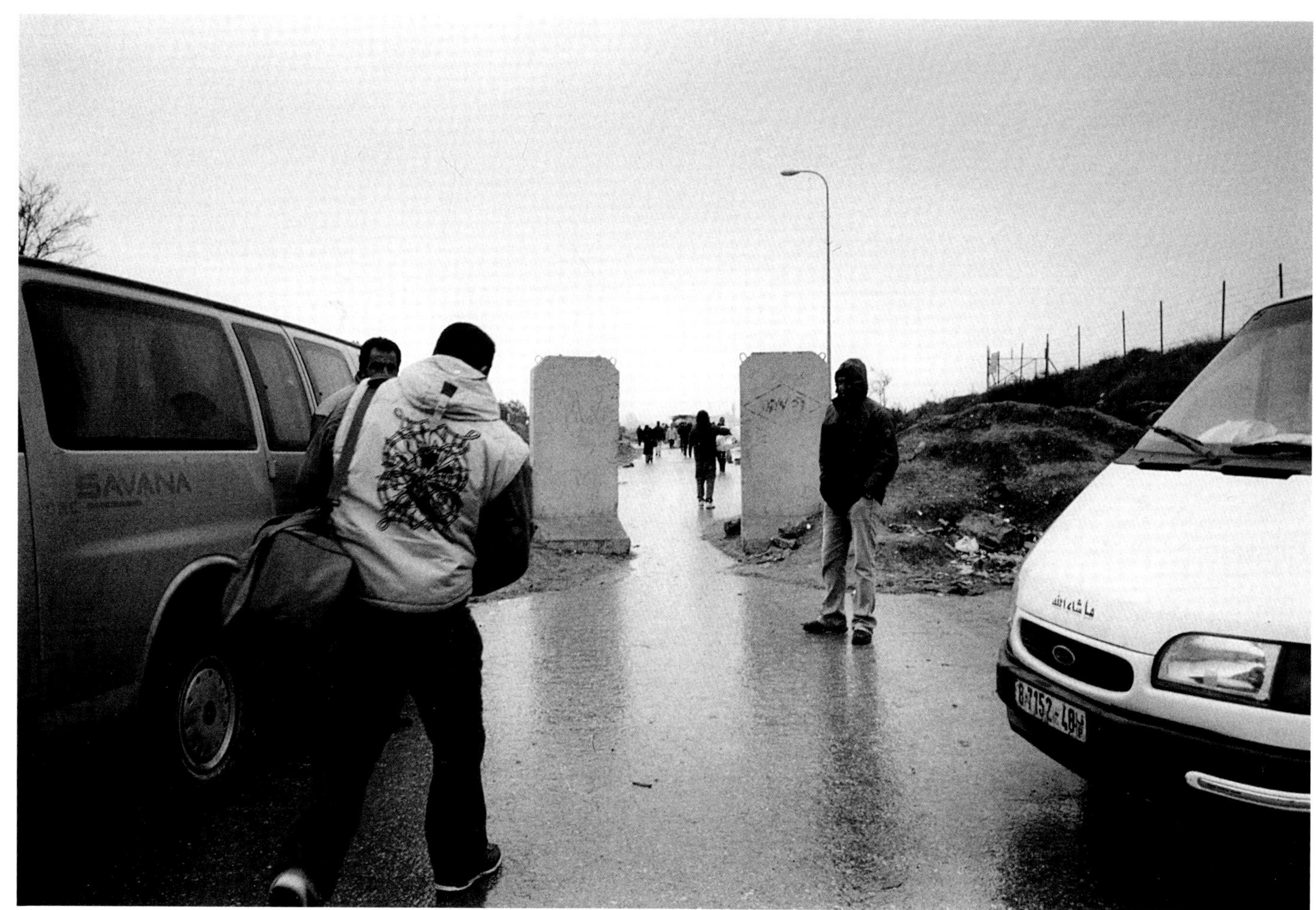

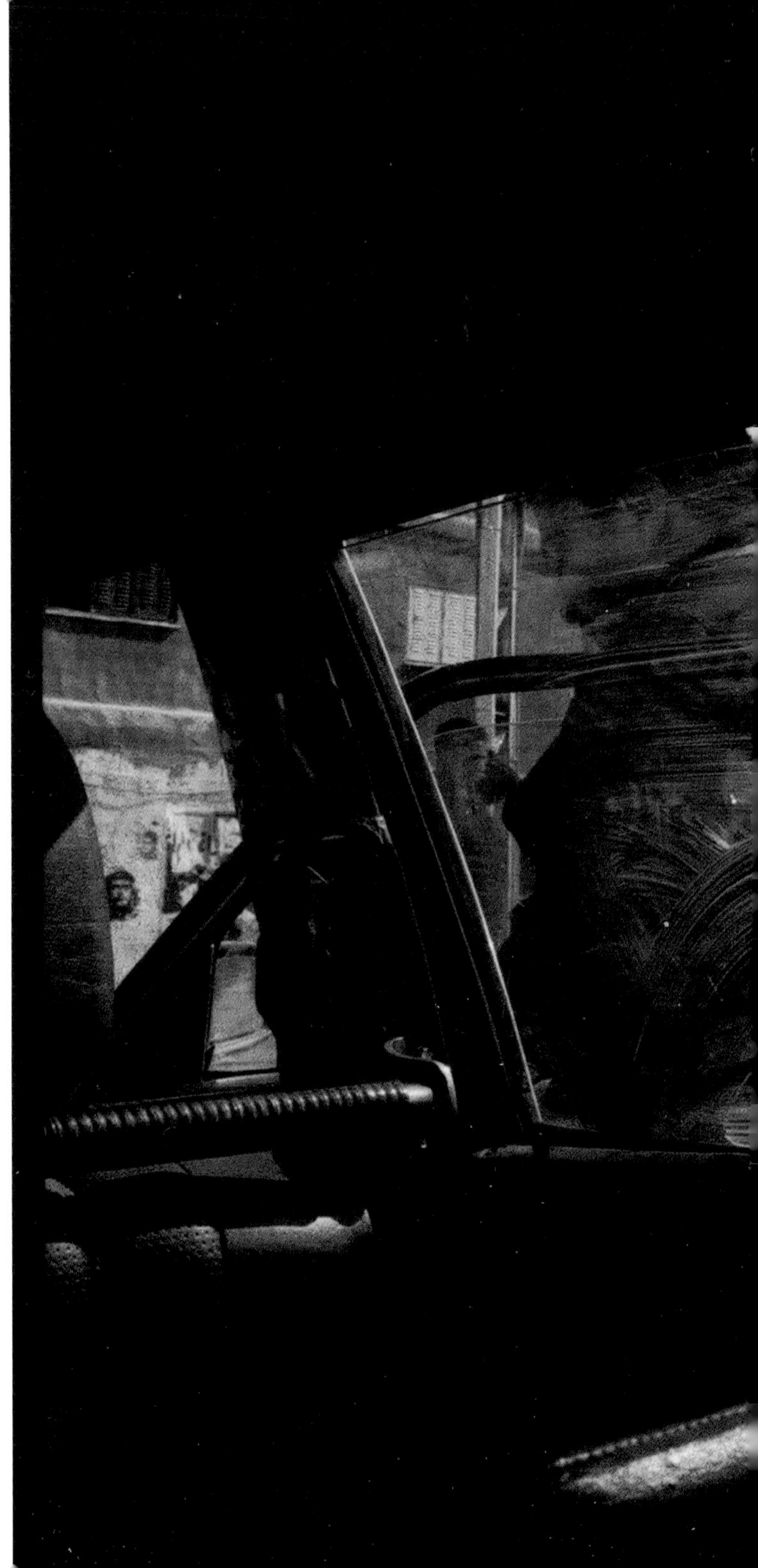

The entrance to the
Dheisheh refugee camp
in Bethlehem that is
home to more than
11,000 Palestinian
refugees.

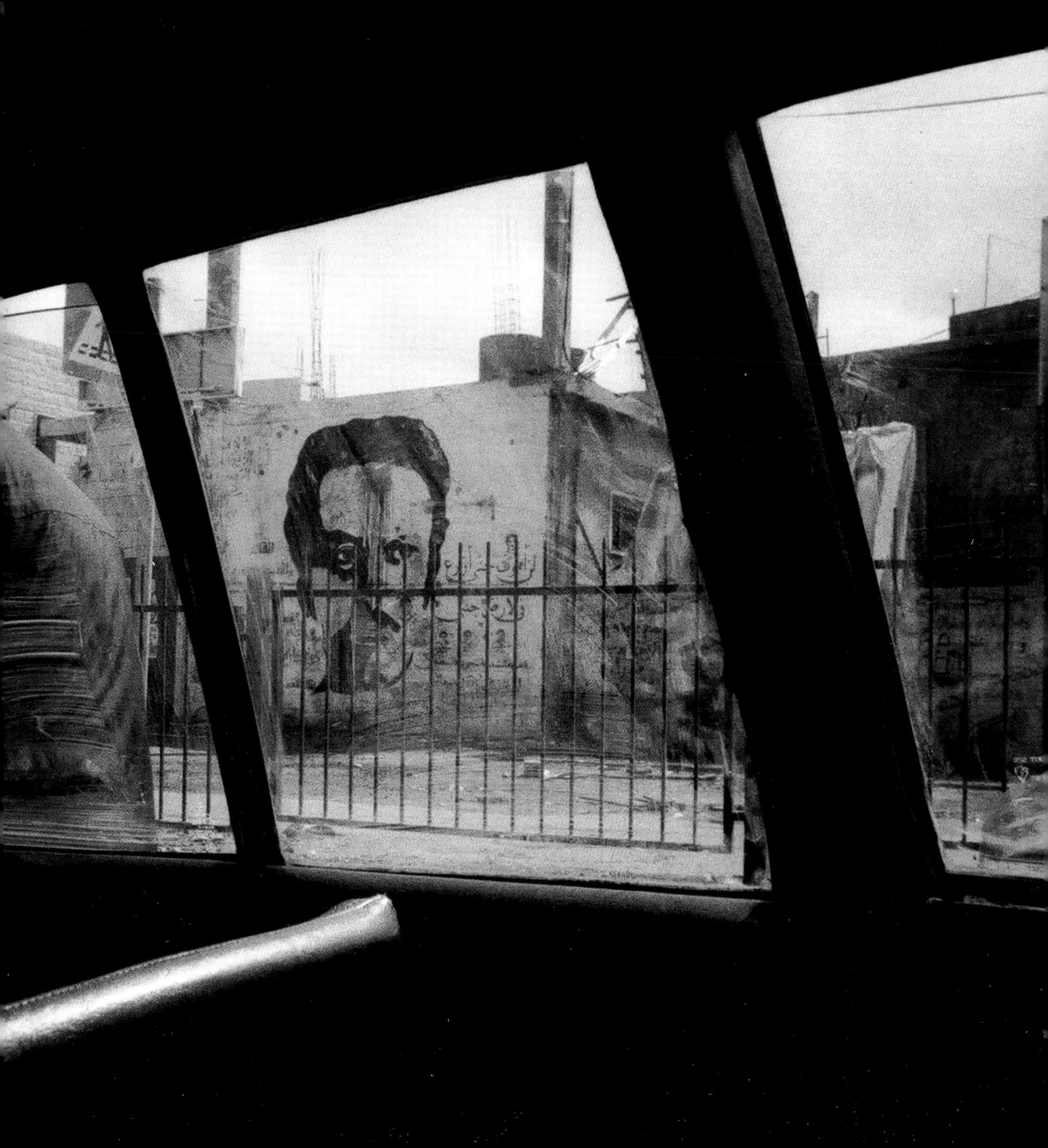

Windows magazine organizes a trip led by Israeli journalist Merron Rappaport to the 8-meter (27 ft.) high wall in Abu Dis (near Jerusalem) for Israelis to learn more about the Barrier and its effects on the ground.

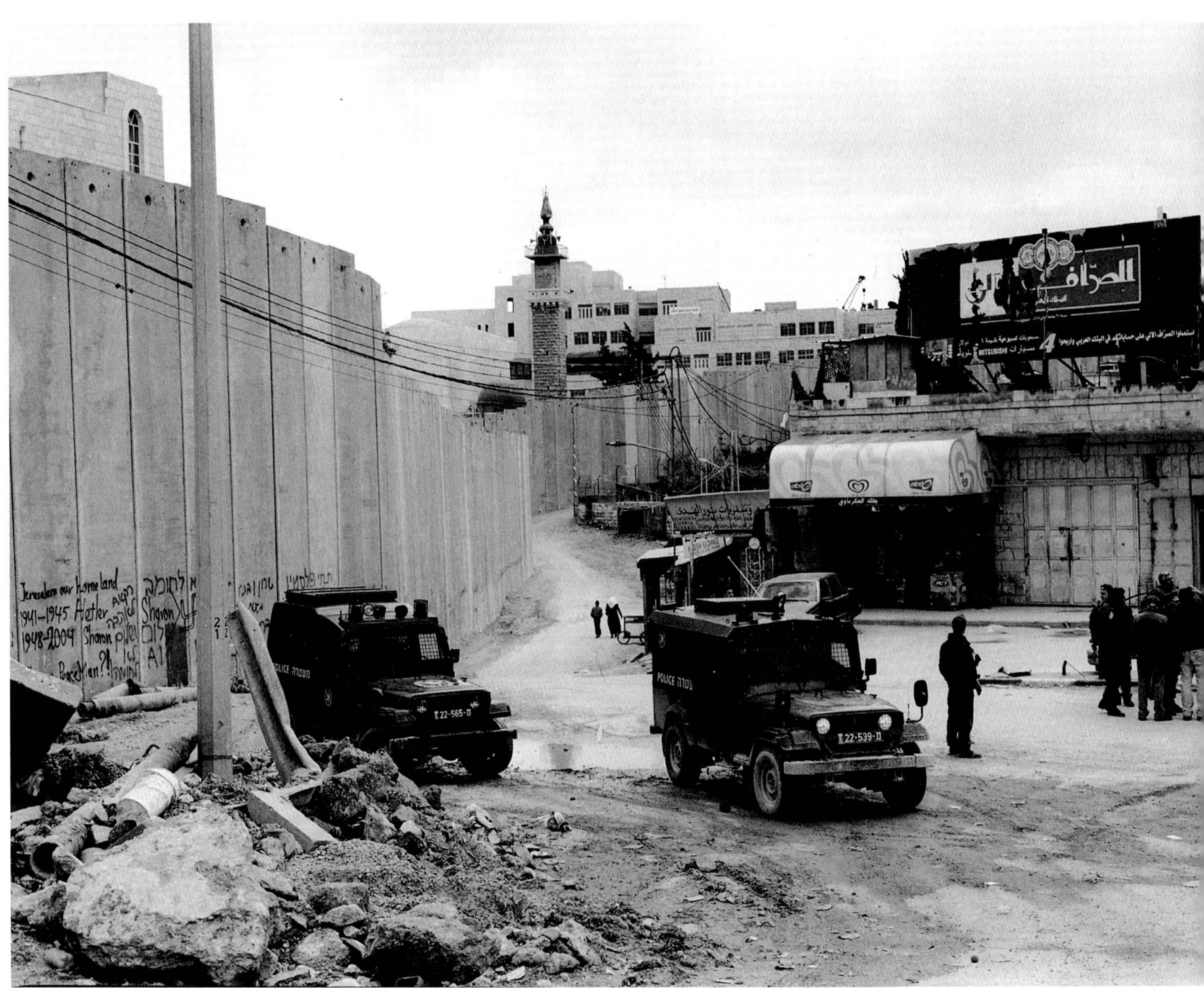

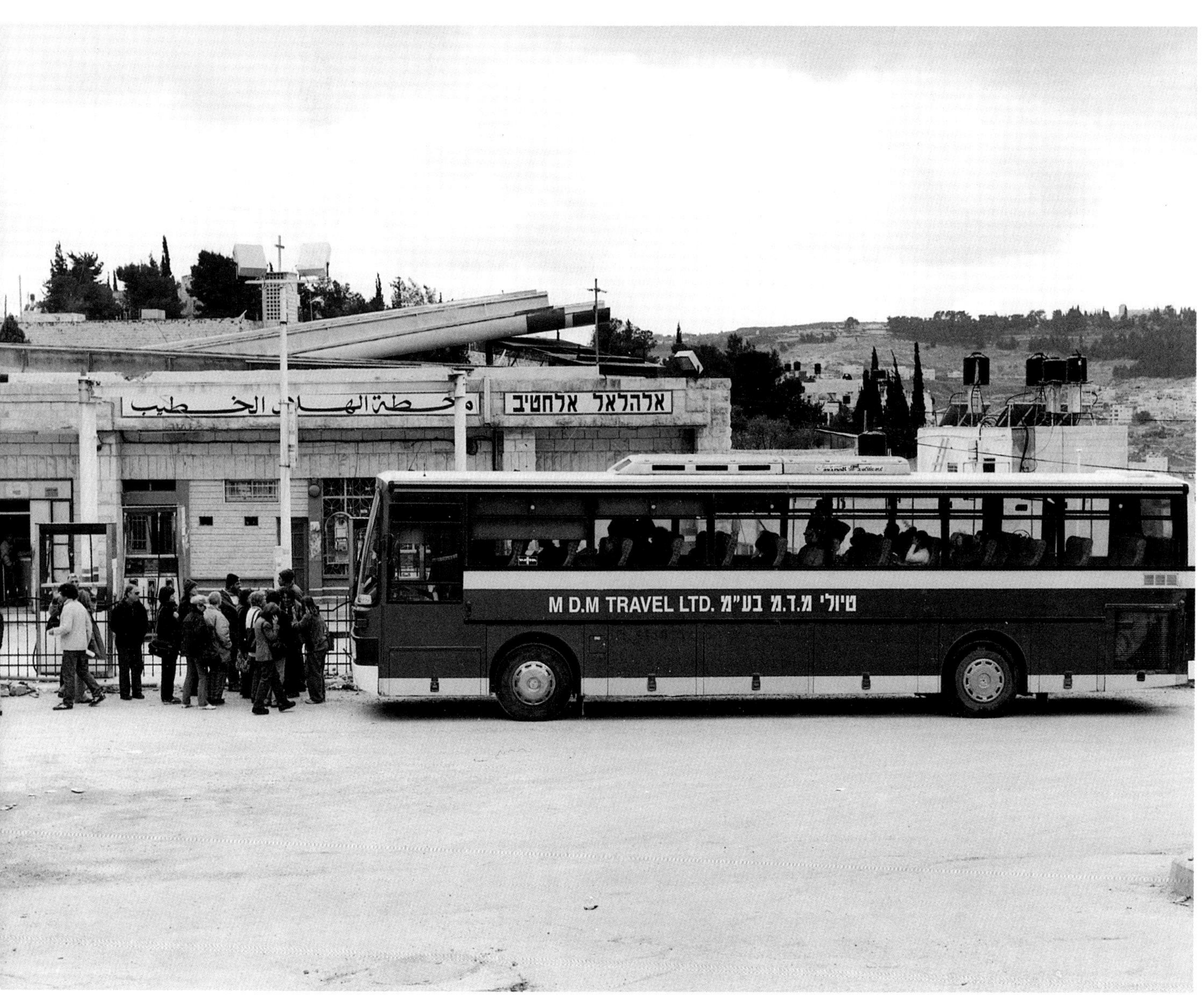
طة الهلال الخطيب
אלהלאל אלחטיב
M D.M TRAVEL LTD. טיולי מ.ד.מ בע"מ

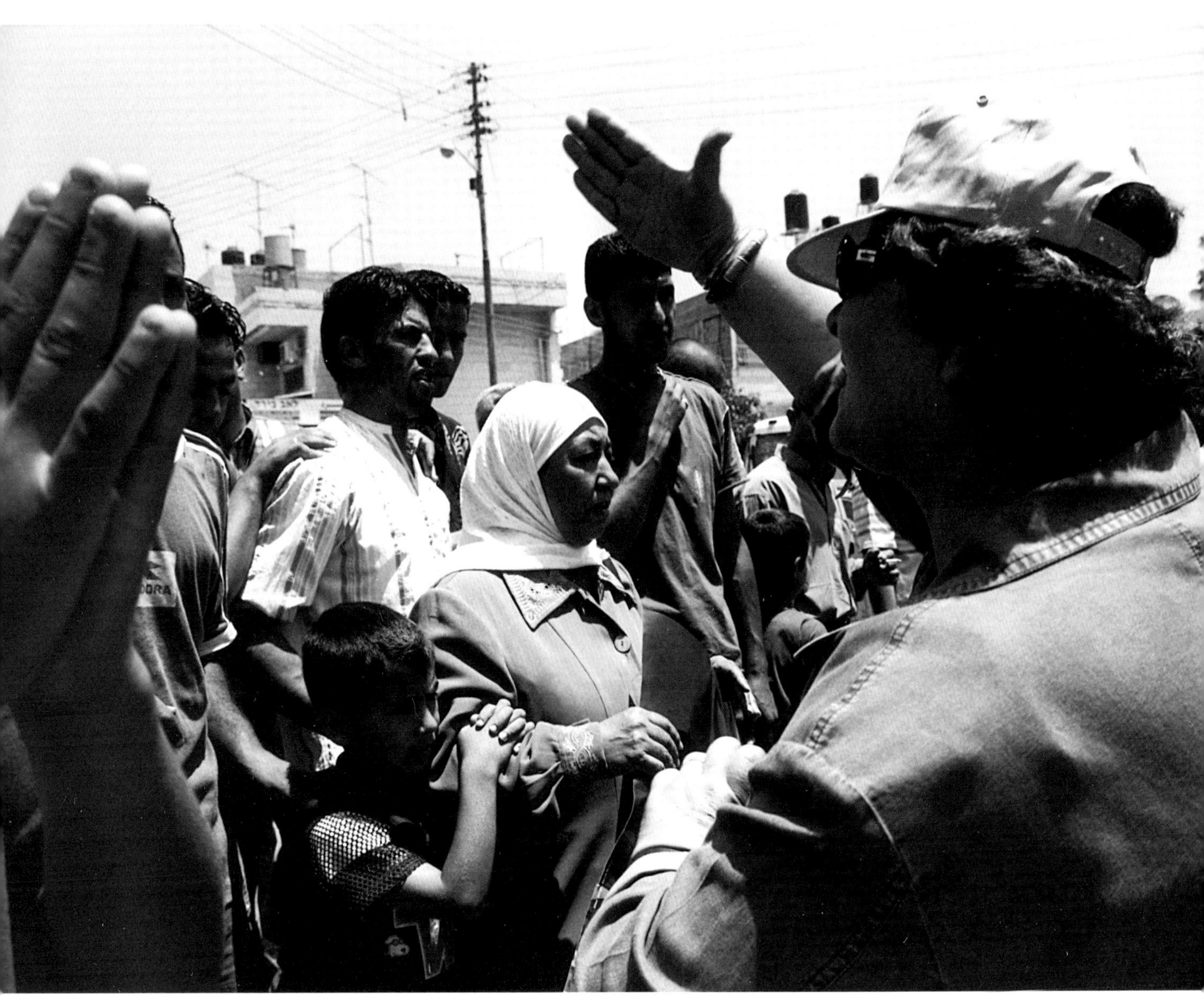

Palestinians and Israelis
together protest in
Aram against the
construction of the
Barrier, June 2004.

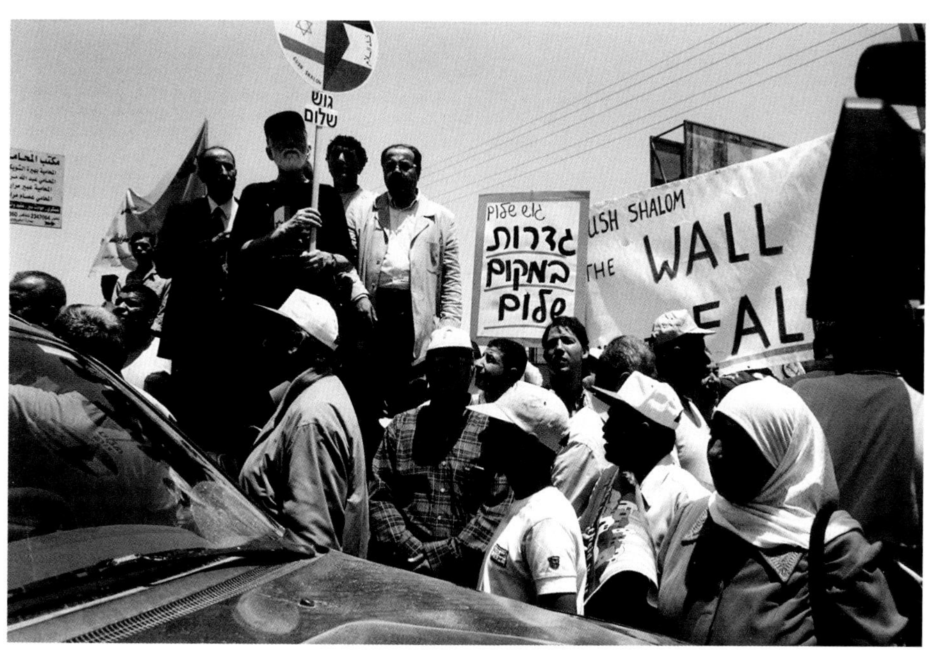

The Palestinians
attempt to restrain the
younger generation
from throwing stones
towards the Israeli
army in Aram.

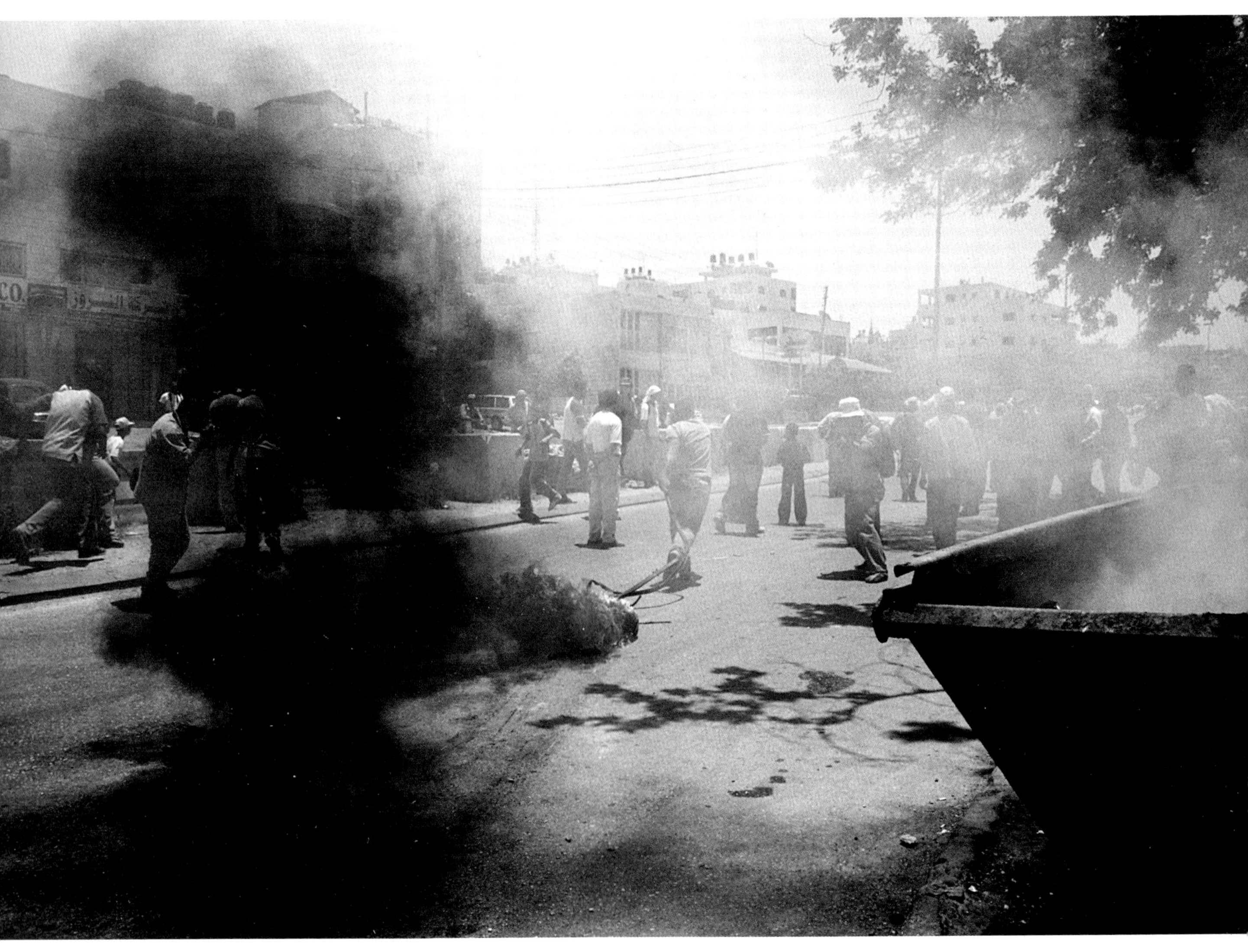

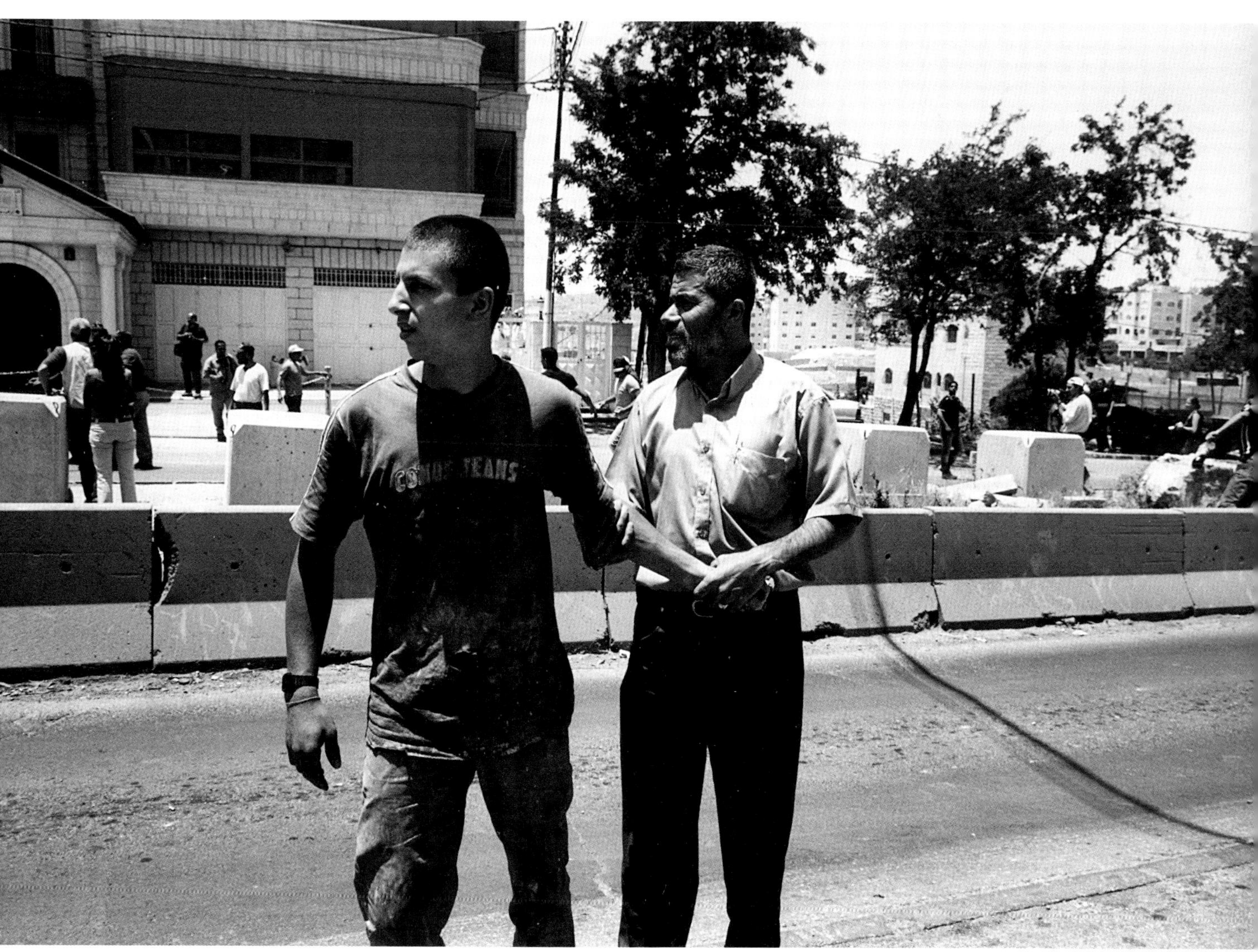

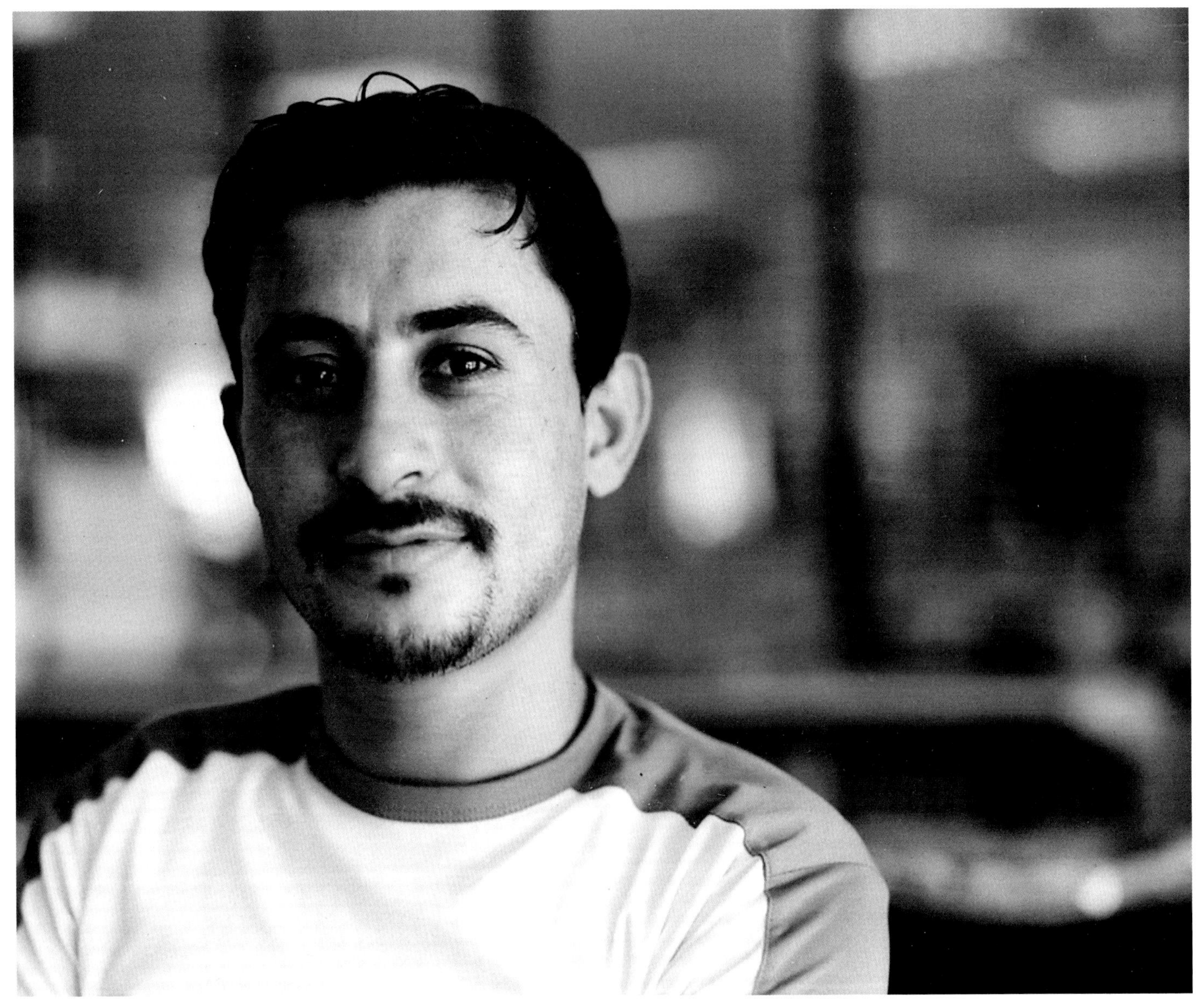

"My greatest fear is the Wall. If they build
it here in Aram, the pastry shop will not
survive and I won't be able to pay off the
debts from my wedding."

Fazal, Aram
Palestinian.

"I'm afraid of death, I don't want to get
killed like my friend."

Mahmoud, Tulkarem
Palestinian.

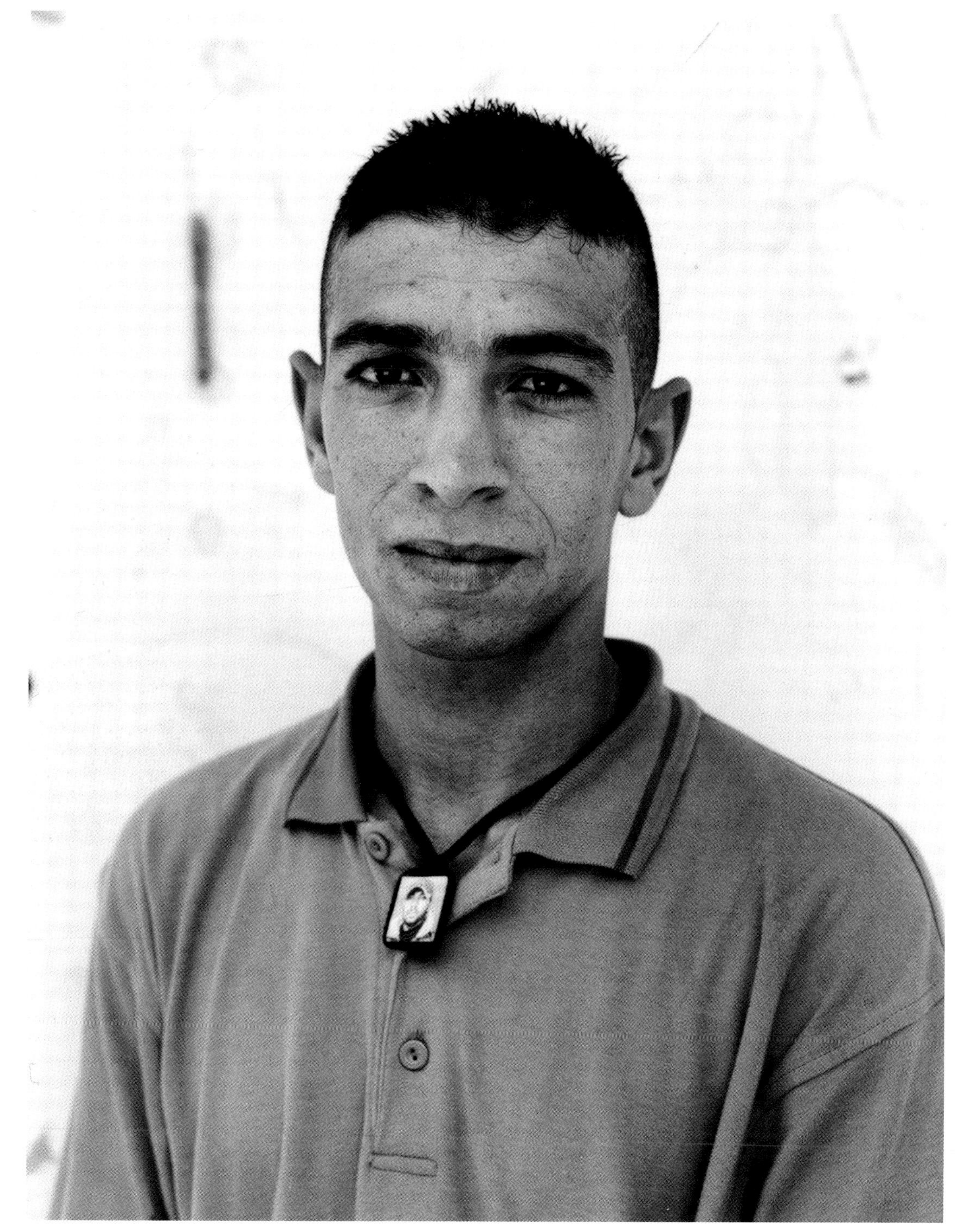

Human rights activists from Machsom Watch observe the Jabarra checkpoint as a Palestinian Israeli businessman from Nazareth waits to enter.

Machsom Watch founded in 2001 is a voluntary group of Israeli women conducting daily observations at military checkpoints to monitor human rights abuses.

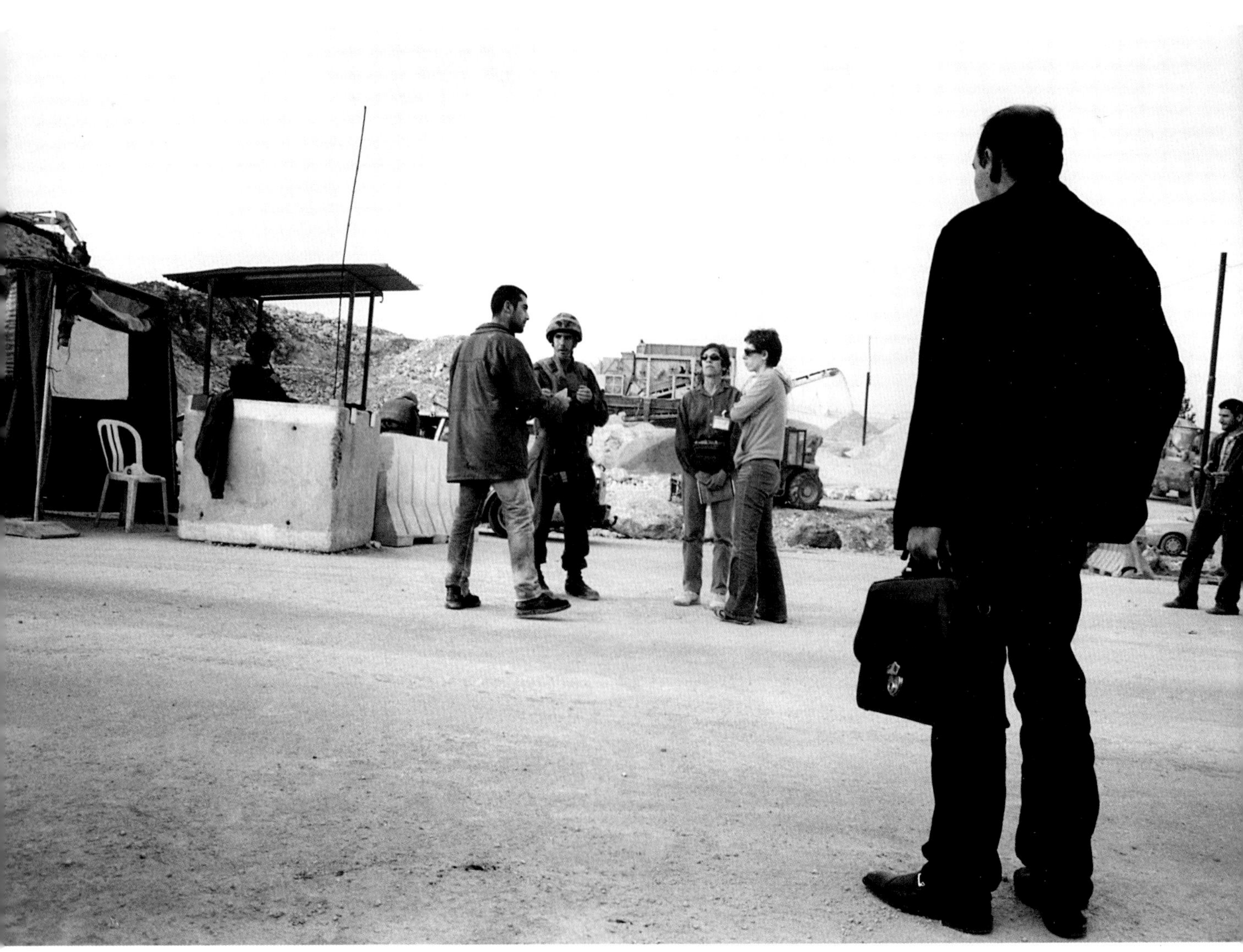

Israeli and Palestinian
board members of the
organization Windows
hold a meeting at the
checkpoint.

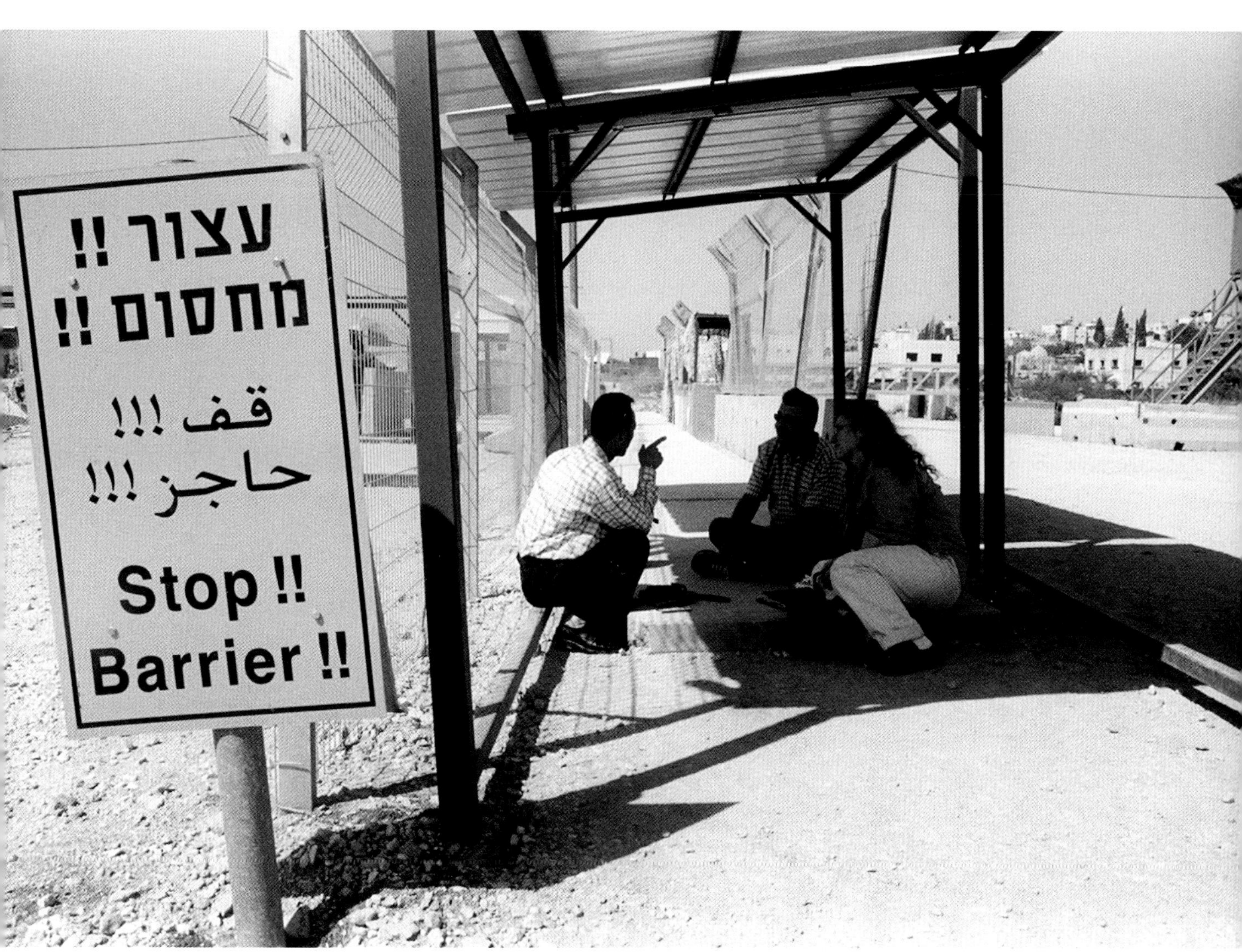

עצור !!
מחסום !!
قـف !!!
حاجز !!!
Stop !!
Barrier !!

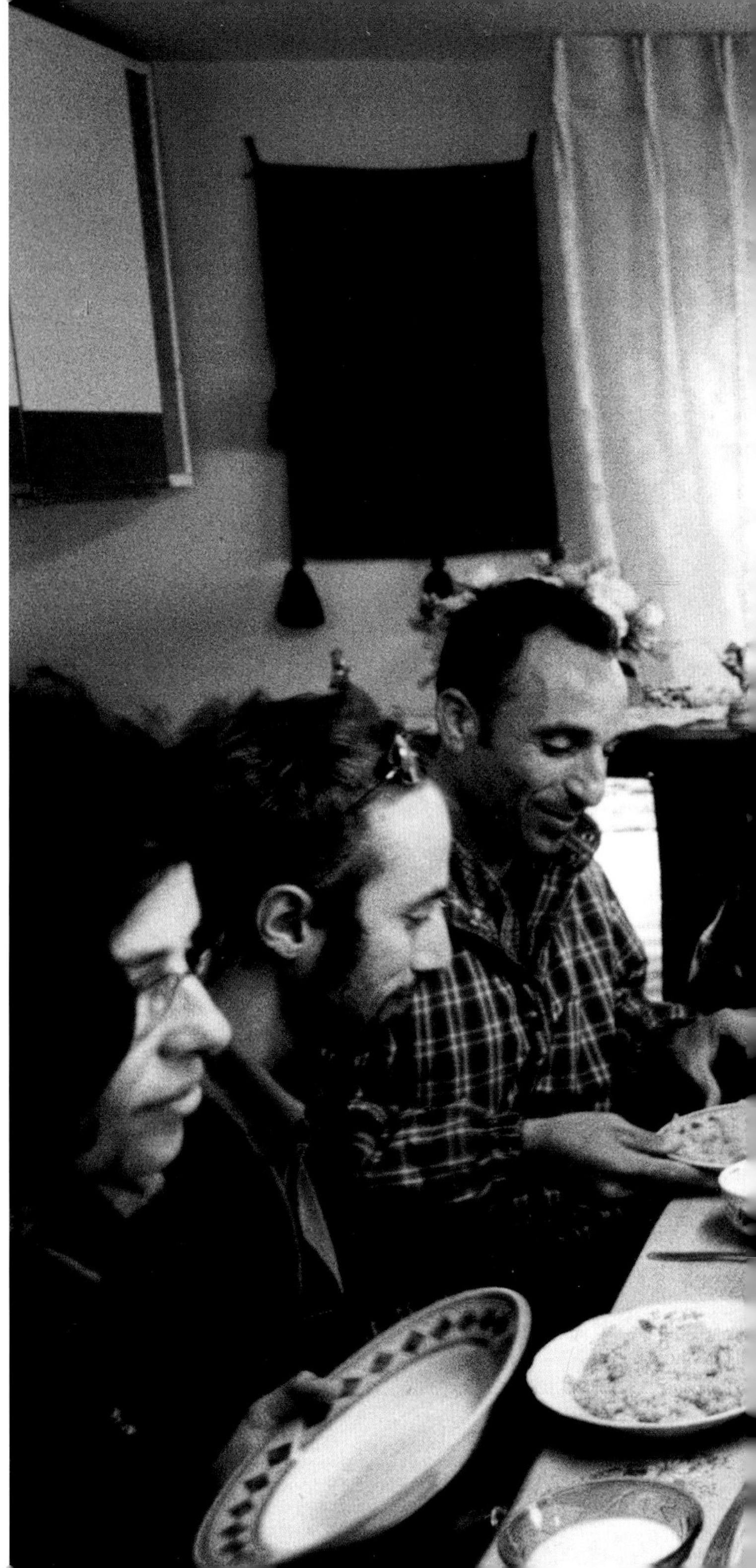

Israeli and Palestinian members of Windows share a meal together at Kanaan's home in Asira, West Bank.

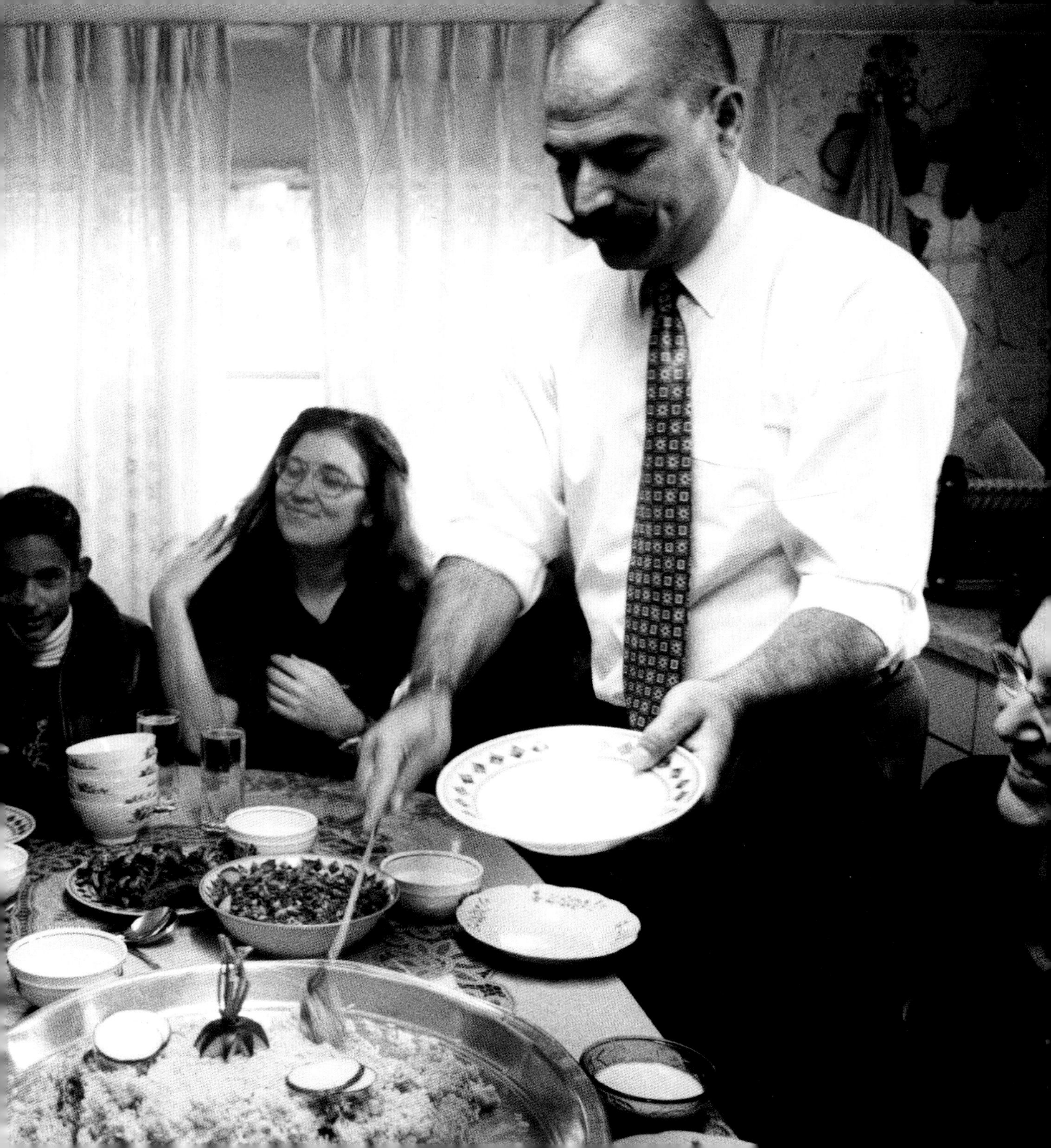

Street scene, Ramallah,
West Bank.

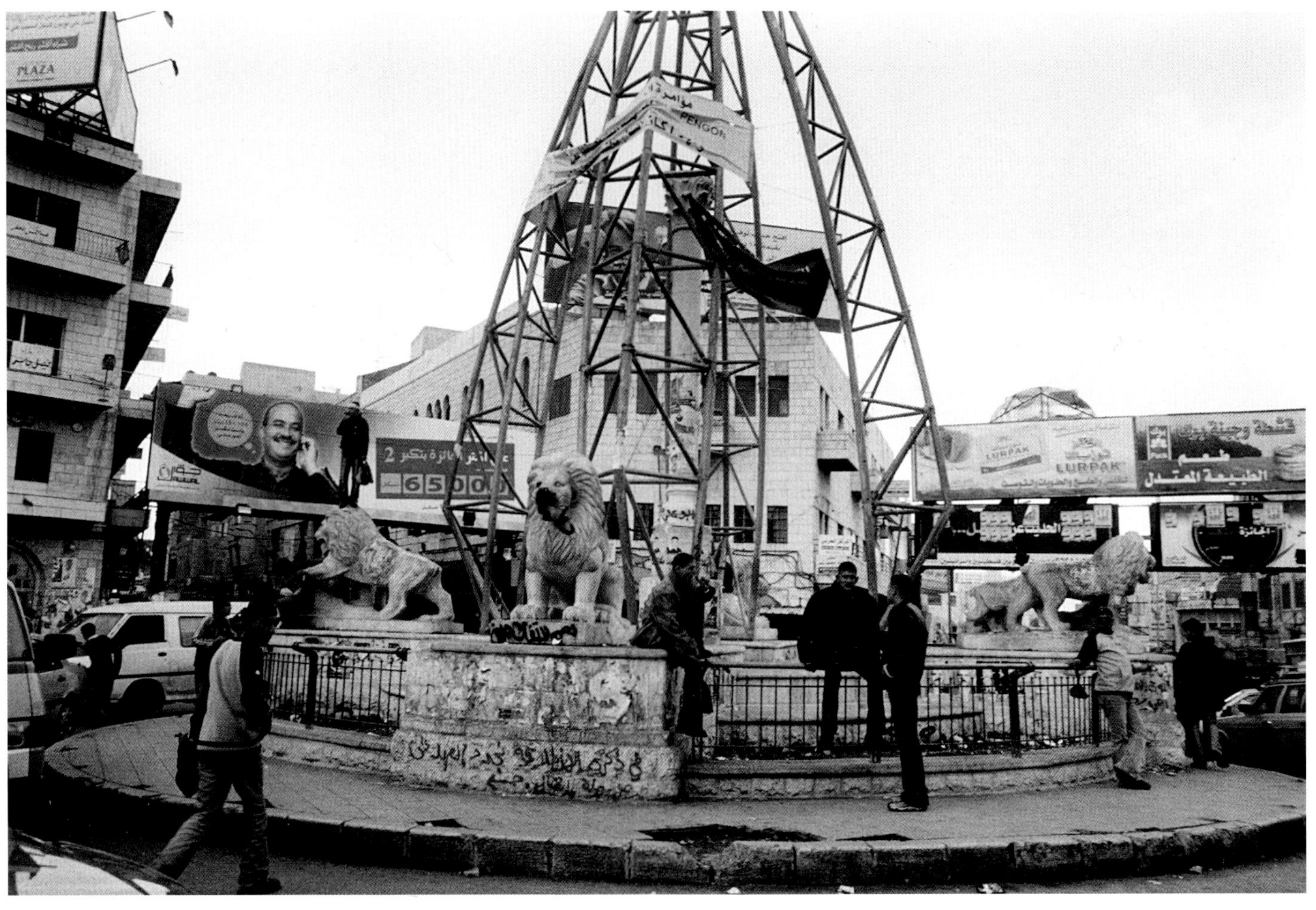

Yasser Arafat's
destroyed compound in
2004 before his death,
Ramallah.

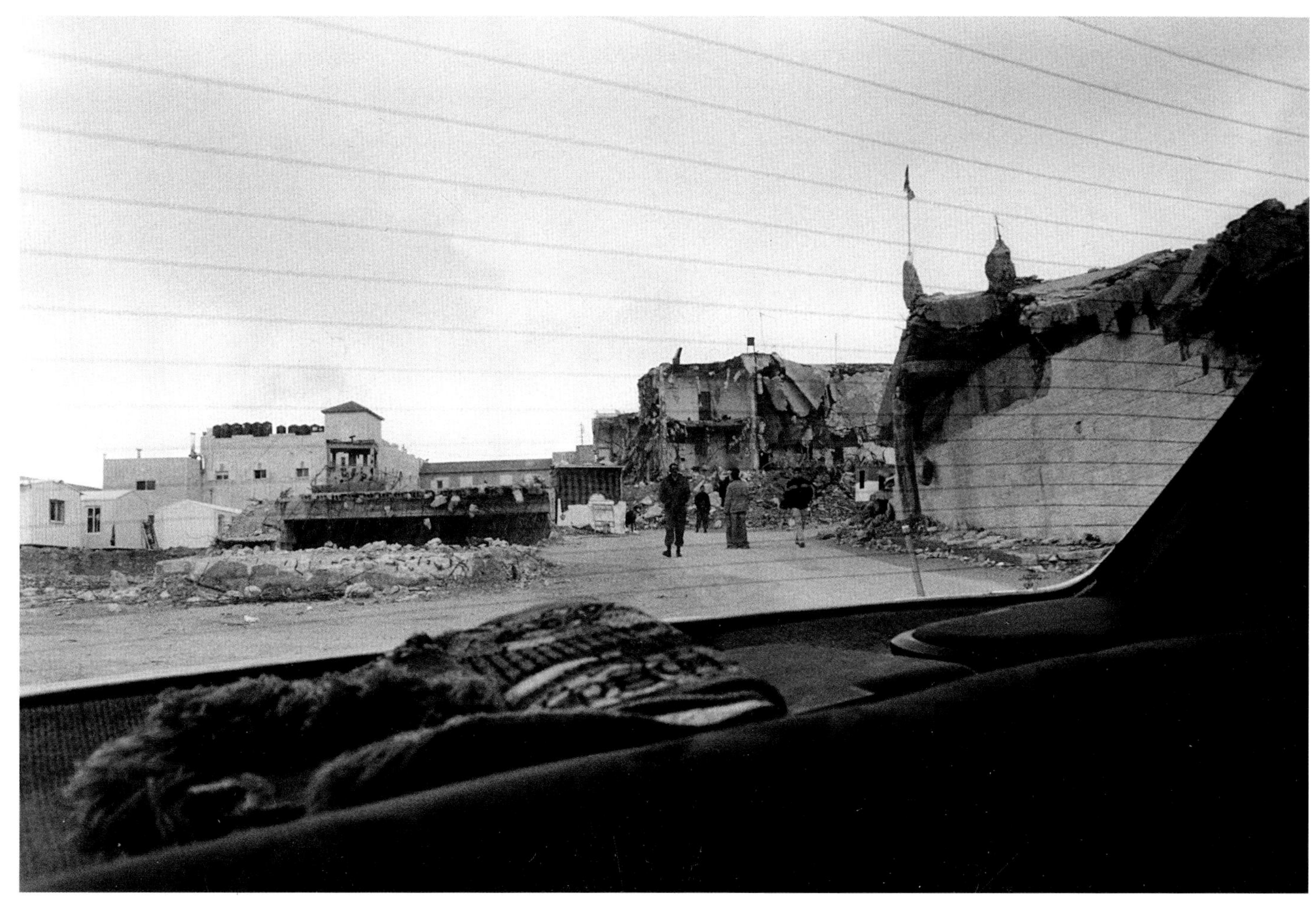

Palestinians passing
under the Israeli army
watchtower at the
Kalandia checkpoint
between Ramallah
and Jerusalem.

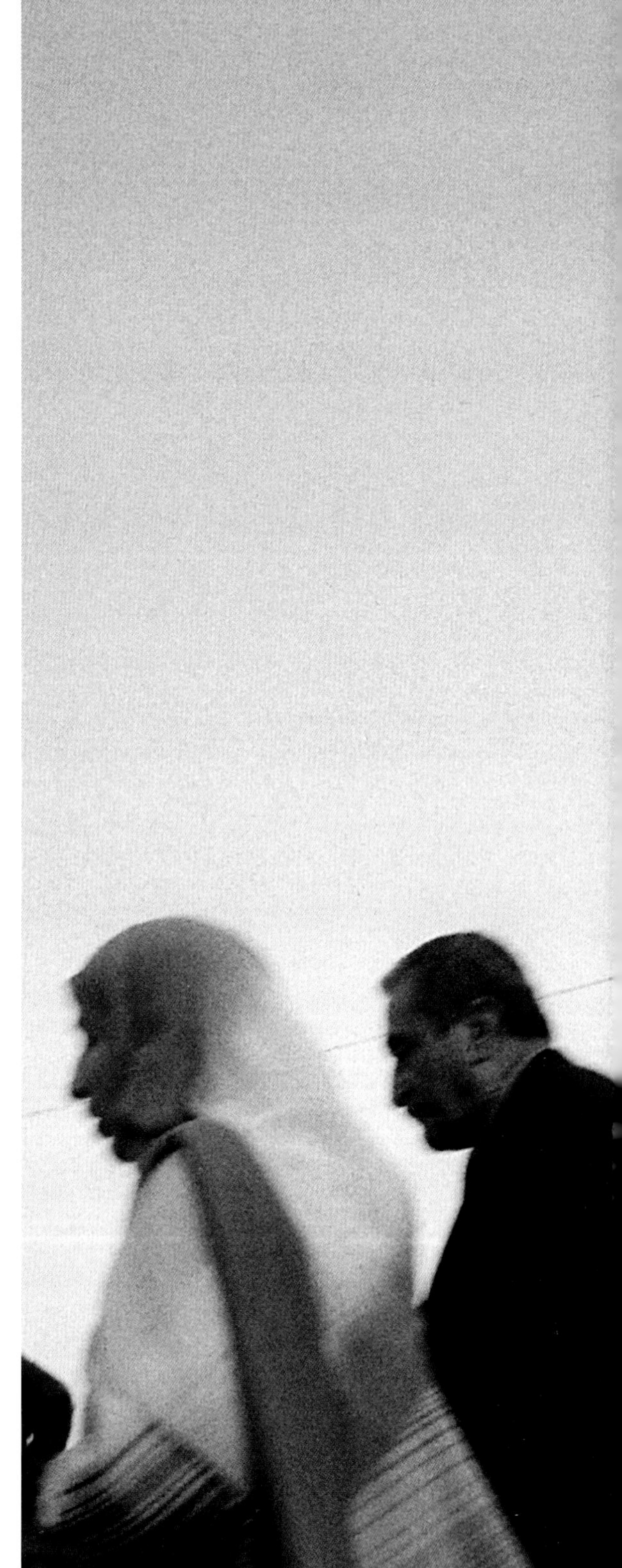

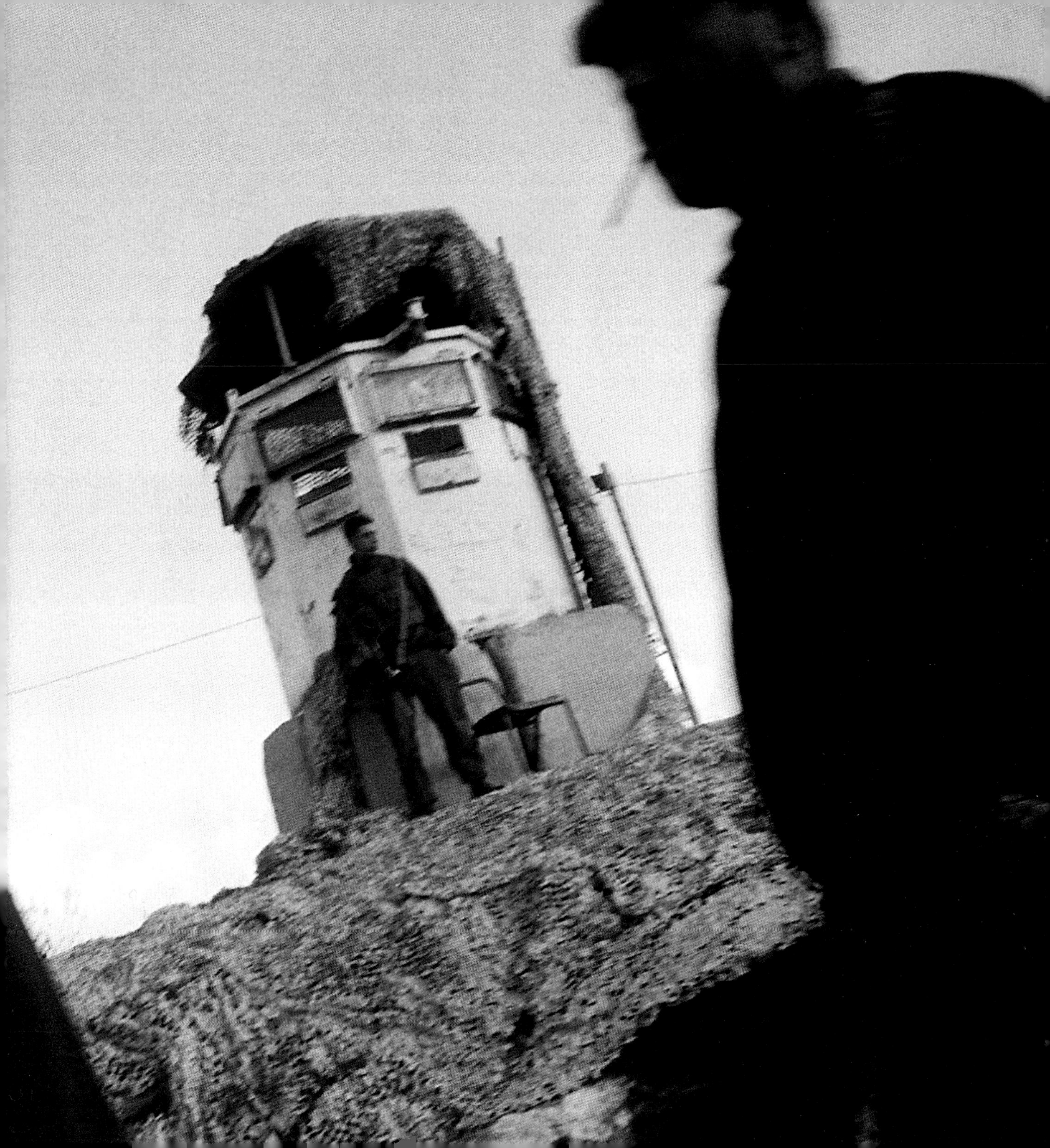

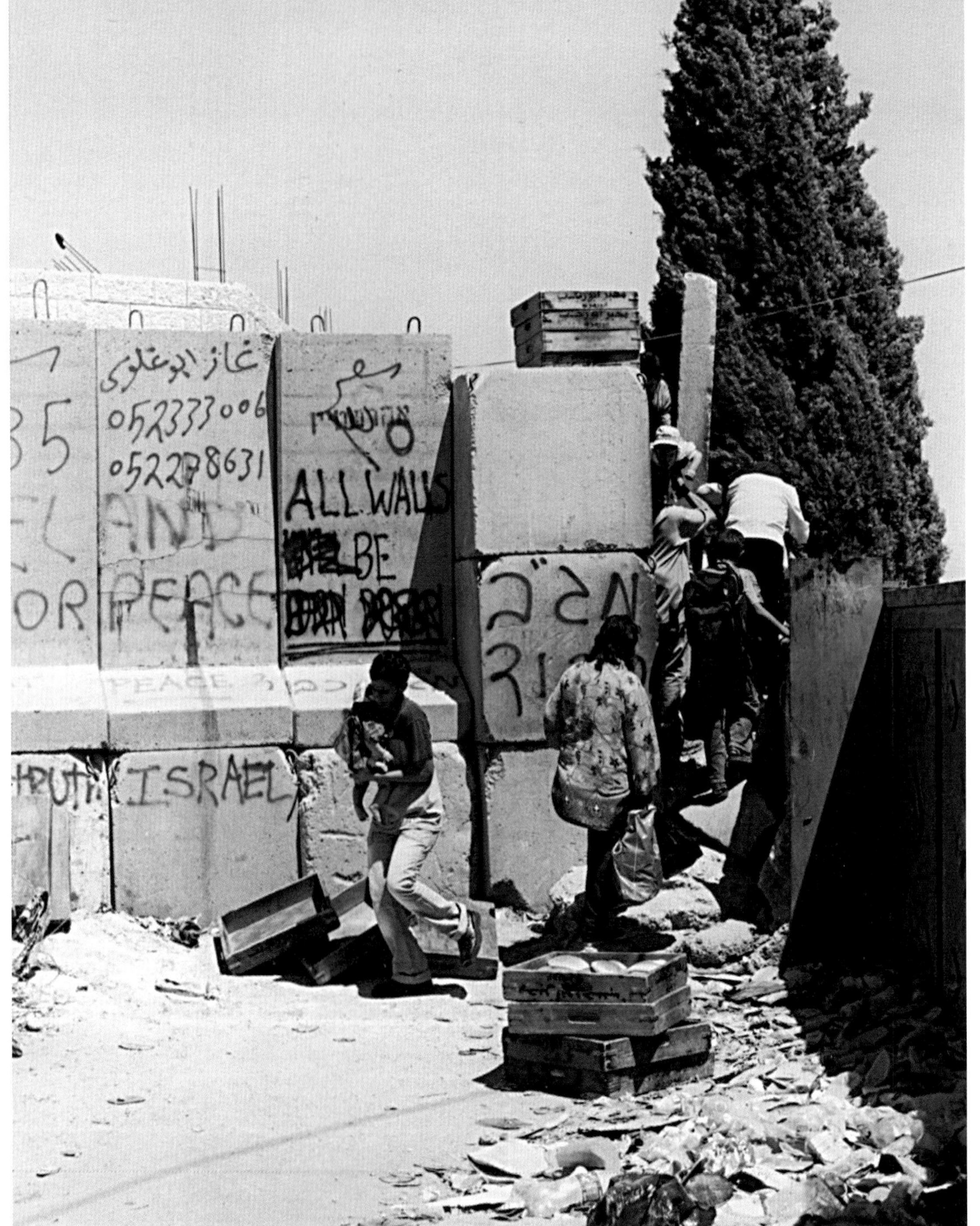

This is the daily routine for hundreds of Palestinians living in the Jerusalem suburb of Abu Dis. In order to reach their jobs, schools, and hospital they must climb over this portion of the old wall, which will soon be replaced by the 8 meter (27 ft.) high new wall.

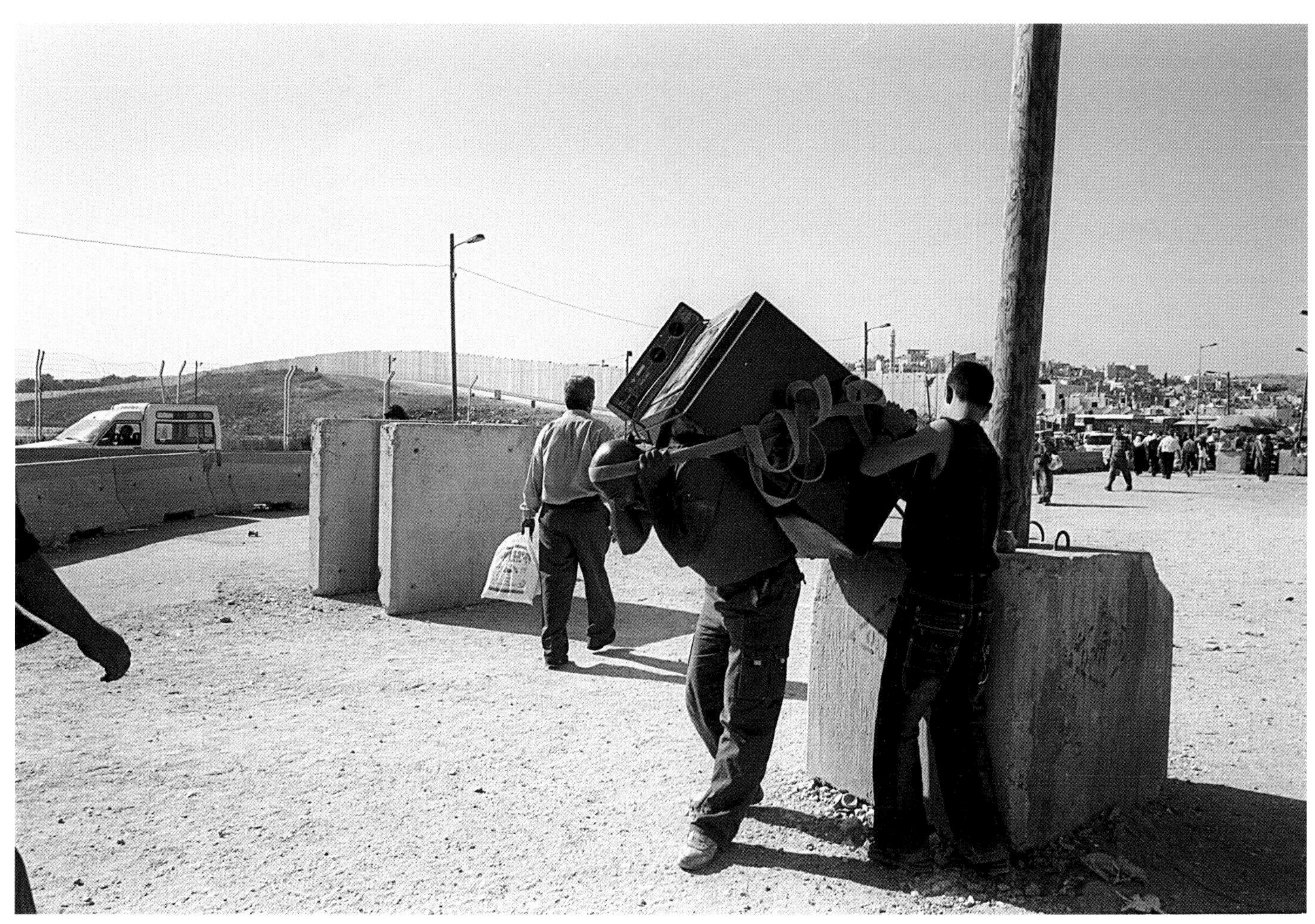

A Palestinian man transports a washing machine on his back across the Kalandia checkpoint.

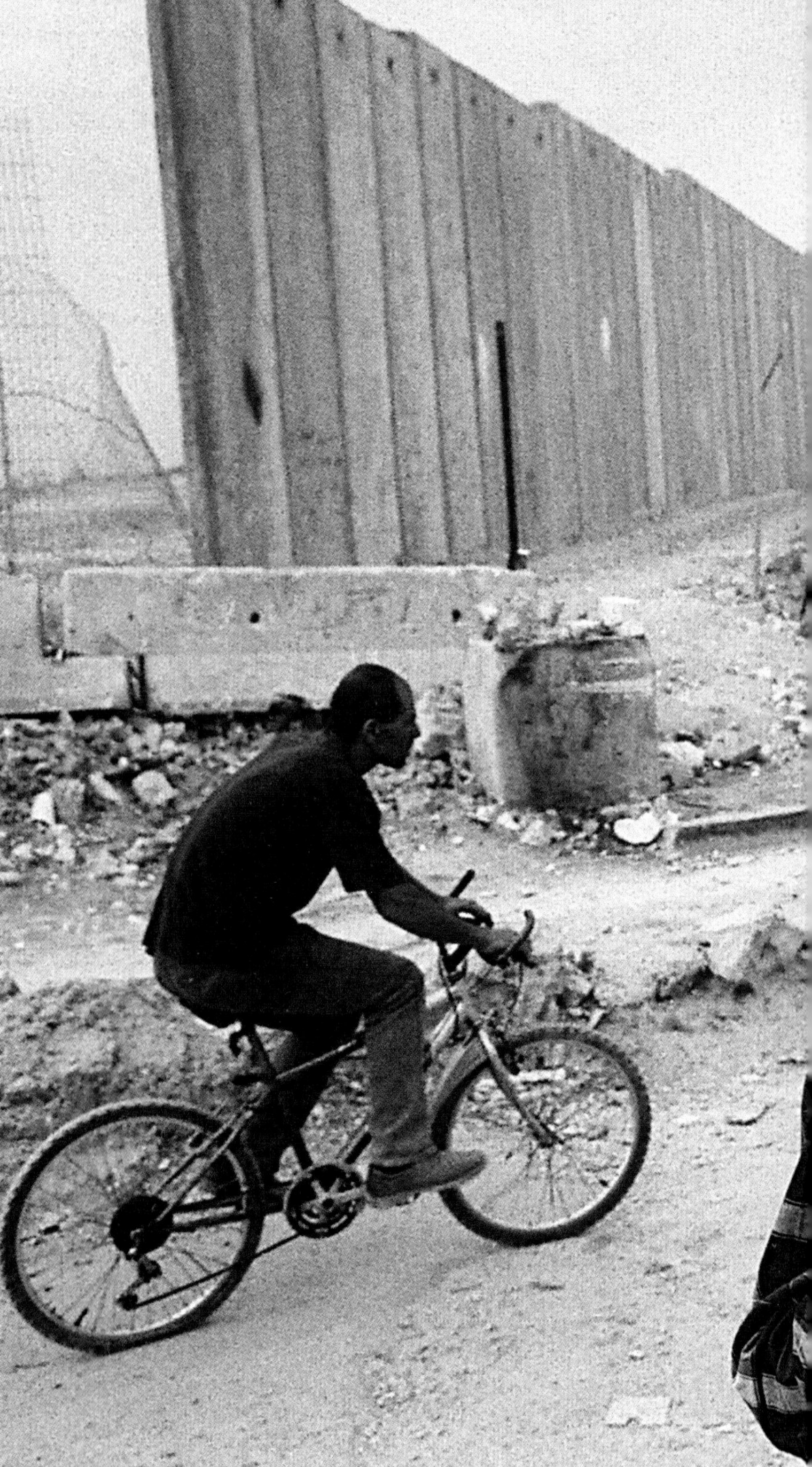

Nizar waits with his
daughter Nawal at the
Kalandia checkpoint.

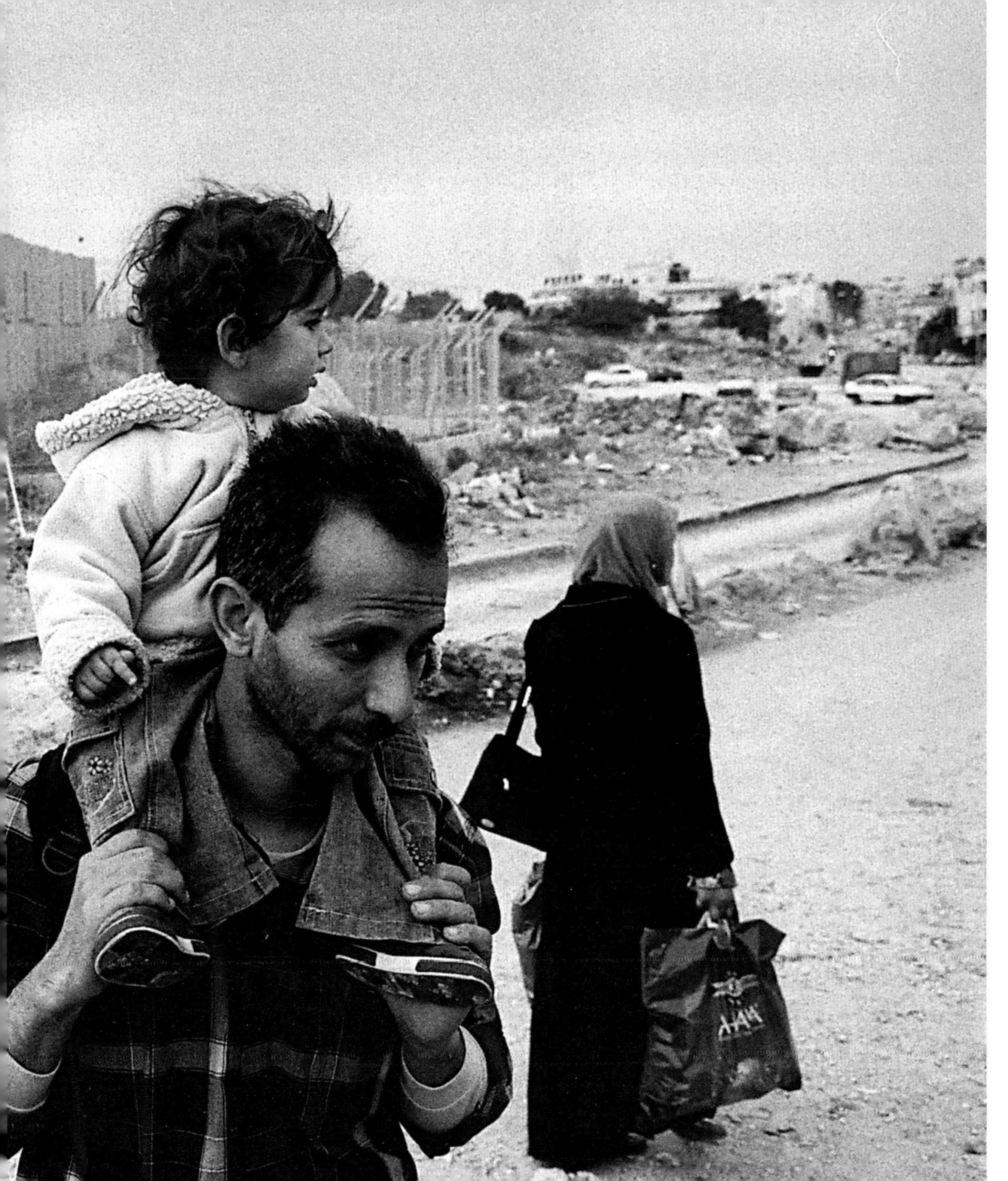

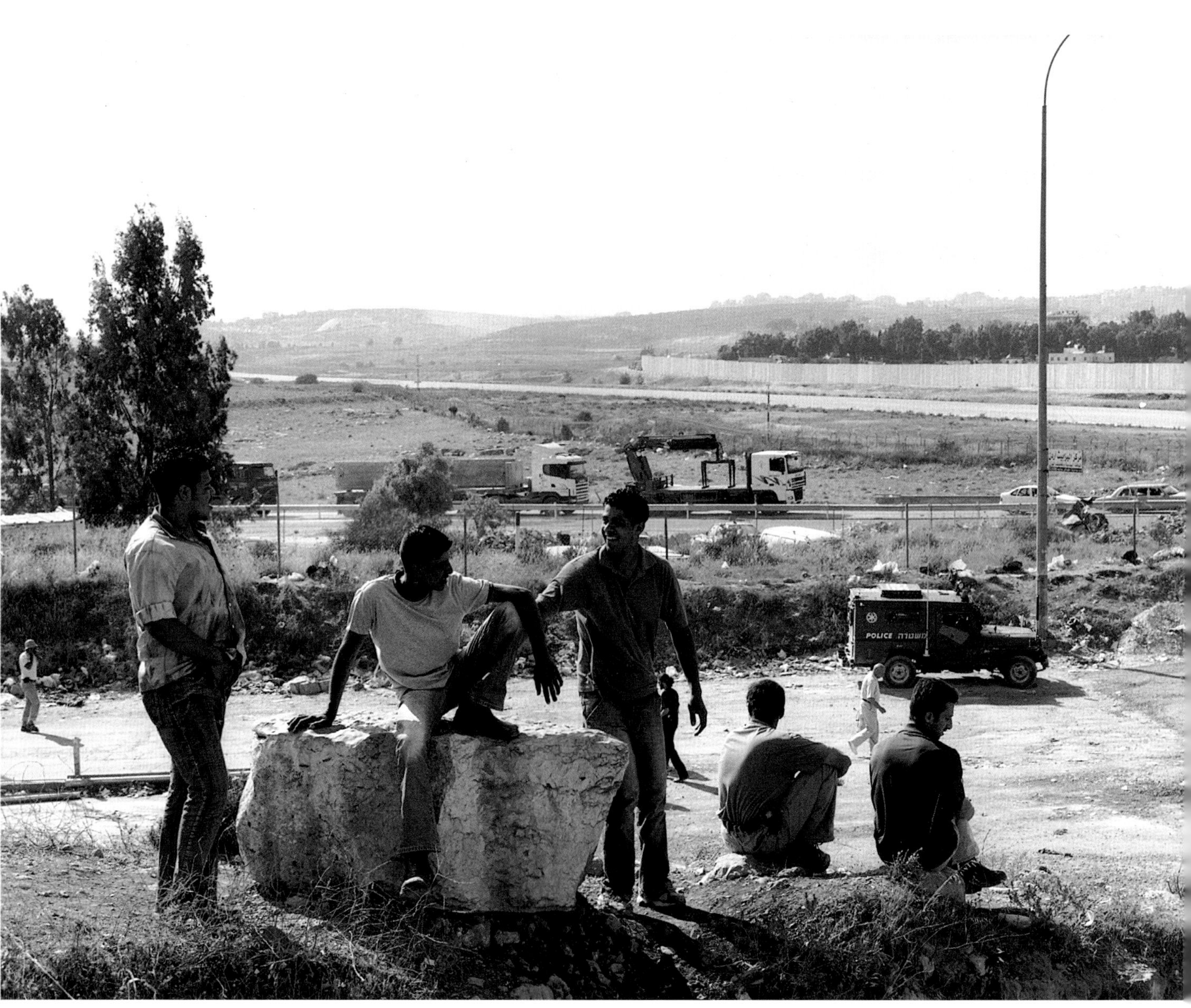

A view of the Kalandia
checkpoint and the
Barrier built where the
Ramallah airport once
stood. All that remains
of it is the airstrip.

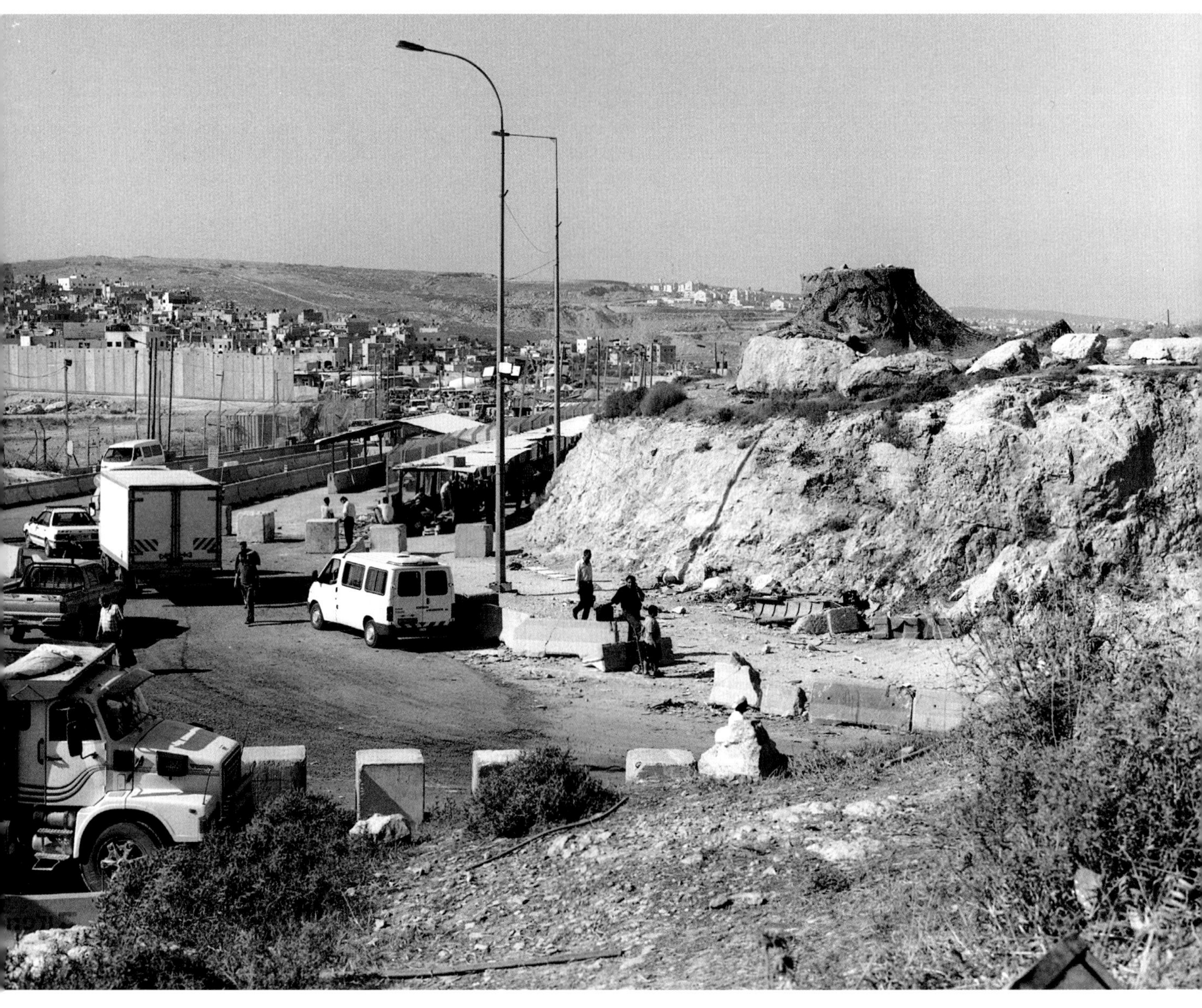

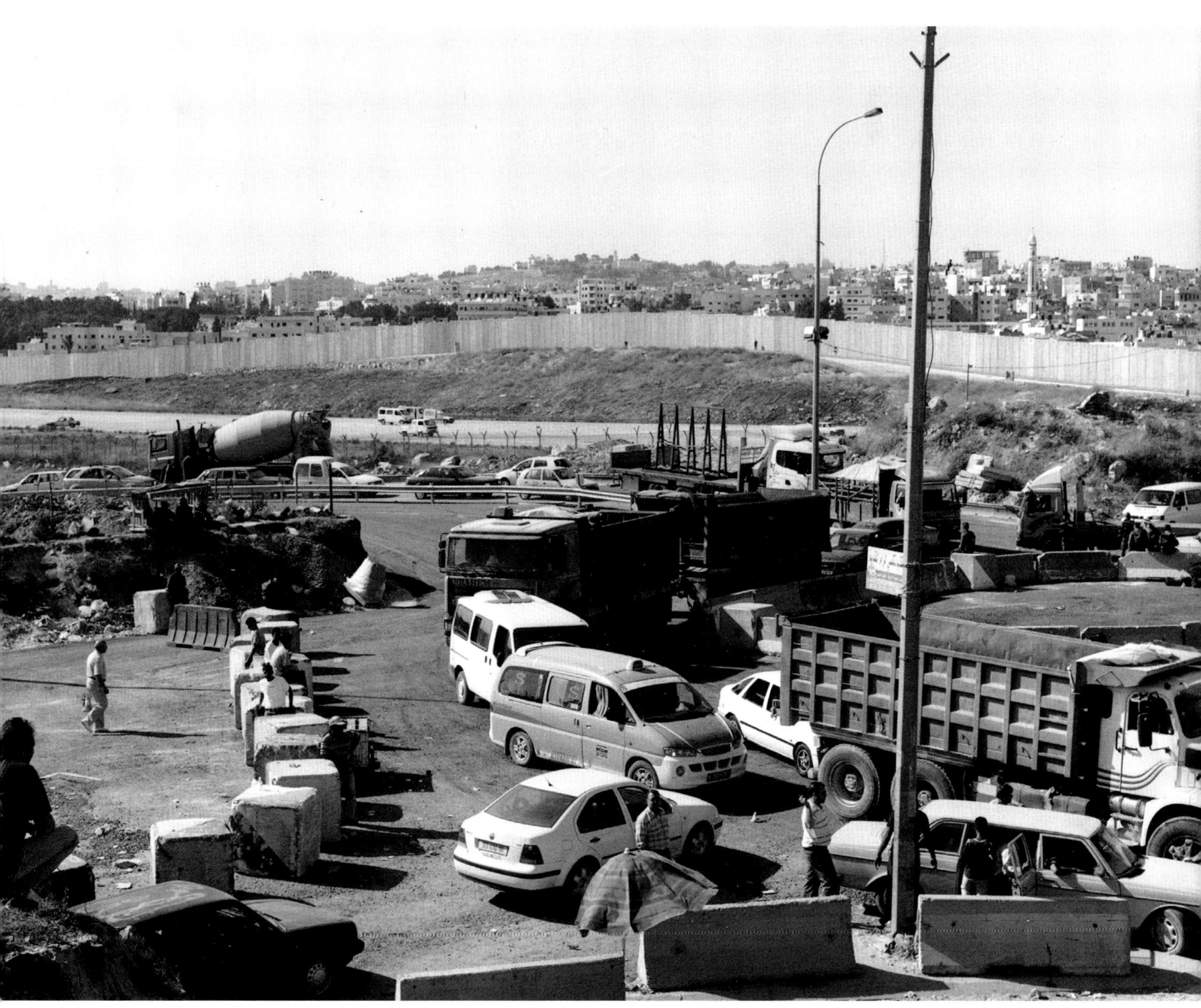

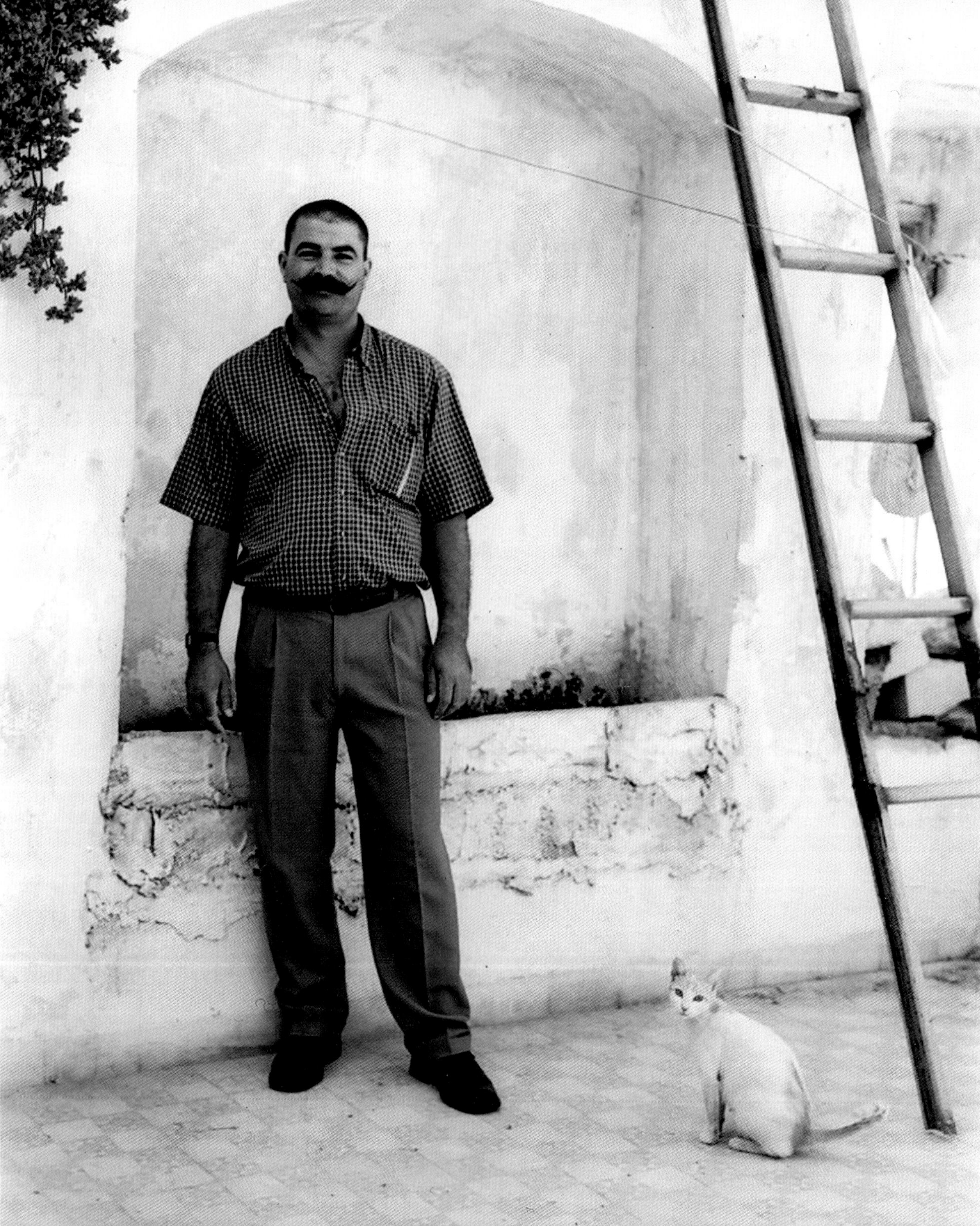

"What has been completely lost here is being treated like a human being."

Kanaan, Asira
Palestinian.

A woman speaks
through the narrow
slits in the wall to her
friend on the other
side, Nazlat Isa.

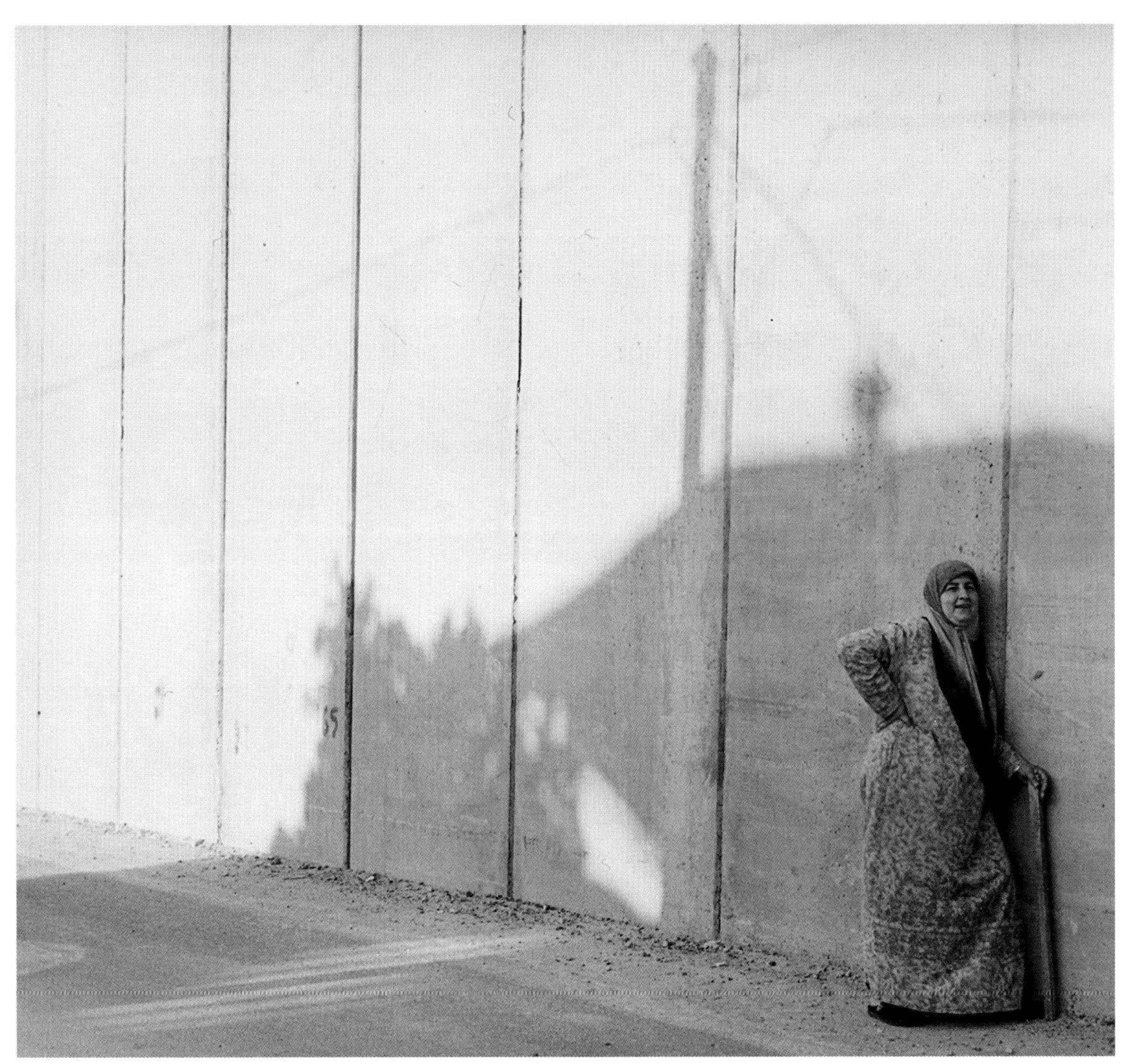

Afterword

With each of Rebecca's pictures I get more and more angry and the anger keeps blocking my words. Nothing comes out to justify the abomination of the wall, the brutality of it, the cruelty to a people who have had to endure a modern diaspora, a crushing occupation, a betrayal by many Arab countries. I'm talking about the Palestinians. Yes, I know the terrible history of all that the Jews have had to endure for centuries. They have had to bear up under so much of what is invidious about humanity. I think I am able to empathize in my own small way with the horrors of the Holocaust and the struggle for a Jewish State and the terror of the Intifada *suicide bombings. But does any of this justify this wall?*
Does it justify the all-too-apparent land grab that it represents…
or the false illusion of security it gives the Israelis?
For me the answer is "no". The wall is a symbol of failure.
The failure of leaders. Of political process. Of religious dreams.
Who knows, perhaps these photographs of the wall's concrete brutality will awaken the outside world to the terrible calamity of the current situation and perhaps individuals will be forced to consider how they can help bring it to an end. Perhaps.
The wall is in your face, folks. What does it stand for?
Can you let it continue to stand?

Terry Gilliam
April 2006

Notes

[1] Tanya Reinhart, *Israel/Palestine How to End the War of 1948*, New York: Seven Stories Press, 2005, p. 7.
[2] http://www.un.org/unrwa/refugees/camp-profiles.html.
[3] http://www.un.org/unrwa/refugees/camp-profiles.html.
[4] For more information on the various reasons why houses are demolished by the Israeli Army refer to the Amnesty report at http://web.amnesty.org/library/Index/ENGMDE150402004?open&of=ENG-ISR.
[5] Reinhart 2005, p. 251.
[6] Reinhart 2005, p. 260.
[7] B'tselem report, *Not All it Seems, Preventing Palestinians Access to their Lands West of the Separation Barrier in the Tulkarm-Qalqiliya Area*, June 2004, www.btselem.org.
[8] David Grossman, *The Yellow Wind*, New York: Picador USA, 1988.